The Artist and Society
in Shakespeare's England

The Artist and Society in Shakespeare's England:

The Collected Papers of Muriel Bradbrook
Volume I

M. C. BRADBROOK
Professor of English Emerita,
University of Cambridge and Fellow of
Girton College

THE HARVESTER PRESS · SUSSEX
BARNES & NOBLE BOOKS · NEW JERSEY

First published in Great Britain in 1982 by
THE HARVESTER PRESS LIMITED
Publisher: John Spiers
16 Ship Street, Brighton, Sussex

and in the USA by
BARNES & NOBLE BOOKS
81 Adams Drive, Totowa, New Jersey 07512

© M. C. Bradbrook, 1982

Editor: Sue Roe

British Library Cataloguing in Publication Data

Bradbrook, M. C.
  The artist and society in Shakespeare's England.
  Vol. 1
  1. English literature – Early modern, 1500–1700 –
  History and criticism
  I. Title
  820.9'003   PR421
  ISBN 0-7108-0391-5

Library of Congress Cataloging in Publication Data

Bradbrook, M. C. (Muriel Clara), 1909–
  Artist and society in Elizabethan England.

  (The Collected essays of Muriel Bradbrook; v. 1)
  1.   English literature – Early modern, 1500-1700 – History and criticism –
  Addresses, essays, lectures.
  2.   Shakespeare, William 1564-1616 – Criticism and interpretation –
  Addresses, essays, lectures. I. Title. II. Series: Bradbrook, M. C. (Muriel
  Clara), 1909-   .
  Collected essays of Muriel Bradbrook; v. 1.
  PR423.B7   1982   820'.9'003   82-6645
  ISBN 0-389-20294-0   AACR2

Photoset by Rowland Phototypesetting Ltd
Bury St Edmunds, Suffolk

Printed in Great Britain by
Mansell Limited, Witham, Essex

Contents

Foreword

Muriel Bradbrook's long and fruitful career, which now spans more than fifty years' research into Elizabethan drama in all its aspects – themes, conventions, stage conditions, social history, literary criticism – as well as studies of Malory, Marvell, Ibsen, Conrad, T. S. Eliot, Malcolm Lowry and Patrick White, has been marked throughout by qualities which are not often found together. A strong sense of history, for one thing, and an ability to do what Eliot held to be the critic's chief task, to bring the writer back to life, are qualities of whose importance she is well aware. As she writes of the eldritch tradition, with its use of savage humour and ridicule, 'Today these are relatively inaccessible; they can be recovered' – if, we should add, one knows our social and literary history well enough; or again, as she begins her British Academy lecture, 'I shall try to recover traces of the archaic spectacular tradition from which Shakespeare first started . . .' (pp. 85, 87). In this mode she belongs to the line of historical scholars of Elizabethan drama which began with Edward Capell, George Steevens and Edmond Malone, continuing to E. K. Chambers, W. W. Greg, Alfred Harbage, and beyond, all of whom had an enviable grasp of English theatre in its totality, from the Middle Ages to the Puritan revolution.

Such knowledge is not easily come by, and her own description of herself as a research student at Cambridge in the 1930s gives an insight into the amount of 'reading and re-reading' involved:

> Sometimes I would read a great play twenty or thirty times, along with all the minor plays that have survived. I know no substitute for laminating the text into one's mind in a variety of moods and settings, the equivalent of the actor's study and rehearsal. (p. 4)

Attending her lectures, as an undergraduate at Cambridge in the early 1960s, I was struck by the way she would enter the lecture-hall as if brooding on some part of her memory, and begin by recalling what exactly, at this time of year, the Children of St. Paul's would have been performing. The fruits of this life-long immersion in the drama can be seen in all her work, of course, but is glimpsed here in a number of casual asides: on the antics or momes in court revels (p. 39), on clowns' extempore rhymes (p. 49 n. 10), on country mummings (p. 79 ff), on the shrew tradition (p. 108), on the prodigal sons (p. 149), or on the Lord Mayor's triumphs (p. 167). This awareness of the totality of drama extends to props and action (pp. 81, 90, 94), and to the place of theatre in a political context. She notes the fact that when Cromwell came to full power, Puritan attitudes to the theatre notwithstanding, he commissioned masques for the entertainment of the French ambassador, and for the wedding of his daughter (p. 63); or the poignant detail that Charles I 'was beheaded at the door of his own theatre' (p. 67). She has always had a fine sense of context, as of the relations between the court and society, demonstrated in her memorable essay on Spenser and the ambivalence of the *vita activa* tradition, which legitimated ambition as the desire to serve the state, but offered no way of controlling corruption and sycophancy (as so often in the Renaissance, one feels, the propagandists legislated for a perfect world, leaving the poets and dramatists to cope with its distorted realities). The grasp of context is not only social and political but topographical, as in her account of Webster's part of London (p. 54 ff), or her comment on the 'great *Prelate of the Grove*' in Marvell's *Upon Appleton House*: 'the Archbishop of York's Cawood Castle lay within sight' (p. 70).

To bring knowledge to bear on the whole context of literature demands a sharp awareness of reality, which has always been one of her strong qualities: she illuminates what it actually means to be a gifted, ambitious, but place-less writer, such as Gabriel Harvey, Spenser, Webster or Shakespeare; or how a writer draws on his extra-literary life: 'Webster, a student of the Middle Temple, wrote no play without a trial scene' (p. 174). Here, as so often, 'background' is energized and brought into relation with the work of art. In the essay on *The Taming of the Shrew* she made me aware for the first time of the novelty heralded in the title by the word 'taming': 'traditionally the shrew triumphed; hers was the oldest and indeed the only native comic role for women'. Shakespeare innovates by keeping Katherine on stage a good deal yet giving her a surprisingly passive role: 'she spends most of the time listening to Petruchio. The play is his; this is its novelty' (p. 108). Her account of the shrew tradition, typically wide-ranging yet concise – we seldom complain of a topic being pursued at too great length, rather the opposite – throws up the important point that 'Katherine is the first shrew to be given a father, the first to be shewn as maid and bride; she is not seen merely in relation to a husband' (p. 111). It takes a scholar to know the theatrical history involved here; it takes a critic to use it.

When she moves into analysing the plays the qualities revealed are those of acumen, sensitivity, the power to see both resemblances and differences. On 'dramatic structure', for instance, a concept often used vaguely, she can make short, penetrating observations, such as this: 'The lament of Hotspur's widow is immediately followed by the appearance of Falstaff's whore; it is one of the telling silent strokes' (p. 128); or this: Falstaff's boast that 'I have a whole school of tongues in this belly of mine', an 'elaborate way of saying that "Everyone that sees me, knows me"', by its metaphor suddenly clothes Falstaff in the robe which Rumour had worn in the prologue' (p. 131). On a work's genre, and the expectations that go with it, she describes Milton's *Comus* as a 'masque against masquing, his plea for temperance in a form traditionally used for extravagant display' (p. 63); and notes of the 'medley plays' that they 'delighted the audience only by an unpredictable mixture of predictable items' (p. 91). In Peele's *Old Wives' Tale*, say, 'there is no need for a plot' (p. 92). The perils of allowing spectacle to dominate in Shakespeare's romances, which made use of the latest theatre technology, are captured in her comment on 'the descent of Jupiter, spectacularly the highlight of the whole play *Cymbeline* but poetically a gap and a void' (p. 101). *Measure for Measure*, that play of puzzles and reversals, is categorized by two surprising references to related genres: 'The essence, as in a modern detective story, is surprise and speed' (p. 145); while the Duke's award of himself to Isabella recalls the dénouement of Gilbert and Sullivan's *Trial by Jury* (p. 146)! This refreshing lack of piety, this readiness to make the necessary judgment whatever the status of the work, institution, or personage involved, have been features of Muriel Bradbook's work throughout her career, as can be seen in many independent reviews, which ought also to be collected.

In the development of her work one can see a move from the internal or literary dimension of the plays into considering their social dimension, and the situation of actors and companies in Renaissance England. I think that one can also trace a deepening of response to human personality. This can be seen sometimes in her comments on writers themselves, as in her remark that Spenser 'never became the poet of intimate relationships' (p. 34); or her characterization of Ben Jonson as 'the most masculine of Elizabethan comic dramatists' (p. 118). She goes on to relate the dramatist's personality to genre in *Epicoene*, noting how the action is tightly controlled by irony:

There are two standards of what constitutes right social behaviour: that of the fops and the Ladies Collegiate and that of the wits, Dauphine and his friends: but there is no free play of sympathy. Satire offers the audience a direct and assured moral judgment, the pleasure of siding with authority: it offers also the covert satisfaction of surveying the baseness which is to be judged. Jonson stands to Shakespeare in this respect as Dunbar stands to Chaucer. (pp. 118–19)

At other times this response to the inner states of personality is used to describe a character in a play: Iago 'appears incapable of relating to anyone reciprocally', and thus seems atrocious (p. 164). If it is a 'psychological truism' that 'the world reflects back upon each individual the image with which he confronts it', then 'Angelo's neglect and contempt for a sexual object once attained is very easily converted to self-hatred when he is exposed' (p. 152). If those two comments are sharply critical – rightly so – then the analysis of Falstaff's 'innocent and unstudied shamelessness' (p. 124), his 'animal, instinctive' self-confidence (p. 126), his 'extraordinary union of the child, the animal, and the criminal' – this brilliant account of Falstaff and his parallel with Hotspur on the one side, Pistol on the other, adds humanity to acumen.

Reading this collection has taught me a number of things, given me insights into writers, plays, traditions, and social patterns. Knowing that I was being invited to introduce it has made me realize more sharply than before how much I, and countless others, owe to Muriel Bradbrook for her work and for her example. The qualities I have singled out – scholarship, a historical sense, sensitivity, candour, an understanding of life – are qualities that any scholar would be happy to emulate.

Brian Vickers
All Souls College, Oxford
Spring, 1982.

Introduction

The essays and lectures collected here – all but one written within the
last twenty years – have been arranged not in the order of their
composition but in chronological order of the events treated. The
opening group epitomizes the social context for Shakespeare's working life, whilst the main group follows him from his beginnings to full
maturity. Here, critical studies, and the lecture to the British
Academy are interspersed with less formal talks on *Henry IV*,
Hamlet and *Othello*, the first two being linked with specific performances of the plays in widely different cultures – Canada and Japan.

The first two essays illustrate the fate of a poet who attempted to
live by Court patronage[1] and after his initial venture in non dramatic
poetry the steps Shakespeare took to avoid it. They introduce what
has been termed 'the Shakespearean moment'

> The 1590s are the crucial years . . . which led directly to the
> greatest moment in English poetry; the Shakespearean moment,
> the opening years of the seventeenth century . . . brought about
> that deep change of sensibility which marks off the earlier from the
> later Elizabethans, which alters the climate from that of *Arcadia*
> and *The Faerie Queene* to that which welcomed *Hamlet*.
>
> Patrick Cruttwell, *The Shakespearean Moment* (1954) p.1.

At this moment power passed to the dramatic form; Webster
stands at the parting of the ways, when, for a man able to choose, the
path led out of drama; the position for Marvell is surveyed from the
post-theatrical interregnum of the Civil War.

There is something of an epitome here also of the course of
Shakespeare's progress in the study and on stage during the past half
century; the survey of that period forms the subject of my introduction. Through the fifty years elapsed since the publication of my first
book, *Elizabethan Stage Conditions* in 1932, at least three shifts

have developed in the reinterpretation of Elizabethan drama in general and Shakespeare in particular. In scholarship, as the pooling of information grew easier, the range of reference grew wider. The history of art, which, especially for the Renaissance, developed after the founding of the Warburg Institute in 1934, has been extended to all forms of Renaissance display, especially the politically tinged forms of masque, tourney and royal entry. Historians themselves have moved from political and constitutional study towards social history; and in the combined schools and joint courses of the newer universities the interaction of these subjects with literary and dramatic history has spread. Simultaneously, scholars and critics have drawn much closer to actors and directors, until now even textual study interacts with the performer's art. Some of this interaction was chronicled by J. L. Styan in *The Shakespeare Revolution* (1977); other of its critical eccentricities were castigated by Richard Levin in *New Readings versus Old Plays* (1979). These two works taken together present two segments of the 'communication explosion' which new means of data retrieval and xerox copying have brought to the scholar, and which the worldwide variety of adaptive performance has brought to the actor. The Annual Shakespeare Bibliography is now computer-aided.

At the third World Shakespeare Conference in 1981, a seminar on translation disclosed a variety of Shakespeares, as multiform as the many Homers of the ancient and modern world. Any branch of study is now likely to develop its own Shakespeare; the psychoanalysts' Shakespeare and the Marxists' Shakespeare have for some time been familiar; more recently, the feminists' Shakespeare has been extrapolated from the plays.

In attempting to sketch the changes in scholarship, criticism, and performance over this last half century, I would term the first phase (that of the late twenties and thirties) the era of poets and scholars; in the second phase, beginning after World War II, the arts, social historians and theatre men build up to the eclecticism of the last decade – a period of do-it-yourself Shakespeare. This lapse from a fixed centre was produced both by the psychological development of audience-response as a guiding factor in criticism, and by a new sense of that total rupture with the past which had been postulated by Sartre – but also by such a traditionalist as C. S. Lewis.[2]

I see the more recent rupture as different from that following World War II. The electronic revolution means that Shakespeare attracts more attention than ever, because paradoxically he provides, if not a fixed centre, a uniquely complex variable – the stabilizing (if Protean) feature in a weightless free-floating cultural dream-world. The 'internal drama' of each spectator (dealt with in my *English*

Dramatic Form and here in the opening of the essay on *The Taming of the Shrew*) is by his art reconciled with an unstable society.

* * *

An easy way of measuring the distance traversed in the first two phases is to set the first *Companion to Shakespeare Studies* (eds. G. B. Harrison and H. Granville-Barker, 1934) against the *New Companion to Shakespeare Studies* (eds. Kenneth Muir and S. Schoenbaum, 1971). Early attempts by literary historians to reconstruct the framework of the Elizabethan public theatre have yielded to the architectural expertise of Walter Hodges or Richard Southern (for ever excluding such speculative work as that of Leslie Hotson or Irwin Smith). Amateur historical excursions give way to the work of Joel Hurstfield. Study of genres spreads to related forms of entertainment in the work of Glynne Wickham, Stephen Orgel and such historical sidelights as Sydney Anglo's *Spectacle, Pageantry and Early Tudor Politics* (1969).

To return to the start of this survey, in 1932 the dominant influence of T. S. Eliot exerted itself not only in the essays on Elizabethan drama published in *The Sacred Wood* (1920), augmented in *Selected Essays* (1932), but more potently in the poetry of *The Waste Land* (1921). By reconstituting in his own visionary poem something like an Elizabethan poetic structure of themes and images, he had transformed the reading of Marlowe, Jonson and Webster as well as that of Shakespeare. The new relevance of the Elizabethans as appropriated in his own lines ('Bad poets imitate; good poets steal') doubled the penetrative power of Eliot's criticial assessments. The clues that led to the original thinking of what was to become *Themes and Conventions of Elizabethan Tragedy* were provided in his essay on 'Four Elizabethan Dramatists'. This revival of *dramatic* poets gave a dimension of close 'internal drama' to his lyric.

Eliot sponsored the work of G. Wilson Knight, which, in the first volume especially, *The Wheel of Fire* (1930), drew out the thematic structure of Shakespeare's tragedies and helped to undermine any naturalistic approach. A little later Una Ellis Fermor introduced the work of Wolfgang Clemen on imagery to English readers; this reinforced Knight. Wolfgang Clemen, *Shakespeare's Bilder*, (1936) cited by Una Ellis Fermor in her own work, was by her encouragement translated and enlarged to *The Development of Shakespeare's Imagery* (1951). Without being polemical, these works modified traditional views.

After World War I literary scholarship had become more technical and institutional, with the advent of two annual biographies (*The Year's Work in English Studies* and *Annual Bibliography of English*

Language and Literature). Periodicals devoted to academic work – which Leavis termed 'the higher navvying' – were countered by literary magazines; but such great data-banks of erudition as the works of E. K. Chambers facilitated the close study of drama in social-historic terms. Cambridge English had been given a strong flavour of social history by the founding fathers, several of whom were historians by training; 'life and thought' replaced the history of the language that still dominated elsewhere. An early and well-known product of this union of literature and history is L. C. Knights, *Drama and Society in the Age of Jonson* (1937).

However, like Leavis, with whom he edited *Scrutiny*, Knights was not interested in performance; he speaks always of 'reading' plays. The study of theatrical conditions was at this time largely theoretical and archaeological, attempting to reassemble lost monuments from the evidence of lawsuits and other records. I myself had the double good fortune of having been taught at school by the sister of an actor who played with the Cassons, and of being able to attend the Festival Theatre of Terence Grey, where experimental performances of classic theatre and the most modern plays were given in the tiny eighteenth-century wooden building with its open stage and sunken pit. I had devised a technique of reading and re-reading an Eliza-bethan text till the shape of its themes and conventions emerged. Sometimes I would read a great play twenty or thirty times, along with all the minor plays that have survived. I know no substitute for laminating the text into one's mind in a variety of moods and settings, the equivalent of the actor's study and rehearsal. In the mid-1930s I spent a year at Oxford, where the only sympathetic minds I encountered were Janet Spens and C. S. Lewis; with him I discussed *Hero and Leander*, Marlowe and Chapman. A little later I was to meet in Cambridge F. P. Wilson who had been evacuated there at the start of World War II; but soon I departed for the Civil Service, where I learnt Norwegian and wrote on Ibsen.

After the war the work of the Warburg Institute began to be applied to the drama, iconography became a department of Renais-sance studying in such pioneer studies as those of D. J. Gordon on Jonsonian masques. Even earlier, in U.S.A., George R. Kernodle had pointed the way in *From Art to Theatre* (1944). This spectacular element soon fed into our theatre itself and influenced live produc-tion. Critics and theatre people tentatively approached each other when the International Shakespeare Conference at Stratford-upon-Avon began in 1946, where it has since met biannually with the members of the Royal Shakespeare Company, at the Shakespeare Institute of the University of Birmingham. *Shakespeare Survey* grew as an annual publication out of these meetings.

Tyrone Guthrie (who believed that 'Theatre is ritual') developed his theatre at Stratford, Ontario, where Tanya Moseivitch's superb building in 1957 replaced the 'big top' in which Shakespeare had been staged from 1953. This masterpiece was copied at Cirencester and Minneapolis, but neither of these theatres emits the vibrations of the original building. In the early 1960s a biannual conference on the Elizabethan Theatre began at the University of Waterloo, Ontario; the lectures have appeared in a series of volumes, *Elizabethan Theatre*.

In England the first university department of drama opened in the fifties at Bristol, with Glynne Wickham as professor; he combined theatrical with literary studies. This brought about alliances with sociology and psychology in the new universities that arrived in the following decade; drama fully recovered its Tudor links with education.

In 1951 I had published *Shakespeare and Elizabethan Poetry*, and in 1955 *The Growth and Structure of Elizabethan Comedy*, depicting the emergence of drama from the cocoon of early Elizabethan non-dramatic poetry. My next study, however, *The Rise of the Common Player* (1962), was more innovatory in exploring the social implications of drama as a performing art. From that time I have become increasingly aware of the dimension of performance and its significance in social history. The first was clearly being illustrated by the general theatrical move away from a naturalist's theatre to one much closer to the Elizabethan stage, both in the remodelled theatre at Stratford, and in the Mermaid Theatre which Bernard Miles installed in a bombed warehouse at Puddle Dock, just below St Paul's.

This meant that many minor works, and the less frequently performed plays of Shakespeare himself could be seen for the first time in centuries. Gradually also the medieval roots of Renaissance drama became clearer. In my undergraduate days the texts of these plays had been neglected for the literary intricacies of the *Gawayne* poet, *Piers Plowman* or the Scottish Chaucerians, but yearly performances of the craft cycles at York and elsewhere revealed their splendid vitality. They are now to be found performed *in situ* as far away as Perran Round in Cornwall where the students of Bristol acted a translation of the Cornish *Ordinalia*. Such late medieval clerks' plays as *Mankind* or *Johan Johan* also attract students; Eliot himself had taken as a model the most famous of the Morality plays, *Everyman*, for his liturgical drama *Murder in the Cathedral* (1936). Here very directly he related the past to the present in the demagogic speeches of the murderers. In *The Fortunes of Falstaff* (1943) Dover Wilson had related the Shakespearean histories of *1 and 2 Henry IV* to the Moral play, and in *Shakespeare's History Plays* (1944) Tillyard saw them as 'the finest of all Shakespeare's Mirrors for Magistrates', fitting the whole sequence very neatly into 'two tetralogies'. What had been a new look in the 1940s became dogma in the 1950s, until *Angel with Horns* (1961) by A. P. Rossiter (died 1957) gave new perspectives to the medieval past and astringently corrected some of the more vapid generalizers. Ritual suited the bare stage and was pursued for its own sake; Rossiter went far beyond stage possibility when he declared that Macbeth, his wife and Banquo 'are parts of a pattern or design; are images or symbols' – not three persons but one event in a poem, with the rest of the cast also in antithesis to the twin protagonists (p. 217).

Thematic or symbolic presentation was better suited to the 'problem plays', which soon followed the history plays as the most popular field for experimental staging.[3] Audiences given these novelties and the plays of other Elizabethans (*Dr Faustus* the most frequently staged) became accustomed to stylish stage formulae; every eccentricity became tolerated as a novelty.

The mood is akin to that I have delineated in my essay on '*Dr Faustus* and the Eldritch Tradition'; it is highly Marlovian, representing the conscious stress of social conflict and became popular with Marxists, especially after the impact of Brecht in the late 1950s. English literature, everywhere a favourite subject in higher education, carried Shakespeare to all the new centres of learning produced by Anglo-American imperial dominance, until all over the world conferences, exhibitions, models of the Globe theatre, festivals, coffee-table books produced the kind of funfair that used to be found only in Shakespeare's home town. In 1964 the fourth centenary in a worldwide cultural celebration evoked hundreds of offerings. By this time the comedies too were beginning to be re-interpreted. C. L. Barber's notable book on Festive Comedy having appeared in 1959 (together with Glynne Wickham's first instalment of his *Early English Stages*), the approach through social history received a new stimulus; but in the theatre Shakespeare's happiest plays were shadowed with darkened and ironic presentation. He had done this to Chaucer, as I have tried to show. His sweet comedy curdled with bitterness proved more palatable than the original bitter comedies of Ben Jonson, who when revived at all was likely to be represented by his most genial entertainments, *The Alchemist* or *Bartholomew Fair*. Bringing out the chill in Shakespeare gave a greater sharpness to the taste for 'alienation' that followed the arrival of Brecht.

However, the part played by all other Elizabethan dramatists in comparison with Shakespeare was a small one. The general shift in taste may be registered once again by comparing two standard collections of non-Shakespearean plays – from the thirties and the seventies.[4]

Black comedy became more acceptable than tragedy where the tragic affirmations were replaced by tragical satire: so the genres blurred. Some versions sprang from stage production, others from 'new readings'. The most notable general form of tragedy, the revenge play, provides the clearest illustrations of these shifts.

E. E. Stoll in 1904, in a book on John Webster, first gave an outline of the conventional elements of the revenge plot as developed in Kyd, Marston, Shakespeare, Tourneur, Webster, and a number of minor plays. Thorndike made some attempt to apply this to Shakespeare. Originally I wrote a chapter on 'Types of Tragedy' including the revenge play for *Themes and Conventions of Elizabethan Tragedy* (it was indeed the main vehicle for treating themes); but as this was thought to make the work too long for publication, it now survives only in my Ph.D thesis in Cambridge University Library. After reading it, Percy Simpson was moved in 1935 to give a British Academy lecture on the theme of Revenge, and in 1940, in *The Revenge Play*, Fredson Bowers mapped out the territory again in a neutral style. Later, Alvin Kernan in *The Cankered Muse* (1959) isolated the tone of bitter tragicomedy inherent in the 'second wave' of revenge plays (Marston, Shakespeare and after); next in *Hamlet and Revenge* (1967) Eleanor Prosser stressed moralistic aspects and surrounded the play with 'evidence' from works of piety and exhortation – although the questioning and ironic tones of *Hamlet* had been the subject of such writers as D. G. James, and Harry Levin.

Recently, three books have explored anew the complexity of this uniquely powerful form. Nicholas Brooke in *Horrid Laughter* (1979) deals with the wry stage effects of what Jacqueline Pearson in *Tragedy and Tragicomedy in the Plays of John Webster* (1980) was to term 'clashing tones'. The undermining of one mood by another, characteristic of tragicomedy, is found to be inherent in the text itself, with its dislocations and disjunctions, its use of self-parody, and of contrasted plot and subplots.

A more comprehensive work by Charles A. Hallett and Elaine S. Hallett *The Revenger's Madness* (1980) attempts to construct on 'an experiental basis' the constellated patterns of traditional elements that earlier writers had merely enumerated. Madness is seen as integral to revenge tragedy – which is therefore naturally disjunctive, based upon 'horrid laughter'. The motifs of the ghost, the revenger's delay, the play within the play, the multiple murders and the death of the protagonist are seen as part of 'the volcano of smouldering rage' which transforms the revenger's vision, altering his subjective constellations, reshaping the world within that is projected as the play-within-the-play (p. 12):

> Once the mind is freed from the restraints that normally control the passions, a fatal chain of events is set in progress. Transformation takes place within the avenger which, though requiring a certain period of time, alters his perceptions of the world to an extent that will enable him to perform heinous deeds and make his own death in atonement for those deeds inevitable. The conventional motifs actually function as dramatic symbols for the various stages of this archetypal experience.

It is disquieting that Marston is rejected as not fitting this pattern, which is best suited to Kyd and Tourneur; but the authors conclude by citing Thomas Goffe, *Orestes* (1623) as evidence that such structure was widely understood.

* * *

Even within the highly specialized field of textual criticism, the effects of performance may be found; the assistant editor of the new Oxford Shakespeare, Gary Taylor, through a chart of the double roles has recently worked out the basis of one of the 'bad quartos' *(Henry V)*. Peter Blayney, who joins an actor's experience to the most precise study of typography, has applied both skills in an analysis of the text of *King Lear*.

Seventeen years ago Charlton Hinman produced the results of his full collation of the First Folio, so that the history of the printing process has replaced a concern with lost originals that had derived from the study of classical texts. The new methods diminish the authority of the earliest text, and indirectly support the eclecticism which now prevails.

The natural license of a pluralistic culture and an egalitarian temper, the abstruseness of the new textual techniques tends to encourage such conjectual absurdities as those collected by Richard Levin. However, the value of his collection is reduced by his prudent refusal to identify the authors. Nor does he point the way to any acceptable alternatives; and he has not produced much effect.

The latest annual bibliography of Shakespeare, *Shakespeare Quarterly* (1980), lists, for example, that in 'Is't possible?' (*Upstart Crow*, University of Tennessee, Fall 1978, 1–23) Wayne Holmes urged that Cassio and Desdemona were lovers but that wearied by her sexual importunities and 'seeing a chance for personal advancement' he had arranged her marriage to Othello. Such 'new readings', like their confident castigation, belong to the world academic scene.

At present three major editions of Shakespeare are in preparation; the American New Variorum, sponsored by the Modern Language Association; the New Cambridge Shakespeare revised – with particular attention to performance and stage history; the new Oxford Shakespeare. Such gigantic enterprises as *The Riverside Shakespeare* (1974), Schoenbaum's *Shakespeare: A Documentary Life* (1975) and his later *Shakespeare: Records and Images* (1981) are challenged by the programme of the Toronto-based *Records of Early English Drama* which, beginning in the later Middle Ages, aims to include Tudor records as well.

Yet at the same time purely linguistic and stylistic studies remain comparatively few. On the other hand concern with translation, with the universal Shakespeare is growing. Winifred Nowottny or Terence Hawkes may explore the oral elements of the language of the sonnets, but it is the non-dramatic language (what used to be termed the subtext) that is the more internationally observed; and of course it invites re-interpretation even more readily. (In the first Japanese translation of *Julius Caesar*, the Emperor indulged in a splendid display of physical prowess at the Forum, using all the Japanese martial arts of defence upon his assailants.)

As I have suggested in 'Beasts and Gods', Shakespeare himself chose the ambiguous art of the theatre with all its Protean risks, abandoning the career of a printed poet. Like Heywood he was a professional who avoided publication, leaving all to fluid activity within the theatre and the minds of actors and audience. If he knew

> Action is eloquence and the eyes of the ignorant
> More learned than their ears,

he also knew the advantage of his own complex art over Spenser's verbal pageants.

In the theatre Shakespeare's words are now more freely adapted in England than they have been since the early nineteenth century; the Shakespearean critic cannot with good conscience retreat into a Gutenberg enclave, or ignore the nonverbal element in the culture that surrounds him. It depends upon the large and small screens. With the whole of Shakespeare, these have adopted only one or two plays of Marlowe or Webster, nor can the Royal Shakespeare company itself afford to stage more than one non-Shakespearean Elizabethan play in any one season.

The notices of Stratford productions in *Shakespeare Survey* enable those who have not seen the plays to follow the season year by year, and trace the rise and fall of a 'deconstructed' Shakespeare. As the repository of past tradition, during the first period of 'rupture' Shakespeare invited very heavy iconoclasm, to emerge unscathed from a series of 'insults'. Nothing that has been done to him approaches what he himself did to the masterpiece of *Troilus and*

Criseyde. *Hamlet* affords the clearest measurement from Michael Benthall's Victorian princeling (1948) to David Warner's undergraduate and on to Michael Pennington's actor (1980). The alienated *Hamlet* evolved into metatheatre, where Hamlet becomes once more the 'sweet prince' only because the property basket is kept in full view to be utilized, whilst backstage the ghost's rusty armour lurks on a stand, a discarded property. The real ghost here is Tom Stoppard's *Rosencrantz and Guildenstern are Dead* and it is exorcised.

A dozen years ago, in his attack on 'the Deadly Theatre' in *The Empty Space* (1968), Peter Brook had invited deconstruction, though not by that name. The need to reflect the theories of Derrida – who is not a literary critic but an anthropologist – derive from the same theatrical power that makes Shakespeare available to his world audience – his flexibility, elasticity or, as one critic has termed it, his 'patience'.

Debunking, deconstruction or dismantling, which Shakespeare himself had practised early in *Love's Labours Lost* and later in *Troilus and Cressida*, having extended through the heroics of the English histories to the affirmative aspects of tragedy, with one reservation (a strong one) Brook praised Brecht's adaptation of *Coriolanus*. Events have not endorsed the literary Marxism of *Tel Quel*, so fashionable when Brook was writing. Brook's *Titus Andronicus* had fired Jan Kott in 1956 in Cracow, but *The Empty Space* has now become theatrical history. In the 1960s there was still an accepted convention to be challenged; in the 1970s that centre was displaced. Brook's *A Midsummer Night's Dream* (1970), based on the circus but true to the spirit of the Elizabethan May game, may be contrasted with Bogdanov's notorious *The Taming of the Shrew* (1978), which attempted too literally and derivatively to copy Brook's later Parisian productions in the ruinous Théâtre du Nord.

Here, a drunken Scotsman entered through the auditorium, fought with an usherette, climbed the stage (the curtain was already up) and proceeded to tear down the scenery. (At this point several foreigners, assuming a riot was about to begin, hastily left the auditorium.) Petruchio, for it was he, exposed the actual scene – broken bits of machinery, *bricolage*; later he entered on a motor bicycle, his Grumio on the pillion having all the appearance of being recruited from the Mafia. This kind of 'happening' belongs to the generation of the fifties and sixties. Now, when the social scene is more bleak, theatres can no longer afford to indulge the black humour of more affluent days, when the 'outcasts of the nursery' vented their tantrums and their guilt vicariously. Alienation is out, and it would appear from the Aldwych Christmas play of 1980, *Nicholas Nickleby*, that warm-heartedness is 'in'.

The senior director at present with the Royal Shakespeare Company, John Barton, has worked with Peter Brook, Peter Hall, Trevor Nunn and Terry Hands; he remains like the Duke of Exeter in his own version of the history plays, *The Wars of the Roses* (1963), a continuity man. He was the first to introduce new lines into *Henry VI*, which he defended by saying the trilogy was not necessarily all Shakespeare's work; in 1976 he added some lines from *The Troublesome Reign* to *King John*.

The necessity for a recreation *de novo* may depend less on the director's wish to vary his material (after the sandpit *Troilus and Cressida*, Achilles in drag) than on creating a suitable vehicle for a particular cast. A powerful actor may insist on being given the part he wants. Or the new machinery may suggest a reading. Thus in Barton's *Richard II* (1973) the new hydraulic staging supplied elevators in midstage so that 'Down, down I come, like glistering Phaethon' became a live image. In 1980 *Richard II* and *Richard III* were presented in diptych (white and gold against black and silver): the characters appeared at first framed in ecclesiastical arches, only to step forward as the human Lancaster and York.

In Barton's series *The Greeks* (1980, Aldwych), which was mainly Euripidean, a new play on Astyanax was devised in the interests of continuity. This series owed much to the Shakespearean histories, and illuminated them in turn, with its fantasy mixed with horror, archaic warriors turning into modern urban guerrillas. The avowed purpose of making the Greek legends live for this generation in its own terms might be illustrated from the latest philosophic work of Derrida's teacher, Paul Ricoeur, *The Rule of Metaphor* (1980), which indicates the function of metaphor as action.

The case against 'Director's Theatre' has been put by John Russell Brown in *Free Shakespeare* (1974). Certainly at the moment the most interesting work of directors and actors of the Royal Shakespeare Company is found in *The Other Place*, the small intimate theatre (smaller than the Elizabethan private houses) where in workshop conditions, actors play within a circle of 120 spectators. *Macbeth* (1976), a splendid *The Merchant of Venice*, and such rarities as Ford's *Perkin Warbeck* or Beaumont and Fletcher's *The Maid's Tragedy*, are given the same concentrated simplicity as the best television productions.

The Shakespearean films for the large screen featured crowd scenes of action – the charge at Agincourt in Laurence Olivier's *Henry V* made Shakespeare's apology lose its point. We *saw* 'the casques that did affright the air'. The latest series of television plays have gone to the other extreme. Single figures, mostly in close-up, predominate. Jonathan Miller, himself a radical director for the stage, began the TV season of 1980 by saying that it was necessary in watching *The Taming of the Shrew* to enter imaginatively the world of the past, when women submitted to their husbands as subjects to kings (later he was to term Cleopatra 'a slut', insulting the text as well as the queen). But he cut the *Shrew*'s induction so that the effect of metatheatre that it confers, the farcical frame to this improbable story, was lost – whereas for the stage *Hamlet* at Stratford it had been intensified.

Miller's televised *The Merchant of Venice* was sharply contrasted with his own earlier production on the stage of the National Theatre. There it had ended with the Kaddish; here the very sensitive question of possible offence was met by the appalling behaviour of the Christians, Shylock's 'Hath not a Jew eyes?' being drowned by loud giggles and uncomprehending horseplay from Solanio and Salerio. In *Antony and Cleopatra*, more perversely, Cleopatra was denied parts of her death scene; 'Husband, I come' was spoken in such a whisper that to those who did not know the line, the words would have been lost; Charmian said 'Downy windows, close' but did not close them; all that was seen was the back of the dead queen's crown (which was not awry) and Caesar's face. This method of undercutting the expected climax has been practised on the live stage (as when in one of the Royal Shakespeare Company's versions of *Richard III* Richard and Richmond addressed their troops simultaneously, drowning each other's exhortation). But lacking the dimension of living theatre, it becomes much more difficult to make 'poetry of the gaps' work for the audience.

* * *

More people may see these television programmes on one night than have attended the playhouse to hear Shakespeare since he first was put on the boards. Our 'delightful Proteus' has provided the five continents with a complex variable, to be endlessly modified, juggled with, and 'insulted' in trials of strength. When the cultural centre is lost, it is the very adaptability, the Protean quality of Shakespeare that makes him viable. He lacks the doctrinal implications that impede other old mythologies; at the same time he releases from individuals repressed passion that is dangerous to them. His sanity enables them to discharge their madness. What Yeats termed 'the filthy modern tide' collectively beats up against his poetry, washing up the debris of the eccentric (in the extrapolation of unlikely themes), the dirty (disguised as psychiatry by unqualified speculators in that mystery) and the aggressive (disguised as biography, or projected on to the sonnets). In the midst of the social hubbub of an international Funfair – Anthony Burgess's syphilitic lecher, feminists crying from the text their new readings of old wrongs, casebooks for examination candidates with answers for all occasions, advertisements using noble lines to sell luxury goods – sometimes the voice of affirmation may not be easy to distinguish. At this moment of time, it is difficult to describe the prevailing sense of uncertainty and insecurity. The new tools which the electronic age has put into our hands can be applied to criticism as to other explorations of data. It is possible in a few seconds to compile a bibliography that would have taken months;[5] but the effects upon the verbal analysis of individual works is at present absurdly rudimentary. Yet the impact on the general lives and responses of Shakespeare's audience will change their habits – at least as deeply as the invention of printing changed the audiences of four hundred years ago.

One way to keep Shakespeare's Protean powers clear is to recall the many different incarnations that he has successively undergone. Adaptations for the Restoration stage carried their own validity for that age; they are not bad Jacobean but good William-and-Mary. As well as listening to the multiplicity of voices in the present – and even trying to meet the very different kinds of audience at their different levels honestly – it is necessary constantly to replenish the sense of Shakespeare who is *not* our contemporary. My own interest has recently been focused on Webster and on the neglected Heywood; and through them on the minor forms of civic drama that in London fed the great mainstream of the public theatre. It is in this direction – and in extending the view of the seventeenth-century stage – that any additions to these collected essays may be expected. The two latest (on *Measure for Measure* and *Othello*) engage with the Inns of Court and City sports.

Heywood, like Shakespeare a full professional actor, composed not a book but a scenario, of which the score has been lost. Like the writers of masques, he used a social dimension of impermanence; as it was not for the Court but the City, this dimension is far harder to reconstitute. Shakespeare will survive the age of the book because of this extra dimension – 'the grace of action' as a contemporary termed it – which makes him much more than a book, and which can be modified in every generation and in any culture. In his case, this extra dimension is welded into the language.

Spenser, too, wrote more than a book, but like Heywood's his extra dimension is not easily recoverable. (Richard Helgerson made an attempt recently in *PMLA*.) By examining these less 'Protean' writers, and estimating the lost dimension of their work, it is possible also to enlarge and correct our response to Shakespeare. There is a wide variety of legitimate interpretation, which gradually shades off into the eccentric, the unacceptably distorted. The best measure of what is acceptable is still provided by such access as we are capable of obtaining to the language of the original composition, the language of the artist as it was spoken in his day. This includes the nonverbal languages of Shakespeare's more primitive arts, and the social context out of which that language grew. 'The Shakespearean moment' was one in which many kinds of language integrated.

In reconstituting the theatrical and social context, a negative point must be established. Linking Shakespeare's work with court performance or the court masque does not mean that *Measure for Measure* is to be read in 'the King James's version' or that we have 'cracked the code' of the royal family's identification with *Cymbeline*. Direct connection between two contemporary events that illuminate each other for us today should not be assumed.

Relating Webster to Penelope Devereux, Antonio Pérez or even the Overbury trial (as I have done) is to relate two elements of what was once the constellated life of London; parts of a common traditional culture are put together for the benefit of a different culture. Only historic myopia and poverty of imagination demands overt identification, as if they fully accounted for one another. The magisterial work of Fernand Braudel supports me here.

On the other hand in building such a social context, events are not picked at random; history is not antiquarianism. If I am not as sure as A. L. Rowse that Antonio Pérez or Emilia Lanier must give the key to some poetry, I feel reasonably confident that the poetry can be read with better insight if the background is filled in with all the facts that external witness offers (the records, in short) and with supporting material that knowledge will select and judgment conjoin. This is a practice that grows with years; I am still learning.

National Humanities Center
North Carolina   M. C. Bradbrook

Notes

1 This is also illustrated by the essay on '*Dr Faustus* and the Eldritch Tradition', reprinted in this present collection, and is implicit in the contrast of Chaucer's *Troilus and Criseyde* with Shakespeare's ('Never clapperclawed with the palms of the vulgar' and probably belonging to the Inns of Court).

2 C. S. Lewis's 'De descriptione temporum', his inaugural lecture at Cambridge, given in 1955, expresses the Christian equivalent of that rupture

with the past that, as experienced by the French, led to the full structuralist theories, to be extrapolated from Lévi-Strauss later.

3 I developed this in two essays which are not reprinted here, on *Measure for Measure* and *All's Well that Ends Well*: the material was incorporated later in book form. However, the essay on *Measure for Measure* in the present collection records a significant shift of point of view on my part towards relating this play to its social setting.

4 R. A. Fraser and Norman Rabkin, *Drama of the English Renaissance* (2 vols., New York, Macmillan, 1976), when compared with C. F. T. Brooke and N. Paradise, *English Drama*, 1580–1642 (Lexington, D. C. Heath, 1933), shows a shift towards the dark plays of Marston, the social comedy of the Carolines.

5 The Annual Shakespeare Bibliography, in *Shakespeare Quarterly*, is now giving upwards of 3,000 items a year and is compiled with computer assistance at the State University of Pennsylvania. Here also a gigantic cumulative bibliography of work since 1959 is being constructed by the retrieval system, and will be ready to print by 1985.

The Emergence and
Retreat of Drama

I

No room at the top:
Spenser's pursuit of Fame

The Shepheardes Calender, printed some time in the winter of 1579/80, itself calendars that moment when one use of lyric manifestly gave way to another. Courtly play of wit to move a suit, win a lady or supplicate a lord was united with the open pursuit of general Fame, as Gabriel Harvey led Edmund Spenser to embark on a joint campaign of publicity which lasted only till late summer, and ended in disaster.

Both achieved Fame; both overreached themselves. By 12 August 1580 Spenser had landed in Dublin, an exile who published no more for a decade, though he carved out an estate for himself and rose to be Sheriff of Cork before the 'the watch word came' that, late in 1598, fired his Castle of Kilcolman; just as Harvey, after thirty years' struggle for university office at Cambridge, finally retired to his native Saffron Walden and thirty years more of obscurity and silence.

Yet however unsuccessful their campaign of self-advertisement – which in Harvey's case had included two rhetorical treatises of 1577, and two small books of verse in 1587, all in Latin – this manifesto of 'the New Poet' established lyric not only as a fit 'kind' for the dignity of print, but for the ennobling of the language, itself a public service.

As a means of self-advancement, poetry was familiar enough, but by the second half of Elizabeth's reign the conventions governing it were both archaic and confused. In English, grave and moral works were allowed for publication, such as *The Mirror for Magistrates* of that supple courtier, Thomas Sackville, who crowned a successful career by achieving an earldom. The general public could not but be edified by being permitted to share advice on government intended for high quarters. Yet the forward youth in search of honour, who employed lyric as an adjunct to social manoeuvres in the ceremonious but chancy game for preferment, would have offended against decorum by publishing his 'toys', made to be slipped into a pocket or dropped through a window. These were but 'the perfume and suppliance of a minute'; and *sprezzatura* or courtly nonchalance forbade the author to claim them even by a signature. An equal mixture of snobbery and modesty dictated that the more truly intimate and fitted to the ear of greatness, the more exclusively such toys should be kept close. The Queen visited at Woodstock in September 1575 Sir Henry Lee, the chief master of ceremonious behaviour, when some of the devices presented to her were written in Italian and in such riddling terms as she alone might comprehend.

Elizabeth herself did not patronize poets directly, for it was no part of her role to pay for her own praises; the duty was delegated to her chief courtiers, whose privilege it was to amuse her. Patronage took the form of grants of office or preferment, more often than fees; patronage of letters had evolved as a method by which, in a society increasingly competitive and unstable, the ambitious could buy, or sell, their talents. Multiplication of secular office encouraged hopes; but rewards grew harder to win, and the poets more remote from these they sought to celebrate. That delicacy and tact by which Chaucer had transformed the mourning of John of Gaunt for his dead wife into a love vision of lost happiness depended on a social assurance which few Elizabethan poets could command; for Spenser, the rainbow grief of the *Death of the Duchess* was replaced by pompous mourning plumes. The total failure of his adaptation *Daphnaida* enhances by contrast his November Eglogue: but even this is a funeral hymn and no more:

> Dido my dear, alas! is dead,
> Dead, and lyeth wrapt in lead:
>   O heavy hearse!
> Let streaming tears be poured out in store.
>   O careful verse!

In *The Shepheardes Calender* Spenser had elsewhere taken Chaucer as his model, but in Chaucer's day the courtly poet made his offering to lord or lady as an act of personal service; the accepted 'man' found grace through his wit by getting up in a little pulpit and reading his verses. In that smaller world, intimate personal feelings were readily transformed into a public guise; the poet was not selling his praises, for he held a place in his lord's train, shared the fortunes of a great household, ate the common bread. Even the mendicant's role was still a dignified one, and to beg an alms involved no social inferiority. But by the early sixteenth century Dunbar was dramatizing his own poverty and want, his grey hair; begging for office had become direct and insistent. Even clowning and licensed jesting sounded a new note of urgency.

Sidney, Ralegh, and other poets of the inner circle at Elizabeth's court could use accents at once easy, intimate and assured; this gave them that superiority which early writers on verse acknowledged.[1] For the crowd of outsiders who sought the patronage of the inner circle, bringing their offering as auxiliaries to their lords, an unwary or ill-timed effort might spell ruin; the plea for recognition, a hopeful assault of flattery conjoined with modest self-display, demanded perfect tact and perfect timing.

The greatest of Elizabeth's subjects, the Earl of Leicester, supported useful books on medicine, history, and rhetoric, or on such practical subjects as horsemanship or chess. Except when their services were required for his own princely pleasures, he was not given to the patronage of poets; but Philip Sidney was his nephew, and Edward Dyer, after 1567, his secretary. The characteristic hope of a literary man in the second half of the sixteenth century was to obtain some office of the crown, or to become a great man's secretary, and possibly, most exciting of all for a scholar, to be sent on a mission abroad in his lord's service. The secretary, half servant, half counsellor, held an office requiring a knowledge of foreign tongues and of oratory. Gentlemen might expect enlargement of their merits from a ready pen; young students of the university might hope also to rise; but first they must learn to advertise themselves.

In his pursuit of Fame, Spenser had Harvey as guide, and Gascoigne as precedent in poetry. Gascoigne in the mid-seventies tried publishing love lyric, satires, entertainments, moral plays

> To hear it said, There goes the Man that writes so well.

Though A Hundred Sundry Flowers (1573) maintained a gentlemanly anonymity, it was expected to be recognized as his. The heroine of the main tale, like Spenser's Rosalind, is placed in a conventional north-country castle; and the audience invited to a pretty guessing-game. The form is that of easy social intercourse, and the little group of three courtly friends whose epistles explain the publication (also announcing further works by their talented companion) appear, as the printer drily comments, to be of one assent in having it printed.[2]

Three years later Gascoigne republished the same work with an entirely new orientation; he dropped the gentlemanly negligence and ungentlemanly betrayal of a woman's favours for a simple, rude but moral role. Even though sponsored, printing had been a faux pas. He also won the chance to present work directly to the Queen, and as an example of his capacities proffered a Hermit's Tale in four different languages, with a sonnet which declared his object quite plainly:

> Then peerless Prince, employ this willing man
> In your affairs, to do the best he can.

Finally, lowering his sights, he made a bid for the favour of Leicester's opponent, his old patron Lord Grey de Wilton, with a moral
satire, *The Steel Glass*. His tale of his own life ends with an allegory
at once pathetic and absurd in which he sees himself as the silenced
singer, born of Plain Dealing and Simplicity, whose tongue was cut
out with the Razor of Restraint. This example counted with Gabriel
Harvey as appears by the *Letter Book*, where a projected Pamphlet
of extemporal Verses upon Gascoigne's death (of course to have been
published by a friend) represents Harvey's first excursion into
English verse.

Gascoigne died on 7 October 1577; by which time Harvey and
Spenser had been some seven years acquainted. Spenser's talents had
already carried him far, for socially his origin was among the
humblest of Elizabethan poets. The son of a journeyman clothmaker,
born in Smithfield and educated as a 'poor boy' at the Merchant
Taylors' school, he proved so apt that when, by 1569, he was ready
to proceed to Pembroke Hall as a sizar (or poor scholar with
servant's duties) he had already translated for publication a small
group of emblematic poems. He ventured to claim kinship with the
Spensers who were minor gentry in East Lancashire; and a Lancashire family, the Nowells, supported him. After graduating, he
could write himself gentleman whatever his father had been; though
defeated in a contest for college fellowships by his schoolmate
Lancelot Andrewes. In 1578 Young, Master of his college, became
Bishop of Rochester, and selected Edmund Spenser for secretary. The
new Master, William Fulke, was chaplain to the Earl of Leicester,
and it was perhaps through Fulke that in 1579 Spenser found himself
promoted as some kind of clerk or secretary in the vast rambling
household of Leicester, who in addition to servants was allowed the
princely retinue of one hundred retainers. Gabriel Harvey was
elected a Fellow of Pembroke a year after Spenser went up as sizar; he
was the son of a prosperous tradesman, and already of some repute
in the little worlds of Cambridge and Saffron Walden. Harvey's
ambition to rise to public office through scholarly eminence would
be encouraged by his famous fellow townsman the Secretary of State,
Sir Thomas Smith,[3] but it would appear that as means to this end, he
became very early convinced of the value of publication.

According to Nashe, this was done at his own expense. Whether
calling on the Nine Muses to lament Smith or lavishly proclaiming
his own presentation to the Queen, Harvey's works show always a
direct and undisguised design to magnify himself as the witty,
familiar, stately, accomplished orator. In Latin he had a singular gift
for saying very little at inordinate length; in English, copious verbos-
ity came as readily. His writings serve to show that the problems of

language with which poets and orators contended were not only those of vocabulary and construction, metre and image; they were even more basically, the social problems of tone and address. In his person, Harvey poses the dilemma of his age; social flux and insecurity were reflected in language to such an extent that the ability to communicate could be diminished, rather than increased, by theoretical attempts to grapple with it. (It is the dilemma of Shakespeare's Brutus.) In the first of his many Cambridge quarrels, one of the fellows of his College 'unjustly and scornfully laid in my dish'

> my common behaviour, that I was not familiar like a fellow, and that I did disdain every man's company. To this, I made him answer, that I was afeared lest over much familiarity had marred all: and therefore, where as I was wont to be as familiar, and as sociable, and as good a fellow too, as any, seeing some to be somewhat far of, and other not to like so well of it, as it was meant, I was constrained to withdraw myself somewhat the more, although not greatly neither, out of often and continual company.

Harvey's writings can still provoke rage after nearly four hundred years; his insults are as insufferable now as when his exultant contempt first penned them. The orator's very considerable powers seem involuntarily geared to produce negative feelings, in which they are singularly efficient. His affectionate jocularity is equally repulsive, as when he writes to Spenser with clamorous exuberance:

> *Liberalissimo Signor Immerito*, in good sooth my poor Storehouse will presently afford me nothing, either to recompence or countervaile your gentle Mastership's long, large, lavish, luxurious, laxative letters withal, (now, a God's name, when did I ever in my life hunt the letter before?).

Spenser's first reactions to Harvey's proferred friendship appear in the January Eglogue.

> It is not Hobbinol wherefore I plain,
> Albe my love he seek with daily suit:
> His clownish gifts and courtesies I disdain,
> His kids, his cracknels and his early fruit.
>   Ah, foolish Hobbinol! thy gifts bin vain;
>   Colin them gives to Rosalind again

'The fool hideth his Talent' is one of Harvey's jottings; and 'gallant audacity is never out of countenance'. Oratory in its most modern, practical, Ramist form, was the study he selected as the readiest way to 'actual commodity and preferment'; in 1574–5 he was appointed Praelector in Rhetoric and among the 'suavissimi adolescentes atque bellissimi pueri' to whom he addressed his orations, Spenser would still have been present. Harvey hastened to display his talent in the full glory of print. The treatises appeared in 1577, in which year he lost by death the support of Sir Thomas Smith (with whom Harvey is even reputed to have claimed kinship; though the humble letters which survive, including one in which he begs Lady Smith to take his sister as a sewing maid, make no such pretence). The Latin elegy on Smith, which presents the Nine Muses lamenting 'in a row' is perhaps too common in form to have influenced Spenser's 'Tears of the Muses'; but the *Gratulationes Valdensium* with which Harvey celebrated the greatest social triumph of his career, his meeting with the Queen at Audley End on 26 July 1578, is an emblematic work that belongs with the heraldic, iconographic mingling of verse and pictorial art traditional at court and which became increasingly significant to Spenser. In one poem, supposed to be on a picture of Leicester, the Earl is provided by Harvey with three mothers, Venus, Charis, and Pallas, as well as three fathers, Apollo, Mercury, and Pluto, doubling Spenser's 'dreadful blunder' (noted by C. S. Lewis) in the 'Hymn of Love', when he gave Love three parents. Leicester presented Harvey to the Queen as one whom he intended to send abroad in his service; Elizabeth gave Harvey her hand to kiss, and observed that he already looked more like an Italian in countenance than an Englishman. Utterly intoxicated by this notice, Harvey, who had spent vast sums upon a gorgeous suit of apparel, not only wrote two long poems, one upon the kiss and one upon his Italian visage, but according to his enemies affected for some time an Italian accent and manner. He does not seem to have been depressed by the Queen's pleading fatigue and retiring before the disputation 'Whether a Prince should prefer Clemency to Severity?' where he opposed the Public Orator, Fleming of King's. Lord Burleigh, the Chancellor, presided, vainly demanding brevity of the speakers; after three hours, he cut them short somewhere near midnight. The scholars, cheered with beer and wine bestowed on them by the courtiers, made their way home by moonlight; for beds in Saffron Walden were not to be had.

This was Malvolio's little moment of glory. Harvey again rushed into print with all the epigrams which had been prepared by visiting scholars; the symbolic discursions on their coats of arms which, together with pairs of gloves of carefully graduated costliness, had been bestowed on leading courtiers; above all his own leading part in the proceedings, the first of his four 'books' being dedicated to the Queen.

Anticlimax followed in a month. Even an appeal from Leicester, through their Master, would not move the Fellows of Pembroke to renew Harvey's fellowship. Speedily claiming kinship with the time-serving Henry Harvey who was Master of Trinity Hall, Gabriel transferred himself in December 1578 to that society and to the study of law – the road by which Sir Thomas Smith had risen to be an Ambassador and Secretary of State. He wrote a 'pleasurable and moral politic natural mixt device' in English verse, which he hoped to present to Leicester.

Next spring he began, as it would seem, to angle for the post of Public Orator himself and to urge publication upon Spenser. The Epistle to Harvey prefixed to *The Shepheardes Calender* is dated 10 April 1579; and in his *Letter Book* Harvey has two drafts of a letter of coy reproach addressed to Spenser, protesting against the surreptitious publication of Harvey's own English poems, one dated summer 1579. In fullness of fancy, he imagines his work hawked at Stourbridge or Bartholomew Fair – publicity at the lowest social level.

> With, what lack ye, Gentleman? I pray you will you see any freshe new books? Look, I beseech you, for your love and buy for your money. Let me borrow an old cracked groat of your purse for this same span new pamphlet. I wisse he is a University man that made it and yea highly commended unto me for a great scholar. . . . What? Will iii.d fetch it?

He accuses his friend of wishing shortly to send him those other servants of Leicester, the common players

> for some new devised interlude or some malconceived comedy fit for the Theatre or some other painted stage where thou and thy lively copesmates in London may laugh their mouths and bellies full for pence or two pence apiece. By cause per-adventure thou imaginest Unico Aretino and the pleasurable Cardinal Bibiena that way especially attained to be so singularly famous.

The last sentence is worth pausing upon. Harvey was an earnest student of Italian affairs; in his rhetorical treatises he shows a fierce jealousy of the Italians' superior reputation for learning. Among Italian writers Aretine, whom he mentions frequently, attained to considerable ascendancy by his literary invective, which he wielded as a political instrument of coercion among the petty Italian princes of his day. Harvey, and some of the later satirists, especially Marston, who was Italian by his mother's side, may have dreamed that they could storm the citadel through satire, more surely than by courting favour through flattery; and if so, the disaster which overtook Spenser would prove only too clearly that there was no room in English political life for such attempts.

Meanwhile Spenser himself was resisting the publication or 'uttering' of his work. On 15 October 1579 he wrote to Harvey from Leicester House, with something not unlike Harvey's social perplexity, but inclining to the pure courtly view

> I was minded for awhile to have intermitted the uttering of my writings: lest by overmuch cloying their noble ears I should gather a contempt of

> myself, or else seem rather for gain and commodity to do it, for some sweetness that I have already tasted. Then also me seemeth the work too base for his excellent Lordship, being made in honour of a private Personage unknown, which of some ill-willers might be upbraided, not to be so worthy, as you know she is; or the matter not so weighty, that it should be offered to so weighty a personage: or the like. The self former Title still liketh me well enough, and your fine addition no less.

In spite of these modest doubts, he is ready to submit to Harvey's judgment and does not feel any doubt at all in urging Harvey to print 'when occasion is so fairly offered of Estimation and Preferment. For whiles the iron is hot, it is good striking'.

On other matters he touches with the lofty tone of the insider, and in sharp contrast to the loquacity of his correspondent:

> Your desire to hear my late being with Her Majesty, must die in itself. As for the two worthy gentlemen, Master Sidney and Master Dyer, they have me, I thank them, in some use of familiarity . . . New books I hear of none but only of one, that writing a certain Book called *The School of Abuse*, and dedicating it to Master Sidney, was for his labour scorned; if at least it be in the goodness of that nature to scorn. Such folly is it, not to regard aforehand the inclination and quality of him to whom we dedicate our books. Such might I happily incur, entituling *My Slumber* and the other pamphlets, unto his honor. I meant them rather to Master Dyer.

Leicester ('His Honor' or 'His Lordship') is proposing to send Spenser to France in his service; and so he composes an elaborate Latin farewell to Harvey, who accepts it as a 'goodly brave younkerly piece of work' but doubts the imminence of the journey. The news from France was ill for Leicester. Late in 1579 Alençon had renewed his suit to the Queen; and to facilitate matters the French Ambassador had betrayed to her Leicester's secret marriage with the Countess of Essex, as a result of which he was disgraced. In January 1579/80 Philip Sidney protested to the Queen against the French match, then prudently retired to the country.

At this point *The Shepheardes Calender*, now dedicated to the same Sidney and of course meant only for his private solace, was allowed by the good offices of an anonymous editor, and with the addition of a handsome 'puff collateral' for Gabriel Harvey, to escape into print. Its range and variety, from the moral to the amatory, and from obvious archbishops ('Algrind') to delicious 'you-know-who's' must have been irresistible; the New Poet achieved fame, and before many years were passed, was quoted (under his proper name) by Abraham Fraunce as a model of rhetoric, and compared to Virgil by William Webbe.

The scene is set in Kent, where Spenser himself had lived in the service of the Bishop of Rochester (who appears in the September Eglogue) – although it was to Wilton and not to Kentish Penshurst that Sidney had now withdrawn. The 'general drift and purpose', in spite of the author's 'labouring to conceal it', would seem to be the pursuit of honour, surveyed from what was traditionally the lowliest of all occupations.[4] Love is given a share of the interest, but no one could have called this a posy of 'flowers', for half the Eglogues are 'grave and moral'. In the October Eglogue, the difficulties of a poet are frankly set forth.

Paradoxically, Eglogues, the recognized 'kind' of poetry for beginners – recalling many learned authors, ancient and modern, but also experimenting in the revival of 'old words' from country speech – are proffered to Sidney, 'most worthy of all titles both of learning and chivalry'. Although offerings made as an act of service could not be anonymous, the author, modestly signing himself Immerito, addresses his 'book' as 'a child whose father is unkenned' and who was 'base begot with blame'; nevertheless he promises 'I will send more after thee'.

The collection was given the name of a well-known popular manual, and in its presentation to the public commended to a known master of rhetoric, 'the most excellent and learned both orator and poet, Gabriel Harvey', with a justification of the new principles of composition and a full apparatus of glossary and synopsis, such as was usually granted only to works of classical standing. Harvey is begged publicly to defend the work against Envy, that is sure to be set afire 'with the sparks of his kindled glory'. A stimulating mixture of humility and audacity, lowly design and high claim is most dexterously blended. The excuse for publishing is that Immerito is 'estranged', that is, gone abroad; and while his hatred of 'promulgation' is stressed, it is hoped that this venture may lead him to print other excellent works which sleep in silence. (This, Immerito had already planned to do.)

Finally in a judiciously placed postscript, Harvey himself is urged to pluck out of darkness those so many excellent English poems of his which lie hid, that they may obtain equal fame with his published Latin works 'which in my opinion, both for invention and elocution, are very superexcellent'. The 'unfriendly friend' who delivered the work to the public had of course to be anonymous; and so the provider of notes and Epistle signs himself E. K. Whether E. K. were a pupil of Harvey or a man of straw[5] (his voice often sounds like Harvey's filled with Spenser's information) the printing of the work, as distinct from its composition and presentation to Sidney, would seem to be initiated by the older man, the result of his firm belief in his novel and experimental method of using the common press to proclaim his own and Spenser's learning and their familiarity with the great.

There can be no doubt, however, about the *Three Letters*, (and *Two Other Letters*) which rapidly followed upon *The Shepheardes Calender*, for Harvey was later to admit the charge that he published them as part of his campaign for advancement. 'The New Poet' at first was allowed one brief letter, chiefly for purpose of advertisement: it was afterwards implied that he did not actually write it.

> Signor Immerito was counterfeitly brought in to play a part in his Enterlude of Epistles that was hissed at, thinking his very name (as the name of Ned Allen on the stage) was able to make an ill matter good.

So Nashe; who especially twits Harvey with the puff, a sanctimonious document, 'by a well willer of the two authors' signed 'Your, and their, unfeigned friend in the Lord':

> For an author to renounce his Christendom, to write in his own commendation, to refuse the name his Godfathers and Godmothers gave him in baptism and call himself a well-willer to both the writers; when he is the only writer himself; with what face do you think he can answer it at the day of judgment?

These letters offer aspiring wits and envious academics the entry to a dazzling little coterie, rather like the modern world of the little magazines. The 'Areopagus' at Leicester House gives judgment on the new versifying; the Cambridge scholar drafts his *Anticosmopolita*, and provides not only views on poetry but a 'pleasant and pithy familiar discourse of the Earthquake in April last' backdated to give an air of spontaneity, and cast in the form of a dialogue with two female stooges, Mistress Inquisitiva and Madame Incredula. Of course this display of learning is to be shown only to the two gentlemen 'you wot of'. Immerito, it is needless to say, rashly lent it to others, while the writer can innocently hope that 'some learned and well advised University man' would undertake to write upon the topic. The letter of the anonymous well-willer (dated 19 June 1580) is devoted to puffing the really remarkable talents of 'Mr. H.' (by the second instalment 'of Trinity Hall', while 'Immerito' becomes 'Edmundus').

> Shew me, or Immerito, two English letters in print, in all points equal . . . two of the rarest and finest treatises, as well for ingenious devising, as also for significant uttering and cleanly conveying of his matter that ever I read in this tongue; and I heartily thank God for bestowing on us such proper and able men with their pen . . .

Harvey having been worsted in the tussle for the Orator's office, the letter on the earthquake concludes with a verbal convulsion intended to engulf the university. An unlucky reference to 'your old Controller' aimed at his chief enemy, Dr Perne, was taken by the Controller of the Queen's Household as a personal attack, and a satirical poem on the Italianate Englishman, a role Harvey had by now discarded, was by the malicious assistance of John Lyly fastened on the Earl of Oxford. Harvey's efforts, as usual, recoiled sharply upon himself.

So, it would seem, and almost at the same moment, did Spenser's. In defence of his lord, he committed the incredible political folly of attacking Burghley (who favoured the French match) and the Duke of Alençon, in 'Mother Hubbard's Tale'. Again a 'rough' satire, like the more moral parts of *The Shepheardes Calender*, and Gascoigne's *Steel Glass*, it was clearly meant for backstairs circulation only, but the fact that it came from Leicester House would be enough. The Earl was not above exposing his favourite nephew as a catspaw to the displeasure of the Queen, and evidently possessed the nicest sense of what she would accept.

Gascoigne's play of Zabeta had been cut out from the princely pleasures of Kenilworth because it gave too frank expression to hopes on the question of the royal marriage. Leicester could not be expected to tolerate a work which might have been interpreted as showing the Queen as the slumbering custodian of royal prerogative, for Elizabeth would certainly have taken steps to show that she was awake. In *The Shepheardes Calender*, along with the magnificent tribute of the April Eglogue, the 'New Poet' in his July Eglogue had already shown the Archbishop (like another Aeschylus) brained by a shell-fish, dropped on his bald head by an eagle. The eagle was King of the Birds, and who was it that had disgraced Grindal? . . . Had either of the fables been read in this literal sense by the royal lady, it seems improbable that her reign would have been adorned by any other works from Spenser's pen. Action was called for; and it was decisive.

It is perhaps a sign of the unexpectedness of the blow that Harvey's draft dedication for Spenser's 'unauthorized' publication of Harvey's English works should bear the date 1 August 1580 – less than a fortnight before Spenser, who like Gascoigne before him had transferred from Leicester to Lord Grey de Wilton, set foot on Irish soil. He had been sent abroad on a mission at last; but instead of tasting the learning and wit of France and Italy, buried in a kind of Elizabethan Siberia. The Razor of Restraint silenced another child of Simplicity and Plain Dealing, this time for a full ten years.

Spenser's apology and justification survive in the poem *Virgil's Gnat*, with its dedicatory sonnet to Leicester.

> Wrong'd yet not daring to express my pain,
> To you (great Lord) the causer of my care,

In cloudy tears my case I thus complain
Unto yourself, that only privy are . . .

In this 'visionary' work, flowery meads and happy ease are invaded by a terrifying Serpent; and in the Gnat's complaint, all the pains of hell and the afterlife depicted.

The fall must have felt most steep and grievous, as Spenser had been withholding some of his works from print out of a sense of decorum. In the exuberant letter of April 1580 he described his plans for *Epithalamium Thamesis*; he had finished his *Dreams* and *Dying Pelican* and begun his *Faerie Queene*; in the usual tell-tale postcript he adds that his real hopes lie in majestic Latin praises of Leicester's family:

> I take best my Dreams should come forth alone, being grown by means of the gloss (running continually in manner of a paraphrase) full as great as my *Calendar* . . . Of my *Stemmata Dudleiana*, and especially of the sundry Apostrophes therein, addressed you know to whom, must more advisement be had, than so lightly to send them abroad . . .

To which Master H. replies that there is little hope to go forward in poetry 'unless ye might make account of some certain ordinary wages, or at the least wise have meat and drink for your days works . . . For I pray now, what saith Master Cuddie, alias you know who, in the tenth Aeglogue of the foresaid famous new Calendar?' Yet after quoting two verses, it is playfully allowed that vulgar sales may purchase gentility:

> Master Colin Clout is not everybody . . . yet he peradventure by means of her [Poetry's] special favour and some personal privilege may happily live by dying Pellicans, and purchase great lands and lordships, with the money which his Calendar and Dreams have and will afford him.

It was clearly not on the published but the unpublished works that Spenser relied; Harvey had not really converted him completely. He had before him the example of Leicester's chief secretary, Edward Dyer, nine years his senior, and so little given to publishing that only half a dozen lyrics have survived. But Dyer had a surer hand, and kept to the realm of delicate compliment. When in disgrace with Elizabeth he concealed himself in an oak tree, and as she passed, touched his lute, on which he played masterly, and warbled out a strain of brief melodious despair. This melted the lady, as no lengthy complaint from Virgil, however dexterously adapted, could melt Spenser's offended lord. The courtly method was open only to courtiers: Dyer, a gentleman's heir, still awaited substantial reward.

Yet in 'Virgil's Gnat' Spenser discovered what poetry could do for himself. He learnt to live in a world of imaginative vision, enlarging its scope beyond the turning seasons, as wild Irish landscape became the background for strange adventures performed in honour of a remote and distant Gloriana. The blow had probably fallen, when in *Two Letters* Harvey gave a more equal share to his friend Immerito, whose name was no longer used as a mere selling device. Soon Harvey was getting more publicity than he relished; for one of his enemies wrote the Latin comedy *Pedantius*, in which he was cruelly caricatured, his very clothes purloined to add to the sharpness of the jest, his manners mimicked and his Latin phrases mauled.

Five years later, new-elected Master of Trinity Hall, in spite of desperate lobbying he found himself dexterously displaced by a Cambridge cabal, using the royal mandate to install their man in his place. Spenser administered consolation, writing loyally from 'Dublin this 18 of July 1586' as 'your devoted friend during life' a sonnet which Harvey was later himself to publish in his own commendation.

> Harvey, the happy above happiest men
> I read; that sitting like a looker-on
> Of this world's stage, dost note with critic pen,
> The sharp dislikes of each condition;
> And as one careless of suspicion,
> Ne fawnest for the favour of the great,
> Ne fearest foolish reprehension
> Of faulty men, which danger to thee threat:
> But freely dost, of what thee list, entreat,
> Like a great lord of peerless Liberty;
> Lifting the good up to high Honour's seat,
> And the Evil damning evermore to die:
> For Life and Death is in thy doomful writing!
> So thy renown lives ever by enditing.

Such was Spenser's augmented vision of what a scholar's life might be; it proclaims, unconsciously perhaps, the consolation which he himself had found. Harvey could never have 'learnt a style from a despair' as Spenser had done. This praise of retired life is entirely public in its address. Emancipated from court and coteries, Spenser had ceased to write for a lord; he now was writing for himself and posterity: Fame was the spur. He spoke with authority, an authority acquired at cost not of learning but of experience. For when he returned in 1590, in the train of Ralegh, he returned as the acknowledged author not only of *The Shepheardes Calender*, 'a masterpiece, if any', but as one who could dedicate his epic to the Queen herself, and claim the rare privilege of a direct reward. Other small early poems appeared in print after the success of *The Faerie Queene*, among them the fatal 'Mother Hubbard's Tale'. This was over-confidence; it was suppressed, but not before, with a glow of fiery insistence, Spenser had cursed the desperate game of court favour:

> Most miserable man, whom wicked fate
> Hath brought to court to sue for hadywist,
> That few hath found, and many one hath missed:
> Full little knowest thou, that hast not tried
> What hell it is, in suing long to bide:
> To lose good days, that might to better spent,
> To wait long nights in pensive discontent:
> To speed today, to be put back tomorrow,
> To feed on hope, to pine with fear and sorrow:
> To have thy prince's grace, yet want her peers':
> To have thy asking, yet wait many years:
> To fret thy soul with crosses and with cares:
> To eat thy heart with comfortless despairs:
> To fawn, to crouch, to wait, to ride, to run,
> To spend, to give, to want, to be undone . . .
> That curse God send unto mine enemy.

He mourned the death of Leicester, and was praised by John Florio for being 'so thankful without hope of reward'. 'The Ruins of Time' perhaps incorporates some of *Stemmata Dudleiana* transposed into English, but from celebration the accent is turned to lament.

> I saw him die, I saw him die, as one
> Of the mean people and brought forth on bier . . .

There is still a little bitterness for the great man's misplaced trust in 'painted faces with smooth flattering' and in 'the courting masker louting low':

> Spite bites the dead, that living never bayed.
> He now is gone, the while the Fox is crept
> Into the hole, the which the Badger swept.[6]

On a courtly topic his uncertainty returned, and Spenser writes some very bad verse. Noble lines are mixed with a dull catalogue of Leicester's brother, sister-in-law and sister-in-law's father. Even the first tribute to Philip Sidney has but one fit phrase:

> Most gentle spirit, breathed from above . . .

Then suddenly, a whole series of emblems of mutability are presented, in tragic pageants, to the memory of 'Philisides'. Grief for Leicester was mixed with the bitterness of worldly disillusion; the despair for Sidney could be expressed only in heroic symbols, impersonal visions. From the time when, as a schoolboy, he had translated sonnets for *The Theatre of Worldlings*, to his latest poetry, Spenser invested traditional objects with symbolic power – most often, as here, with alternate colouring of grief and joy, festivity and lament. In many of his shorter poems, these two moods alternate; the most powerful alternation is presented in 'Colin Clout's Come Home Again', where the returned exile sets down, in a manner he might have learnt in youth, a 'reconciliation of contraries'. It may seem absurd to compare this splendid maturity with Harvey's painful drivel, but the structural principle is that of *The Scholar's Love* – a 'blazon' followed by a 'recantation' or 'correction'. However far Spenser developed as a poet, there was a sense in which he remained bound to the formative, shattering experience of his twenties. The poem begins with Hobbinol asking Colin for his story and ends with the praise of love and of a still unrelenting Rosalind; and though it may be that after twelve years these names shadow new incarnations of love and friendship, yet the shepherd Colin keeps his old blend of modesty and audacity. Festal and melancholy colourings are in turn thrown over the landscape, as the song renders first a mood of bedazzlement at courtly richness, splendour, fertility, magnificently summed in praises of Elizabeth:

> Her words were like a stream of honey fleeting
> The which doth softly trickle from the hive,
> Able to melt the hearer's heart unweeting,
> And eke to make the dead again alive.
> Her deeds were like great clusters of ripe grapes,
> Which load the branches of the fruitful vine . . .

then sharply reverts to the familiar cut-throat competition for favour:

> Where each one seeks with malice, and with strife
> To thrust down other into foul disgrace,
> Himself to raise; and he doth soonest rise
> That best can handle his deceitful wit
> In subtlest shifts and finest slights devise,
> Either by slandering his well deemed name,
> Through leesings lewd and feigned forgery,
> Or else by breeding him some blot of blame,
> By creeping close into his secresy:
> To which him needs a guileful hollow heart,
> Masked with fair dissembling courtesy.

All Arts of the Schools are out of place, and those who profess them 'but instruments of others' gain'. The court is judged all the more firmly because the judgment is neither 'moral' nor 'satyrical' but given as a piece of observation, coolly drawn by a stranger, a Gulliver in Lilliput. Although the poem was sent to Sir Walter Ralegh, it is a vision fashioned for Spenser's self; he maintained his own blend of the world without and the world within, yet his vision was still social rather than purely personal. He never became the poet of intimate relationships. *Amoretti* is a competent exercise, 'Epithalamion' a festal triumph. His mood, now of brilliance and now of shadow, threw bright gleams or drab lowerings upon a landscape sometimes filled with gay processions, sometimes desolate and forlorn, reflecting a deep and inward, though a generalized response to the frustrations and uncertainties of his whole life. But he had gained absolute assurance of tone, and a vantage point from which he could address rivals like Ralegh and Essex with equal dignity.

In 'Prothalamion' the latest Vision of London is an exile's, built upon an accepted bitterness of rejection:

> . . . I (whom sullen care
> Through discontent of my long fruitless stay
> In Prince's courts and expectation vain
>
> Of idle hopes, which still do fly away
> Like empty shadows, did afflict my brain)
> Walked forth to ease my pain
> Along the shore of silver streaming Thames . . .
>
> But ah! here fits not well
> Old woes, but joys to tell
>   Against the bridal day, which is not long:
>   Sweet Thames! run softly, till I end my song.

The melancholy figure who introduces this 'spousal verse' confers more than a tonal contrast as he submerges private grief in the triumph of two young students, descending to meet their brides from the water gate of the great house where Spenser himself had spent his most hopeful years, and where now Leicester's stepson, Essex, held court. The swans of 'Prothalamion' revive perhaps something of the early lost 'Epithalamion Thamesis', and certainly the vision of Leicester's lost heir, Philip Sidney:

> Upon that famous River's further shore,
> There stood a snowy Swan of heavenly hue,
> And gentle kind as ever fowl afore;
> A fairer one in all the goodly crew
> Of white Strimonian brood might no man view.

The submerged image of the swan singing at his death lies drowned beneath the murmuring of the liquid Thames, yet the end of the poet's song is hinted in that dark momentary shadow at its beginning; this was indeed to prove his latest verse. The kind of masque or procession which it celebrates was given dramatic form in Jonson's *Hymenaei*, with its celebration of Concord; but in Spenser, where the full experience is transmitted by rhythm rather than statement, it remains more accessible to the present age.

Spenser is again celebrating a return to 'merry London, my most kindly nurse' and need not be grudged his present claim to alliance with the Spencers of Althorp – a great house indeed, though hardly, as he boasts, of 'ancient fame', being but recently risen from simple graziers to the point where they could annex the glories of the medieval Despencers. This last relic of vanity fits in well enough with the worldly splendour of 'Prothalamion'; the Spencers were even disposed to admit 'affinity' – to the extent at least of one feminine member of the house, Lady Strange.

His old friend Harvey too clung to his dreams. He, who had thought of gaining public eminence by his pen, was sunk and overwhelmed, in a seven-years' cheap pamphlet war with young Tom Nashe. 'Saint Fame for me, and thus I run upon him!' cried his trumpet-tongued adversary. As time progressed, he became ever angrier and loftier, and was always promising a crushing reply from a certain noble gentlewoman, whose style, when quoted by him, was peculiar in the extreme.[7] What finally emerged instead was a stream of the coarsest obscenities, put into the mouth of a college servant; for Nashe's cool assurance and quickness left Harvey helpless as a Spanish galleon before an English man-o'-war. At this point, the bishops Whitgift and Bancroft ordered that 'all Nashe's books and Dr Harvey's books be taken, wheresoever they may be found, and that none of their books be ever printed hereafter'. But this final humiliation did not come to Harvey till June 1599, when Spenser had lain for nearly six months in his grave at Westminster.

The story of Spenser's bid for Fame is a happier one than those of most Elizabethan poets. 'Unhappy Mr. Gascoigne' had died unsatisfied: Dyer gained no office, sold his patrimony and ended overwhelmed in debt: Lyly, after some years of glittering fame and others of diminishing hope, finally wrote to the Queen:

Thirteen years your Highness' servant; but yet nothing.
Twenty friends, that though they say they will be sure, I find sure to be slow.
A thousand hopes, but all nothing, a hundred promises, but yet nothing.
Thus, casting up the inventory of my friends, hopes, promises and times; the summa totalis amounteth in all to just nothing.

But Lyly had remained at court, to suffer the fate of the butterfly; Spenser had endured the brazen world he depicts in *A Short View of the State of Ireland*. (In many early poets, their prose represents a 'shadow side' – dogmatic and admonitory in Chaucer, harshly efficient and repressive in Spenser.) 'Fame' for him was wedded to

'Eternity'; in the glowing alembic of his verse, he transmuted his brazen world and delivered a golden one.

Notes

1 As Sidney in his *Apology*: 'I have found in divers small learned courtiers a more sound style than in some professors of learning'.

2 See R. M. Adams, 'Master F.J. as original fiction', *PMLA* (1958), 4, for a full discussion of the conventions of the anonymous introduction.

3 Author of *De Republica Anglorum*; the famous Greek scholar, friend of Cheke and Ascham, Regius Professor of Civil Law; he rose to be Secretary of State, Privy Councillor and Ambassador to France. The most notable Elizabethan example of pure scholar turned successful politician.

4 From the Miracle plays onwards, the shepherd was used as a type of humble poverty. At the end of the Parnassus plays, disappointed scholars retire with tarbox and scrip to keep sheep on the hills of Kent.

5 The identity of E.K. has of course been endlessly debated. Harvey was certainly capable of composing an epistle to himself, as his *Letter Book* shows. It seems almost incredible that any third party could bring forward, even to refute, the charge of pederasty, as E.K. does in notes on the January Eclogue. The result was what might be expected; it is rebutted, (and therefore repeated) by William Webbe.

6 A line echoed by Yeats:

> 'No Fox can foul the lair the Badger swept
> (An image out of Spenser and the common tongue).'
> ('The Municipal Gallery Revisited', *Last Poems*)

7 An even more distorted fancy has produced in the *Letter Book* a series of letters purporting to be by Harvey's sister Mercy, repelling the dishonourable advances of a noble lord, culminating in the detection of the correspondence by Harvey himself, who sends a letter of high moral reproof and lofty scorn to the wicked lord. The letters of Mercy are utterly improbable as the actual effusions of a young girl. In *Three Letters* Harvey proudly publishes the schoolboy efforts of his brother John, touched up by himself as he admits; his megalomaniac habits mixing with family loyalty supplied a weakness Nashe exploited to the full.

II

Beasts and Gods: the social purpose of *Venus and Adonis*

The player's challenge

Precisely because it is of a different kind, there has been very little attempt to see *Venus and Adonis* as the work of one whose nature was already subdued, like the dyer's hand, to the popular stage-writings of his day. In this Shakespeare has succeeded in what was surely his initial intention, to make a second reputation for himself. To appear in print was to make a dignified bid for Fame; the author at once achieved recognition and respectful notice, even among those who despised, or affected to despise, the work of the common stages. In a few years the students of St John's College, Cambridge, in the person of Judicio would commend William Shakespeare the poet – 'Who loues not *Adons* loue or *Lucrece* rape?' – while they gave a pulverizing defence of William Shakespeare the playwright to Kempe:

> Few of the university pen plaies well, they smell too much of that writer *Ouid*, and that writer *Metamorphoses*, and talke too much of *Proserpina & Iuppiter*. Why heres our fellow *Shakespeare* put them all downe, I and Ben Ionson too.[1]

This elegant poem, redolent of Ovid, joins Marlowe and Shakespeare; for like *Hero and Leander*, it is witty and challenges abstinence on behalf of the flesh. Both poets had also been joined for rebuke, though each for very different reasons, in a work which appeared a few months before *Venus and Adonis*. Shakespeare's first venture into print, while not a direct reply to Greene's *Groats-worth of Witte*, may be regarded as a response provoked by this piece of vilification. Because I would see Greene's attack as more sustained and even more insulting than it is usually thought, I would suggest it produced a degree of irritation that writing alone could cure.

Shakespeare's intention is signified by the dedication to the Earl of

Southampton, and by the motto. He was dissociating himself from baseness:

Vilia miratur vulgus . . .

is more characteristic of Ben Jonson (who translated it 'Kneel hinds to trash') than of the tolerant Shakespeare; it betrays the spirit in which the work was published. *Venus and Adonis* furnishes a literary equivalent of the application to Herald's College for a coat of arms:

mihi flavus Apollo
Pocula Castalia plena ministret acqua.

The gulf that lay between popular playwriting and courtly poetry may be measured in that scene of *Histriomastix*, where the artisan players presented Troilus boasting to Cressid:

Thy knight his valiant elboe weares,
That When he shakes his furious Speare,
The foe in shivering fearefull sort,
May lay him downe in death to snort.   (ii. i)

They were dismissed in disgrace and an Italian lord observed:

I blush in your behalfes at this base trash;
In honour of our Italy we sport,
As if a Synod of the holly Gods,
Came to tryumph within our Theaters.   (ii. i)

If both Shakespeare's poem and Greene's pamphlet are read, not in terms of their classical background but as pictorial imagery, they seem to me to provide a coherent pattern – a disparagement, or rhetorical invective, against the common player; and a counter-challenge of nobility, by a common player. Greene in scorn affixes the beast's mask upon his enemy: Shakespeare counters this by evoking a goddess, and celebrating the triumphs of the senses and the flesh in divine, human and animal forms.

The antics and the upstart crow

It may be well here to recall a few dates:

3 September 1592: Death of Robert Greene.
20 September 1592: Registration of Greene's *Groats-worth of Witte*.
8 December 1592: Registration of Henry Chettle's *Kind-Harts Dreame*,
    containing an apology for printing the *Groats-worth of Witte*.
18 April 1593: Registration of Shakespeare's *Venus and Adonis*.

To which might be added the conclusion of T. W. Baldwin, based on an examination of the literary sources, that *Venus and Adonis* was written 'most likely just a few weeks or at most months before' registration, and the fact that it was announced in the letter of dedication as Shakespeare's first work in print.[2]

In a passage which ever since the eighteenth century has caused much throwing about of brains, Greene had addressed three gentle-men-playwrights (Marlowe, Nashe, Peele):

> Base minded men all three of you, if by my miserie you be not warnd: for vnto none of you (like mee) sought those burres to cleaue: those Puppets (I meane) that spake from our mouths, those Anticks garnisht in our colours. Is it not strange, that I, to whom they all haue beene beholding: is it not like that you, to whome they all haue beene beholding, shall (were yee in that case as I am now) bee both at once of them forsaken? Yes trust them not: for there is an vpstart Crow, beautified with our feathers, that with his *Tygers hart wrapt in a Players hyde*, supposes he is as well able to bombast out a blanke verse as the best of you: and beeing an absolute *Iohannes fac totum*, is in his owne conceit the onely Shake-scene in a countrey.[3]

Greene puts Shakespeare among the lowest and most scurrilous type of actor, the antic or mome; these grotesque characters with animal heads and bombast figures came into court revels with mops and mows, for dumb shows of detraction and scorn. In the first unbridled Christmas festivities of Elizabeth's reign, cardinals, bishops and abbots appeared at court in the likeness of crows, asses, and wolves; in 1564 Cambridge students pursued the Queen to Hinchingbrooke with a dumb show presenting the imprisoned Catholic prelates – Bonner eating a lamb, and a dog with the Host in his mouth – a dumb show from which the Queen rose and swept out, taking the torch-bearers and leaving the players in darkness and disgrace.[4] Such antics were no longer in favour at court; but they were seen in country merriments and in the afterpieces of the common stages. The players had brought their enemy Gosson on the stage in some such monstrous form. 'We will have, if this fadge not, an antique' (*Love's Labour's Lost*, v. i. 154–5) suggests that even village players rated the form below a show.

In 1570 first appeared *A Marvellous History entitled, Beware the Cat*, a 'Christmas Tale' attributed to William Baldwin. He describes how he had been at Court with Edward Ferrars, King Edward VI's Lord of Misrule, and some others; they lay abed together discussing the play of *Æsop's Crow* which the King's players had been learning, and which Baldwin discommended, saying:

> it was not Commicall to make either speechlesse things to speake: or brutish things to commen resonably. And although in a tale it be suffer-able . . . yet it was vncomely (said I) and without example of any authour

to bring them in liuely personages to speake, doo, reason, and allege
authorities out of authours (ed. 1584, A4⁴⁻ᵛ).

This introduction to a queer, ribald collection of witch stories
about Irish cats – by turns horrific and bawdy, and like the shows at
court, with a strong anti-papal bias – implies that a play of *Æsop's
Crow* first gave speaking parts to antics. It might have been remembered, and thus might have given point to Greene's earlier rebuke to
the actors:

> why *Roscius*, art thou proud with *Esops* Crow, being pranct with the
> glorie of others feathers? of thy selfe thou canst say nothing, and if the
> Cobler hath taught thee to say, *Aue Caesar*, disdain not thy tutor, because
> thou pratest in a Kings chamber: what sentence thou vtterest on the stage,
> flowes from the censure of our wittes.[5]

Whether Greene's upstart crow be, in the literary sense, Æsop's
crow, or as Dover Wilson would have it, Horace's crow,[6] he is
primarily neither, but an antic taught to speak by poets and unnatur-
ally spurning his teachers. Garnished in the 'colours' of Greene's
rhetoric, as in the colours of brilliant playing suits, if his plumes were
pulled, he would appear a mere crow of the old kind. Yet there is one
of these crows who has not only learnt to speak verses but to write
them; with him, the beast form is an inward one, for like all players,
he is treacherous and cruel; by concealing his predatory nature
within, he is transformed from crow to tiger. As an antic took to
speech so a player has now taken to writing; Shakespeare, like the
original crow, violates decorum.

The kind of player Greene suggests is one who had begun as a
tattered, gaudily dressed stroller, with the slipperiness, the capacity
for betrayal, of all wandering tribes – gipsies, fiddlers, minstrels,
tinkers. The disparagement laid on him is akin to that of the
mock-blazon devised for the Duttons when they claimed the
academic title of Comedians:

> Three nettles resplendent, three owles, three swallowes,
> Three mynstrellmen pendent on three payre of gallowes,
> Further sufficiently placed in them
> A knaves head, for a difference from alle honest men.
> The wreathe is a chayne of chaungeable red,
> To shew they ar vayne and fickle of head;
> The creste is a lastrylle whose feathers ar blew,
> In signe that these fydlers will never be trew . . .[7]

Greene's bespattering is of this kind, with bestial comparison, and
social denigration. Its theatrical, not its literary echo, is cruellest.
Three years before the appearance of Greene's *Groats-worth of
Witte*, Martin Marprelate had been brought on the common stages

to be lanced and wormed in the form of an ape; and when the shows were banned, Lyly lamented:

> He shall not bee brought in as whilom he was, and yet verie well, with a cocks combe, an apes face, a wolfs bellie, cats clawes, &c.[8]

Several years after, at the end of *Poetaster*, Jonson showed Tucca gagged and vizarded, Fannius fitted with fool's coxcomb and cap, and in the epilogue proclaimed:

> Blush, folly, blush: here's none that feares
> The wagging of an asses eares,
> Although a wooluish case he weares.
> Detraction is but basenesse varlet;
> And apes are apes, though cloth'd in scarlet.   (v. iii. 626–30)

There were plenty of hybrids as extraordinary as the crow with a tiger's heart. Greene was not writing for scholars; the context evoked a direct visual memory for his readers. Stage pieces would naturally spring to mind, though a Latin phrase might follow for the few.

The structure of Greene's *Groats-worth of Witte*

This passage on Shakespeare, the highest point of Greene's invective, is not detachable from the rest of the pamphlet, in which the poet tells his life-story as the tale of the prodigal Roberto, born in a rich mercantile city [Norwich], disinherited by his father, cheating his brother, and cheated later by a drab. As Roberto sits lamenting under a hedge, he is accosted with smooth and consoling words:

> But if you vouchsafe such simple comforte as my abilitie may yeeld, assure your selfe, that I wil indeuour to doe the best, that either may procure you profite, or bring you pleasure: the rather, for that I suppose you are a scholler, and pittie it is men of learning should liue in lacke.   (p. 33)

The stranger, so civil in his demeanour, turns out to be a player:

> A player, quoth *Roberto*, I tooke you rather for a Gentleman of great liuing, for if by outward habit men should be censured, I tell you, you would bee taken for a substantiall man. So am I where I dwell (quoth the player) reputed able at my proper cost to build a Windmill. What though the world once went hard with me, when I was faine to carry my playing Fardle a footebacke; *Tempora mutantur*, I know you know the meaning of it better than I, but I thus conster it, its otherwise now; for my very share in playing apparell will not be sold for two hundred pounds. Truly (said *Roberto*) tis straunge, that you should so prosper in that vayne practise, for that it seemes to mee your voice is nothing gratious.   (pp. 33–4)

This player with the ungracious voice goes on to say he is famous for acting Delphrigus and the King of the Fairies, that he has thundered in the Twelve Labours of Hercules, and played three scenes of the Devil in *The Highway to Heaven*. Moreover, he is author as well as player – a 'countrey Author' 'passing at a Morrall' who wrote *The Dialogue of Dives*; finally, for seven years he was absolute interpreter of the puppets. His repertoire was on the level of the Antic, though more respectable.

> But now my Almanacke is out of date:
> > *The people make no estimation,*
> > *Of Morrals teaching education.*
> Was not this prettie for a plaine rime extempore? if ye will ye shall haue
> more.   (p. 34)

This caricature of an untrained player-poet, who is none the less wealthy, and can speak ingratiatingly, must not be taken for an individual likeness. For apart from anything else, some of it is stock stuff, borrowed from Nashe's preface to Greene's own *Menaphon*:

> Sundry other sweete gentlemen I know, that haue vaunted their pennes in priuate deuices, and tricked vp a company of taffata fooles with their feathers, whose beauty if our Poets had not peecte with the supply of their periwigs, they might haue antickt it vntill this time vp and downe the Countrey with the King of *Fairies*, and dined euery day at the pease porredge ordinary with *Delphrigus*. But *Tolossa* hath forgot that it was sometime sacked, and beggars that euer they carried their fardels on footback . . .[9]

Nevertheless, there was one especially noted player-poet when Greene was writing; one who according to a later tradition had been a schoolmaster in the country, and therefore might well have been supposed to begin with morals teaching education; this is the player-poet alluded to by name later as a so-called Comedian who is fit only to antic it up and down the country. The player with the ungracious voice might have been recognizable to contemporaries; for it is worth noting that Chettle begins his apology with a tribute to Shakespeare's acting ability ('excellent in the quality he professes'). The kind of play in which this player began is the kind which in Shakespeare's 'lost years', before the arrival of the University Wits, must have provided the repertory of all common players.

Greene used the popular method of detraction, taking a pre-existing formula, and working in an ascription or two which would fit a particular person – a method of denigration by suggestion, still practised, for example, in the speeches of learned counsel or of politicians who know their art. Seaside photographers of the past invited sitters to pose with their heads stuck through a cardboard cutout, so that they appear to be taking part in a comic donkey race or rowing on a choppy sea. So, in this kind of caricature, the personal touch and the public property are conjoined; the individual is dressed in an ass's head or a calf's skin and the joke depends on contrast between the human and the dummy parts. Clowns who sought voluntary ridicule at an Elizabethan fair would compete at the sport of grinning through a horse-collar; here ready-made detraction was clapped on a selected victim.[10]

In the *Groats-worth of Witte* Greene makes two contrasting uses of beast-fables, literary equivalent of the antic show of scorn. The cheating courtesan gives Roberto a 'caveat by the way, which shall be figured in a fable' of the Fox and the Badger, directed against the red-haired fox who was also the red-haired Greene. The whole work ends with a 'conceited fable of that old Comedian Æsop' told by Greene; in this farcical afterpiece to his tragic story, the improvident Poet appears as the Grasshopper, while the provident Ant represents the Player, who refuses succour in time of need:

> Packe hence (quoth he) thou idle lazie worme,
> My house doth harbor no vnthriftie mates:
> Thou scorndst to toile, & now thou feelst the storme,
> And starust for food while I am fed with cates.
> Vse no intreats, I will relentlesse rest,
> For toyling labour hates an idle guest.   (pp. 48–9)

Here is the 'forsaking' and cruelty of which Greene has already complained – and in his letter to his wife, he reveals he was like to have died in the streets.

It is when, in the course of the narrative, Roberto's time for repentance comes that the narration turns into confession, and Greene speakes for the first time in his own person:

> Heere (Gentlemen) breake I off *Robertoes* speach; whose life in most parts agreeing with mine, found one selfe punishment as I haue doone. Heer-after suppose me the saide *Roberto*, and I will goe on with that hee promised...   (p. 39)

Having thrown off the vizard, Greene gives his precepts, and appeals to the gentlemen playwrights; in exactly parallel manner, having presented the unnamed player-poet in the narrative, he then attacks a similar figure, but directly and by name, in the confession. Some link may be supposed between the two. The construction of this pam-phlet is not as haphazard as it at first appears.

Chettle's reply to Greene

In the epistle to the 'Gentlemen readers' prefixed to *Kind-Harts Dreame*, Chettle makes handsome apology to Shakespeare as player, as citizen and as poet:

> my selfe haue seene his demeanor no lesse ciuill than he exelent in the qualitie he professes: Besides, diuers of worship haue reported, his vprightnes of dealing, which argues his honesty, and his facetious grace in writing, that approoues his Art.[11]

Shakespeare is cleared from the imputation of being an antic, or a dishonest skipjack player, and though he has not published, he is allowed by report facetious grace in Art. But against this must be set a tribute to Greene in the body of the work, where his ghost appears to protest against the cruel imputations that are being put about after his death:

> the fifth, a man of indifferent yeares, of face amible, of body well proportioned, his attire after the habite of a schollerlike Gentleman, onely his haire was somewhat long, whome I supposed to be Robert Greene, maister of Artes; of whome (howe euer some suppose themselves iniured) I haue learned to speake, considering he is dead, *nil nisi necessarium*. He was of singuler pleasaunce the verye supporter, and to no mans disgrace bee this intended, *the only Comedian of a vulgar writer in this country* [my italics]. (p. 13)

Kind-Harts Dreame is a reply to the general case against players, a humble plea for the liberty of honest, if lowly, wanderers. The pamphlet consists of five newsletters from five apparitions (including Greene, and Richard Tarlton the clown, who defends harmless pastime) seeking to deliver a 'bill invective against abuses now reigning' to be borne by Piers Penniless' Post to the infernal regions. The fiddler, the juggler, the simple-hearted narrator come from London fairgrounds. There is little chance that William Cuckow or Kind-Hart the toothdrawer could be taken for anyone but themselves; that is perhaps the purpose of the very full description they are given.[12]

That Greene's name is often attached to scurrilous pamphlets and that he appears so often coupled with Tarlton,[13] whose jests were exceptionally bawdy, may appear surprising to anyone who remembers the inoffensiveness of his romance and the delicacy of much of his work: though it should be recalled that Chettle said he had expunged from the *Groats-worth of Witte* a certain accusation against Marlowe, which to publish 'was intollerable'.

The whole chain of scurrilous invective and lachrymose repentance put out under Greene's name shows his sales-value for printers;

in the *Groats-worth of Witte*, from the first appearance of the player
with falsely 'civil demeanour' to the afterpiece of the Ant and the
Grasshopper, Shakespeare might not unjustly consider himself to be
bearing the brunt of a widely-read invective. That the attack cut deep
may be easily supposed. Years later, even Polonius remembered that
'beautified' was a vile word. After extracting an apology from
Chettle, Shakespeare went on to safeguard his reputation with a
work whose elegance and modishness was recognized within the
walls of Greene's own college and university. His 'facetious grace in
writing' was publicly shown by a work of learning (Art). Its un-
abashed celebration of the delights of the flesh gave an answer more
convincing than a directly aimed reply to the terror-stricken repentance of the poor wretch who, by his own confession, had been guilty
of all the faithlessness and promise-breaking with which he charged
the players.

Venus and Adonis

Venus and Adonis, sumptuous and splendidly assured, was designed
not to answer Greene, but to obliterate the impression he had tried to
make. In this it seems to have succeeded. Yet, because Shakespeare
was a player, there remain a few traces in the poem of the very
different Venus he had known upon the common stages – the Venus
of the first actor-playwright, Robert Wilson, a contemporary of
Tarlton. It is a vindication of the goddess, no less than of the player.

   Love appears as a character in each of Wilson's three plays, as well
as in some others which Shakespeare may have known.[14] On the
stage she is more often condemned than praised, especially by
Wilson, who marries her to Dissimulation, and sets her to woo
Contempt. The language of scorn employed by Adonis is mild
compared with that of Contempt, who first seduces Venus from
Mars and then leaves her to lament:

> So flies the murderer from the mangled lims,
> Left limles on the ground by his fell hand.
> So runnes the Tyger from the bloodles pray,
> Which when his fell stomacke is of hunger stancht,
> Thou murdrer, Tyger, glutted with my faire,
> Leaust me forsaken, map of griefe and care.[15]

There may be a faint echo in the final prophecy of Shakespeare's
mourning Venus; a more curious similarity is that Contempt, like
Adonis, is described as being most incongruously smaller than
Venus; if Shakespeare's Venus can tuck Adonis under her arm,

Wilson's Contempt is described as a sort of false Eros, a 'little Goosecap God', a 'little little seeing God'. Greene himself had written a lyric in which Adonis seems almost confused with Eros:

> In *Cypres* sat fayre *Venus* by a Fount,
> Wanton *Adonis* toying on her knee,
> She kist the wag, her darling of accompt,
> The Boie gan blush, which when his louer see,
>   She smild and told him loue might challenge debt,
>   And he was yoong and might be wanton yet.[16]

The climax of Wilson's *The Cobler's Prophecy* is the denunciation of Venus by other gods and her degradation from heavenly rank, since she is known to be but 'Venus alias Lust'; and so is given only 'the detested name of Lust or Strumpet Venus'.

Shakespeare's goddess is admonished by Adonis:

> 'Call it not love, for Love to heaven is fled,
> Since sweating Lust on earth usurp'd his name . . .
> Love comforteth like sunshine after rain,
> But Lust's effect is tempest after sun:
> Love's gentle spring doth always fresh remain,
> Lust's winter comes ere summer half be done;
>   Love surfeits not, Lust like a glutton dies;
>   Love is all truth, Lust full of forged lies.   (793–804)

The same attitude prevailed on the private stage, for in Court plays Venus was in conflict with Diana's nymph, Elizabeth. The comedies of Lyly gave Shakespeare a model, especially for the one which was shortly to follow *Venus and Adonis*, in the winter of 1593–4, *Love's Labour's Lost*.[17] This was eventually published 'as it was presented before her Highness this last Christmas', the first of Shakespeare's plays to achieve this honour. In his poem Shakespeare also addressed himself to the courtly group, Lyly's select audience. Socially Greene and Lyly were poles apart, and to turn from the one to the other was to step from tavern to presence chamber.

Many of Lyly's plays, especially *Midas* and *Campaspe*, are like Ovidian romance in dramatic form, yet they lack its vivid sensuous expansiveness. Lyly's was an artificial world; his 'natural' objects were a collection of rarities brought together by simile. The Venus of Lyly may, like Shakespeare's, fall in love with a fair boy *(Sapho and Phao)*, but she remains a voice only, a speaking part undefined by sympathy, in a series of rhetorical statements:

> O Cupid, thy flames with Psyches were but sparks, and my desires with
> Adonis but dreames, in respecte of these vnacquainted tormentes . . .
> (iv. ii. 14–16)

In *Gallathea* Venus loses Cupid to Diana, and in *Sapho and Phao* to Sapho; in *The Woman in the Moon*, she is shown at her worst, inspiring the heroine with nymphomaniac fury. Venus in Lyly always represents lust; the cool impersonality of his style, no less than the need to consider his royal patroness, would not admit the true goddess. Cupid is a more important figure than Venus for Lyly; desire not passion presides. The fragile elegance of his dialogue combined with an underlying stratum of conventional morality, in spite of its airy mockery and sophistication. Elizabeth, in the person of Sapho, triumphed over Venus:

> Venus, be not chollerick, Cupid is mine, he hath giuen me his Arrowes, and I will giue him a new bowe to shoote in. You are not worthy to be the Ladye of loue, that yeelde so often to the impressions of loue. Immodest Venus, that to satisfie the vnbrideled thoughtes of thy hearte, transgressest so far from the staye of thine honour! . . . Shall I not rule the fansies of men, and leade Venus in chaines like a captiue?   (v. ii. 57–67)

Except by Adonis, Shakespeare's goddess is never condemned in the moralizing manner of Wilson or Lyly. The poem is finely balanced between accepted animalism and a strange pathos. Although at the end she flies away to Patmos, in the poem itself Venus displays all the helpless weakness as well as the beauty of the flesh. She sweats, pants, weeps, swoons – or pretends to swoon[18] – runs like a country lass with no power to save her lover from the boar, though by an instinct of prophecy she foretells his death and the inevitable woes of all who love. She frantically compares herself with the boar; her wooing is paralleled with the hunt. The little hunted hare, the snail who 'shrinks backward in his shelly cave with pain' and the wounded hounds embody more poignant forms of pain and fear than Venus herself. Proud horse and raging boar provide splendid cartoons of lustihood and fury. As he transformed the squalid Venus of the stage, so Shakespeare transformed the grotesque animal forms of his detractor into genuine instinctive creatures, conceived in full naturalistic detail. *Venus and Adonis* is a great work of release, an assertion of natural energies. The artificial beasts of the mime, like the artificial world of Lyly, have been exorcized and left behind; instead, the true animal world – including the human animal – appears, so palpable and so warmly evoked that Shakespeare's contemporaries were quite swept away. Many a Gull besides Gullio was beautified with Shakespeare's feathers:

> Marry I thinke I shall entertaine those verses which run like these:
> > Euen as the sunn with purple-coloured face
> > Had tane his laste leaue on the weeping morne, etc
> O sweet Mr Shakespeare, Ile haue his picture in my study at courte.[19]

Venus and Adonis is at once a claim to social dignity for its author, a justification of the natural and instinctive beauty of the animal world against sour moralists and scurrilous invective, a raising of the animal mask to sentient level, the emancipation of the flesh. Since, however, he did not continue this kind of poetry after the *Rape of Lucrece*, it may be that without the stimulus of Greene's attack Shakespeare would not have been moved to write Ovidian romance, or, if he wrote, to insist at once upon the dignity of print, with all that this implied of a bid for Fame.

Of Shakespeare it might be said,

> Cet animal est très mechant,
> Quand on l'attaque, il se défend

— not with the common style of disclaimer but with positive demonstration of new and dazzling capacities. In *Venus and Adonis*, a lofty form and classic authority is invoked to display the continuity of animal, human and divine passion; the 'vulgar' are rejected only in their narrow prejudice, for the natural at all levels is celebrated.

The player has shown his capacity to move in a world of gorgeous paganism, to write upon a noble model, and to deal with love in aristocratic boldness and freedom. The dedication to Southampton, with its modest apology for 'these unpolished lines' is at once disarming and 'gentle', the tone courtly but unaffected. This could not be calculated; it is the natural consequence of that civility of demeanour which Chettle had so admired.[20]

Notes

1 *Second Part of the Return from Parnassus*, ed. J. B. Leishman (London, Nicholson & Watson, 1949), I, ii, 301–3 and IV, iii, 1766–70.

2 T. W. Baldwin, *On the Literary Genetics of Shakespeare's Poems and Sonnets* (Urbana, University of Illinois Press, 1950), pp. 45–8.

3 *Greene's Groats-worth of Witte*, ed. G. B. Harrison, Bodley Head Quartos (London, 1923), pp. 45–6.

4 E. K. Chambers, *The Elizabethan Stage* (4 vols., Oxford, Clarendon Press, 1923) I, 128 describes the Hinchingbrooke affair; p. 155, the mumming in Coronation year, which happened on Twelfth Night. For late examples of similar shows, see Sheila Williams, 'The Pope-Burning Processions of 1679, 1680, and 1681', *Journal of the Warburg and Courtauld Institutes*, XXI (1958), 104–18.

5 *Francesco's Fortunes* (1590), B4ᵛ-CIʳ. See Chambers, *op. cit.* IV, 236. *Francesco's Fortunes*, a version of Greene's life-story preceding his *Groats-worth of Witte*, contains further abuse of the players. Ferrars actually presented masks of cats and bagpipes before Edward VI in 1553

(A. Feuillerat, *Documents Relating to the Revels*, Bang's Materialien, no. 44 (Louvain, 1914), p. 145).

6 J. Dover Wilson, 'Malone and the Upstart Crow', *Shakespeare Survey*, 4 (1951), 56–68 returns to Malone's view that Greene accused Shakespeare of plagiarism. I would still incline to that set out in Peter Alexander's *Shakespeare's Henry VI and Richard III* (Cambridge, Cambridge University Press, 1929), for reasons which the present article will indicate.

7 Chambers, *op. cit.* II, 98–9. The Duttons were nicknamed 'Chameleons' because they changed their livery and allegiance so often. Cf. *The Defence of Coneycatching* where Greene is accused of saying 'as they were comedians to act, so the actions of their lives were chameleon-like: that they were uncertain time-pleasers, men that measured honesty by profit, and that regarded these authors not by desert but by necessity of time' (Chambers, *op. cit.* III, 325. This refers to actors in general).

8 *Pappe with an Hatchet*. See Chambers, *op. cit.* IV, 229–33 for this and other examples of the stage attack on Martin Marprelate.

9 Chambers, *op. cit.* IV, 236. Such borrowing is constant; for example, in his *Farewell to Folly*, Greene borrows the description of a morris dancer, in burlesque style, from Laneham's Letter on the Princely Pleasures of Kenilworth.

10 C. R. Baskervill, in *The Elizabethan Jig* (Chicago, University of Chicago Press, 1929), p. 67, quotes a 'box' rhyme into which any names could be fitted that the reciter desired:

> 'If I had as fair a face
> As John Williams his daughter Elizabeth has
> Then would I wear a tawdry lace,
> As Goodman Bolt's daughter Mart does:
> And if I had as much money in my purse
> As Cadman's daughter Margaret has,
> Then would I have a bastard less
> Than Butler's maid Helen has.'

Ready-made rhymes may have been used by Clowns in their 'extempore' afterpieces. This one was heard in Oxfordshire in 1584.

11 Ed. G. B. Harrison, Bodley Head Quartos (London, 1923), p. 6.

12 Such care was not misplaced. Nashe in writing to his printers to deny his authorship of 'a scald trivial, lying pamphlet, cald *Greens Groats-worth of Wit*' says of the very knight of the Post whom Chettle uses in *Kind-Harts Dreame*: 'In one place of my Booke, *Pierce Penilesse* saith but to the Knight of the Post, *I pray how might I call you*, & they saye I meant one *Howe*, a Knave of that trade, that I never heard of before' (*Works of Thomas Nashe*, ed. R. B. McKerrow (5 vols., London, A. H. Bullen, 1904–10), I, 154).

13 *Tarlton's News out of Purgatory*, supposedly published by Robin Goodfellow, and *The Cobbler of Canterbury*, with an invective against *Tarlton's News*, both collections of fabliaux, appeared in 1590. *Greene's Vision* (1592) denounces *The Cobbler*, which had been attributed to Greene. *Greene's Newes from Heaven and Hell* (1593) presents

both Tarlton and Greene, who ends as 'the maddest goblin that euer walked in the moonshine' (was Robin Goodfellow a nickname for him perhaps?).

14 *Three Ladies of London* (1582?), *The Pleasant and Stately Moral of Three Lords and Three Ladies of London* (1590), and *The Cobbler's Prophecy* (before 1594). Wilson was a member of Leicester's Men and afterwards of the Queen's Men, *The Rare Triumphs of Love and Fortune* was played before the Queen by Derby's Men at Windsor, 30 December 1582; published 1589. Love appears also, with Death and Fortune, in the Induction to *Solyman and Perseda* (anonymous, company unknown, published 1592).

15 *The Cobbler's Prophecy*, eds. A. C. Wood and W. W. Greg, Malone Society Reprint (Oxford, 1914), 1540–5. Armado compares his own wooing to the roaring of the Nemean lion! (*Love's Labour's Lost*, IV, i, 81–6).

16 From *Perimides the Blacke-Smith* (1588). See T. W. Baldwin, *op. cit.* p. 88.

17 I do not know whether it has been noted how completely Trachinus' speech in praise of the court against academics (*Sapho and Phao*, I, ii, 6–25) agrees with the arguments of Berowne in *Love's Labour's Lost*. In an article in *Shakespeare's Styles*, eds. P. Edwards, I.-S. Ewbank and G. K. Hunter (Cambridge, Cambridge University Press, 1980) I have argued for its indebtedness to John Clapham's *Narcissus* (1591), a warning fable addressed to Southampton.

18 Wilson's Venus also pretends to swoon when rebuked by Mars, in order to win her lover to penitence.

19 *First Part of the Return from Parnassus*, ed. J. B. Leishman (London, Nicholson & Watson, 1949), III, i, 1028–33.

20 Cf. Herbert Howarth, 'Shakespeare's Gentleness', *Shakespeare Survey*, 14 (1961), 90–7; the view of the social purpose of *Venus and Adonis* is similar to that expressed here.

III

Webster's power game

More clearly than any other of Shakespeare's contemporaries, except possibly Marlowe, John Webster speaks to the present age. Both here and in America his plays may be seen on the public stages, on television or as opera, adapted to modern settings and even reflecting contemporary events (at the Kennedy Center in Washington, a modern dress performance of *The White Devil* evoked the Manson murders).

The same highly individual form shapes this play and its successor *The Duchess of Malfi*: an Italian courtly scene of Renaissance magnificence and horror, where lust, ambition, poison, madness and murder fuse in action at once more exotic and more intimate than the English stage had known.

The power of great men is here evinced in personal domination of their circle, although in his first, collaborative tragedy, *Sir Thomas Wyatt*, Webster had used material from Stow, the chronicler of London, to present a Shakespearean model of tragic history, with contemporary political import. In the plots of his two masterpieces, the power game works through personal relationships, played in a close circle of patronage and intrigue. In a recent talk at Cambridge, the Archbishop of Canterbury cited Webster's characters as the supreme examples of unbridled egoism.

What kind of people then are these? The fire of life burns high; they are fuelled by a spirit more powerful than that which consumes ordinary mortals. More like the lives of devils and angels than of human beings, theirs are devoid of daily triviality. The world they live in, like that of the drug addict, is compulsorily attractive or repulsive. Their moods shift abruptly, yet the nervous staccato rhythms of their speech reveal individuality with great precision, since Webster's language is no more diluted by the commonplace than his princes are restrained by precepts of morality.

At the centre of the scene stand women, servants, spies, pimps,

infants – the people things are done to, or those corrupted and
betrayed by necessity. As he combines the exotic with the intimate, so
Webster uses familiar moralizings, only ironically to undermine
them.

The technique is explained by Flamineo, confidential secretary,
pander, and murderer, at the end of one of his most Protean displays:

> It may appear to some ridiculous
> Thus to talk knave and madman and sometimes
> Come in with a dried sentence, stuff'd with sage:
> But this allows my varying of shapes –
> Knaves do grow great by being great men's apes.   (iv. ii. 243–7)

Self-mockery spurs Flamineo onward; at his death, morality and
jests mingle in tragic self-affirmation,

> 'Tis well yet there's some goodness in my death,
> My life was a black charnel; I have caught
> An everlasting cold; I have lost my voice
> Most irrecoverably . . .   (v. vi. 269–72)

Webster follows his fellow dramatist and collaborator, Marston,
in breaking the traditional frame of the earlier Elizabethan revenge
play; it is no longer a working out of divine law, nor even, as in
Marston, the strategy of survival resorted to by the alienated and
dispossessed, nor in Bacon's phrase, 'a kind of wild justice', but an
assertion of the individual will, particularly the right of the head of a
noble family to wipe out in blood any stain upon his honour. Since
the central figures are not the avengers but their victims, the princely
murderers are guilty men, of whose guilt their hired assassins
partake. In the opening scene of *The Duchess of Malfi* Ferdinand in
parting from his sister invokes the Spanish code of family honour:

> You are my sister,
> This was my father's poignard: do you see?
> I'd be loath to see't look rusty, 'cause 'twas his.   (I. i. 330–2)

The part of Ferdinand was created by Burbage, who a decade
earlier had created Othello; the modern reading of Ferdinand's
sexual fixation on his sister makes sense on the modern stage, but in
'A Hispanist looks at *Othello*'[1] the Spanish code-demanding death
for an offending wife, sister or any other female transgressor against
the common blood, has been applied to Shakespeare. It could be
more readily applied to Webster's tragedy, since his princes are of the
house of Aragon. Each meaning has worked on the stage; for
Webster's is an art of performance, and may be played on modern
instruments as well as the originals.

In 1958 his editor F. L. Lucas could say that less was known of

Webster than of the great Greek dramatists; but now, thanks to the researches of Mary Edmond, he can be placed in a particular part of London, in a well-defined social group, with particular political and religious affiliations.

A satirist writing in 1616 had jeered at 'the playwright-cartwright' – Webster was the son of a wealthy coachmaker, also named John Webster, of the parish of St Sepulchre-without Newgate. Born probably four hundred years ago, in 1580, his mother the daughter of a blacksmith, and his wife the daughter of a saddler, he eventually succeeded his father by patrimony in 1615 as a member of the powerful Company of Merchant Taylors, one of the twelve greater livery companies that ruled the City of London.

It would have been an act not merely of eccentricity but of ostracism for John Webster the elder to send his son anywhere but to the Merchant Taylors' school. He himself assisted the scholars to appear in festal chariots. At Merchant Taylors', a strong tradition of playacting had been established by Richard Mulcaster; the earlier dramatists Thomas Lodge and Thomas Kyd both attended the school, and probably went to court with 'Mr. Mulcaster's boys'.

Mulcaster believed in teaching modern literature, beginning with English: 'I love Rome, but London better, I favour Italy, but England more, I honour the Latin but I worship the English.' The tradition of the school was strongly Protestant; Webster's use of a politicized Roman church as the ultimate symbol of evil is not unexpected. His diabolic cardinals are even darker figures than his infatuated princes; and in his early play *Sir Thomas Wyatt* Queen Mary appears quite unhistorically in the dress of a nun.

From Merchant Taylors' Webster went to New Inn, an Inn of Chancery, whence at Michaelmas 1598 he was admitted to the Middle Temple; there he would learn of the spectacular downfall and expulsion of its leading poet, John Davies, author of *Orchestra*. After the Christmas Revels, where he had been assigned the role of the Fool, Davies made a mad assault on his friend Richard Martin, who had played the Prince, breaking a bastinado over Martin's head as he sat quietly at dinner. Here was a lesson in the consequence of treacherous revels which no dramatist could ignore. Davies retired to write *Nosce Teipsum*, a notable exercise in the plain style.

> I know my life's a pain and but a span
> I know my sense is mocked with every thing:
> And to conclude, I know myself a Man,
> Which is a proud and yet a wretched thing.

John Davies was not a thinker, but relied on resonant common-places that had been proved upon his pulses, as T. S. Eliot pointed out in *Of Poets and Poetry*; his verses reshape writers like de Mornay and Montaigne, the writers that Webster used for his tragic ironies. Webster's dramatic sequences usually include a trial scene. *Sir Thomas Wyatt*, composed with Dekker and others, shows the trial of Lady Jane Grey and turns on the question 'What is treason?' His latest plays, *The Devil's Law Case, A Cure for a Cuckold, Appius and Virginia*, differing in other ways, each culminates in a court scene, where the inadequacies of justice are more obvious than its functioning.

At the Middle Temple Webster would have met John Marston, with whom he was to collaborate; Thomas Overbury, whose *Characters* he was to edit after Overbury's murder; and one of his admirers and his successor in tragedy, John Ford. Marston helped to set up the choristers' theatre in St Paul's where two successful City comedies by Webster and Dekker were staged in 1605. It seems probable that his father sent Webster to the Middle Temple for a legal training that he might deal with important customers and trading ventures – for the leading London tradesmen were already merchants and financiers rather than craftsmen, with international interests.

Webster would thus have gained an entrée to circles where the great might be encountered, yet as the son of a tradesman from nearby Smithfield he would learn the bitterness of being put in his place by well-born fools. His comedies satirize the City but also the court gallants who attempt to court the City wives; like the merry wives of Windsor, the band of London women prove more than a match for their suitors.

It would appear that Webster celebrated the literary successes of 1605 with too great abandon, perhaps at the local festivity of Bartholomew Fair; for, as Mary Edmond has discovered,[2] he was on 18 March 1606 married by special licence at the church of St. Mary Islington to 'Sara Gammell'. This was in Lent, a season when marriages were not normally permitted; Islington was a northern village famous for its curds and cream, a resort for citizens in summer time. Less than two months later, on 8 May, the baptism of John Webster, son of John Webster of St Sepulchre's, was recorded at the parish of St Dunstan in the West, 'out of the house of Simon Peniall'. Simon Peniall, recently Warden of the Saddlers' Company, had as eldest daughter Sara, baptized at St Bride, Fleet Street, 20 April 1589. John Webster had copied Shakespeare in more ways than one; his wife was aged just 17 when their child was christened and her name (like that of Shakespeare's bride twenty-four years earlier) had gone misrecorded through embarrassment or tact.

In consequence perhaps of this shock to two sets of pious parents, no more plays were produced for six years; but Webster confessed himself a slow writer, and was twitted for it by his enemies. However, Ben Jonson, who in his *Conversations* (1619) castigated the majority of playwrights, never mentions Webster, whose next set of plays coincided with the mayoralty of a Merchant Taylor known as a patron of drama, Sir John Swinnerton.

The Webster households adjoined the dreaded prison of Newgate, where both Ben Jonson and John Marston sojourned at different times. John Webster the elder in 1605 had witnessed the charitable deed by which a fellow Merchant Taylor paid for the common bellman to call the condemned to repentance on the night before their execution. This figure is personated at the execution of the Duchess of Malfi by Bosola the spy, in the last of his many disguises.

Ritual and formalized scenes of grief bind together the disjunctive events in both Webster's tragedies. In *The White Devil* Duchess Isabella's nightly devotions to her husband's picture, by means of which she is poisoned, the winding of Marcello's corpse, its dirge of the natural pieties of robin redbreast and wren (contrasted with the cruelty of the churchmen who deny burial rites to a man who died in a quarrel) offer fixed emblems or pageants.

By contrast, the vivid, Protean, acting of the leading part, Flamineo, by the young Richard Perkins earned Webster's highest commendation. The play did not succeed at his neighbourhood theatre, the Red Bull, a square innyard where Queen Anne's Men performed with Webster's friend Heywood as their leading dramatist. So Webster himself had the work published by another neighbour, Nicholas Okes, who specialized in playbooks.

The Duchess of Malfi, performed at Blackfriars by the King's Men two or three years later, succeeded from the first; for Webster essentially belonged to the indoor theatres. His disjunctive speech allowed the actor to create the part from within himself; it was adapted also to the more intimate response of a smaller audience; it contained the germ of character development.

The Duchess herself develops from the proud defiance of

> If all my royal kindred
> Lay in my way unto this marriage:
> I'd make them my low footsteps . . .   (I. i. 341–3)

to the equally proud mastery of her fears at the sight of the cords and coffin borne into her 'last presence chamber':

> I have so much obedience, in my blood,
> I wish it in their veins, to do them good   (IV. ii. 169–70)

According to Thomas Middleton, the audience had wept. The sight of the Duchess's still living body melts her brother and converts

Bosola, the hired spy and assassin; this miracle proclaims her justification.

If any explanation could be found for the flowering of Webster's genius in the years 1611–14, it would probably lie in his reading. The external event most likely to precipitate tragedies of court corruption was Overbury's murder. Robert Carr, the King's favourite, had become entangled with Frances Howard, Countess of Essex, during her youthful bridegroom's absence abroad; on his return in 1609, the storm broke.

Webster dedicated his memorial poem for Prince Henry to Carr at the end of 1612 much as Overbury gave him the Character of 'The Wife' – to provide him with models of virtue that would deter him from his course. But Frances gained her divorce in September 1613, the month in which Overbury was murdered in the Tower. Overbury's father was a member of the Middle Temple, and in 1615 Webster edited the *Characters*, and Ford wrote a poem on Overbury. In 1616 Robert and Frances Carr, Earl and Countess of Somerset were found guilty of the murder of Sir Thomas Overbury, and were sentenced to death; being later reprieved by James.

Carr as Lord Chamberlain had been the patron of all poets who aspired to the court. Chapman wrote a poem on the marriage and dedicated his Homer to Carr; Ben Jonson wrote him complimentary verses. His story had exposed the rottenness of the court so effectually that perhaps it silenced Webster, who had been composing his great plays during the period of rumours between the first quarrels between Essex and his wife and the murder of Overbury (1609–13). Life had overtaken art.

The thirty-two *Characters* which Webster added to the collection of Overbury for the sixth edition depicted a little world – it is essential to read each character as part of a group. They are distinguished not as Vices and Virtues in the classical style of Theophrastus but as inhabitants of a contemporary world, the only idyllic one being the 'fair and happy milkmaid'. They are closely related to Ben Jonson's plays and to the verbal games of the young lawyers at the Inns of Court. For the idea is to present an analysis of character that calls for a judgment. As practice in whitewashing a client or blackening an adversary, *Characters* would afford useful models for the young pleaders; but as drama, they depend on a social background that no longer survives. These *Characters* were the first of a vogue which lasted through the century, to be utilized by Clarendon in his great *History*; other young men beside Webster contributed to the Overbury collection, which was reprinted again and again.

Eight years after the success of *The Duchess of Malfi*, Thomas

Drue was to write a play on *The Duchess of Suffolk*, whose story strikingly resembles Webster's and who had appeared among Foxe's Martyrs. After the death of her husband, this royal lady had also married her steward; both had been driven from England to suffer, with their infants, great hardships, till restored by the accession of Elizabeth I. In the same year as the great success of Drue's play, Webster published his own *Duchess of Malfi*, in which therefore he must have retained some proprietory interest. Both could be seen as part of anti-Spanish feelings that prevailed in the City of London, at the same time when a Spanish marriage was being proposed for the Prince of Wales.

On the death of his father, shortly after the first production of *The Duchess of Malfi*, Webster should have inherited a substantial patrimony; his later plays appear as occasional works, written largely for the benefit of his friends in Queen Anne's Men, more especially when they moved to their own indoor theatre, The Cockpit, the first playhouse to appear on the historic site of Drury Lane, and, as it survived to the Restoration, the prototype of modern theatres in England.

In publishing *The Devil's Law Case*, obviously another showpiece for Perkins, Webster dedicated it to Sir Thomas Finch, grandson of Queen Elizabeth's Vice-Chamberlain. The reason for the dedication, however, was not his lineage, but his address, for Sir Thomas lived in Drury Lane, and evidently supported the new theatre against local opposition.

The play contains a set of farcical enlargements or caricatures of some features of the author's own life; the hero is a rich young merchant who seduces a nun! In her recent study of Thomas Middleton, *Puritanism and Theatre* (Cambridge, 1980), Margot Heinemann defined his 'City Tragedy' as a 'dramatization of social mobility, its presentation of sex and marriage, its ethical and religious overtones' (p. 173).

Webster had preceded Middleton by a decade in his concern with the role of women in society, the relation of marriage to money affairs. In Middleton's greatest tragedy, *The Changeling*, the exotic element is provided by the subplot of the madmen, chiefly the work of a collaborator Rowley (who also collaborated with Webster and who led Queen Anne's Men), developed from the masque of madmen in Webster's *Duchess of Malfi*. In Middleton the character development is firm, much of the writing in prose, the tone studiously restrained.

Webster's latest publication was the Lord Mayor's Triumph which he devised in 1624 for the installation of Sir John Gore, Merchant Taylor. Middleton, the usual pageant writer, was in hiding after the scandalous success of his anti-Spanish play *The Game at Chess*. For *Monuments of Honour* Webster did some careful work on the history of his company to find examples of men who had risen from humble beginnings to positions of power: this is 'the Merchant Taylors' honour', exemplified in their motto, *Concordia parvae res crescunt*, 'By unity the smallest things grow great'.

The eight kings who had been free of the Merchant Taylors, seated in the Chariot of Honour, repeat this in chorus; but the dominant feature of the whole procession was the figure of the late Henry, Prince of Wales, dead twelve years since, but remembered as a steady opponent of his father's pro-Spanish policies. Riding also in the procession was the figure of Anne of Bohemia, Queen of Richard II, who had been free of the company, but whose ensign would surely recall that other Queen of Bohemia, so beloved of the Londoners, the Princess Elizabeth, now exiled in the Netherlands after being driven from her country. These silent but eloquent forms constituted a rebuke to the ignoble policies of James's last years. England was passing from the age of Shakespeare to the age of Milton; indeed, just as Webster would walk in the procession in his Merchant Taylors' livery, so among the senior schoolboys of St Paul's following the Mercers' Company, there might have been seen the future author of *The Tenure of Kings and Magistrates*.

Notes

1 By Edward M. Wilson in *English and Spanish Literature of the Sixteenth and Seventeenth Centuries* (Cambridge, Cambridge University Press, 1980). Cf below, p. 166.
2 See *Times Literary Supplement*, 24 October 1980.

IV

Marvell and the masque

Throughout the sixteenth and seventeenth centuries different poetic forms moved into the foreground or receded into the background, not only according to the practice of poets but according to the social influences and pressures that worked, now through one poetic channel, now through another. Between the flowering of Elizabethan poetry and the arrival of the Augustan city, the shift from lyric and narrative to dramatic poetry and its reversal follow the ebb and flow of popular sympathy and concern. Dramatic poetry was at first deeply influenced by the rhetorical patterns of Senecan lament and Petrarchan sonnet; when in mid-Jacobean times power ebbed from this great form and the poetry of meditation developed, lyric became the exploratory and sensitive tool. With the deepening of social conflict, poets turned to 'the paradise within', each evolving his own blend of themes and images.[1] In the reign of Charles I, particularly that part known as 'the eleven years' Tyranny', when he ruled without a parliament (1629–40), the political effects of courtly poetry were achieved through pastoral and masque.

The masque, an expansion of language beyond that customary in the public theatre, depended on song, dance, spectacle, company and occasion. Inigo Jones had triumphed over the rejected Jonson, so that spectacle and variety, rapidly changing and elaborate scenes provided a nonverbal language of ambiguity, while the actual words were 'frozen' in set patterns of praise. Ancient ruins and modern architecture, grotesque antimasques in great profusion leading by vistas to the great transformation scene were used by the architect and engineer to convey all the wonder, elevation, and rapture which the poets had termed 'delight'. The power and glory of the masque lay in its costumes, its whirling light effects, its rapid shifts of scene, its ever more complicated cloud machines, bringing heaven down to earth.[2]

The king's Arcadia, almost a little Versailles before Louis XIV, was presided over by Charles and his queen (who attended Blackfriars and even, with her French ladies, enacted *The Shepherd's Paradise*). However, the more refined their courtly games, the more Charles and his circle cut themselves off from ambitious young men who renounced court ambitions – like George Herbert, who built a temple to which in later years Crashaw added the steps, Knivet the gallery and Christopher Harvey an adjacent synagogue.

Among the products of Herbert's university and of his college, Trinity, was Andrew Marvell, whose roots were in the Puritan north, but who, as an undergraduate, ran away to join the Jesuits (from whom he was recovered by his father). Marvell, who saw the case for both sides in the growing conflict, was to remain a patient builder of bridges, a moderate thinker in an age when moderation was an active notion unrelated to neutrality. He drew the narrow elegance of Caroline courtly life back into poetry of much wider scope, if of more inward and solitary concern.

Marvell's lyrics, the best of which tend to be about retirement, apply the Arcadianism of Charles' court to the situation created by its collapse. When on 6 November 1632, Gustavus Adolphus was killed in Germany, one writer of court masques wrote a lament, only to be answered by another:

> Tourneyes, Masques, Theaters better become
> Our *Halcyon* dayes; what though the German Drum
> Bellow for freedome and revenge, the noyse
> Concerns us not, nor should divert our joyes;
> Nor ought the thunder of their Carabins
> Drowne the sweet Ayres of our tun'd Violins[3] . . .

Marvell wrote when the thunder of Carabins had been heard in England, when another king had been killed, in circumstances unparalelled, by his own subjects. From a Yorkshire garden, among haymakers and neatherds, he addressed his country:

> O Thou, that dear and happy Isle,
> The Garden of the World erewhile,
> Thou *Paradise* of four Seas,
> Which *Heaven* planted us to please,
> But to exclude the World, did guard
> With watry if not flaming Sword,
> What luckless Apple did we tast,
> To make us Mortal, and the Wast?
>
> ('Upon Appleton House' 41: 321–8)

The court masque has amply shewn itself to be the predominant dramatic form of the reign of Charles I.[4] In spite of the previous efforts of Ben Jonson, it was no longer literary, but a ritual of dance, song, and display – 'Power conceived as art' – in which the king and queen, appearing in person, enacted the harmony they claimed to dispense over their kingdom. For this, the disguise of a shepherd or shepherdess (in costly robes), as representing the humblest level of their subjects, enabled the central figures to create a suggestion of unity – even if we are reminded by Henrietta Maria not so much of the old Shepherds' Play as of the Petit Trianon. The two central figures dispensed a godlike power; to be efficacious, the monarchy must be the centre of the rite.

> But *Ceres* corn, and *Flora* is the Spring,
> *Bacchus* is wine, the country is the *King*.
> (*The Last Instructions to a* Painter ll. 974–5)

wrote Marvell many year later, uniting in this couplet the chief figures of Nabbes's masque, *The Glory of the Spring*.[5]

Charles would present a Christmas masque to his queen, she would return him one at Shrovetide. Their marital felicity and irradiating virtue as 'Hymen's twin, the Mary–Charles',[6] constituted a political act; 'to control the way the people saw the monarch was to control their response to the royal policy as well'. Unfortunately these politics of display were confined to the court and the visiting ambassadors. Moreover, this celebration of cosmic harmony often gave occasion to great disorder – manoeuvring for places and precedence, pilfering and pillaging, although Charles himself, unlike his father, remained a model of decorum. He was intensely concerned with his own image; his role modulates, no doubt at his own dictation, from heroic lover to triumphant emperor, to the stellified successor to Jove, to the ruler of the ocean (and imposer of ship money), finally to the patient, long-suffering, Christlike Philogenes of the last masque, danced when war with the Scots had already begun.[7]

The courtiers were in turn offered homage by their servants, the musicians and the players in the antimasques. These latter might be critical – those in *The Masque of Peace*, for instance, criticize Charles's licensing of 'projectors' – but all such dissidence was 'purged' before the dazzling epiphany of the finale.

Charles was a small man, but at the centre of *Salmacida Spolia*, at the apex of a throne was 'his Majesty highest in a seat of gold' which had the effect of giving him physical predominance. The scene might be diminished to scale, the torchbearers might be children. The costumes, costly but fantastic, gave, as it were, a new identity to the masquers. To move out of the frame into the dancing place was itself a wonder, a sort of incarnational descent of the god.

Thomas Carew's *Coelum Brittanicum* (Shrovetide, 1633) displaces all the heavenly deities, in their bestial forms of the zodiac, to replace them by the British monarch.[8] It opens with the impresa of the Lion and the Lily, for the king and queen. Various claimants to divine rule, including Pleasure and Five Senses, are banished before the masquers emerge from a hill which grows out of the earth. After the masquers' dance

> the scaene againe is varied into a new and pleasant prospect cleane differing from all the other, the nearest part shewing a delicious garden with severall walks and perterra's set round with low trees, and on the sides against these walkes, were fountains and grots, and in the furthest part a Palace, from which went high walkes upon Arches, and above them open Tarraces planted with Cypresse trees, and all this together was composed of such Ornaments as might expresse a Princely Villa.
>
> (*Poems*, p. 181)

The final scene, in which the gods were displaced, showed Windsor Castle and the new stars, of which one, more great and eminent than all the rest, figured His Majesty.

Here can be seen the sort of images that Marvell was to use in 'A Dialogue Between the Resolved Soul and Created Pleasure', for different ends, and in 'Upon the Hill and Grove at Billborough', to ends quite opposed to those of the masque.

Carew's pastoral dialogues in miniature form develop the roles of individual masquers; they transform the social rite into a more personal one. *An Hymeneall Dialogue between Bride and Groom* (with Chorus) opens:

> *Groom:*   Tell me (my love) since Hymen ty'de
> The holy knot, hast thou not felt
> A new infused spirit slide
> Into thy brest, whilst thine did melt?
>
> *Bride:*   First tell me (sweet) whose words were those?
> For though your voyce the ayre did break
> Yet did my soul the sence compose
> And through your lips my heart did speake.
>
> (*Poems*, p. 66, ll. 1–8)

The two pastoral dialogues present shepherd and nymph enjoying each other, but each within a little frame of dramatic situation – the intruding Thyrsis, or the singers who present the aubade of parting lovers. These lyrics were set by Walter Porter or Henry Lawes (he gave one of the pastoral dialogues to two tenors or trebles, with thorough bass).

The mention of Lawes is sufficient to recall that it was his brother William who published Milton's *Comus*, as well as supplying the music and apparently playing in the original performance, at which those experienced masquers, the youthful Lady Alice Egerton (who had danced in *Tempe Restored* at court), and her two brothers took the leading parts. Milton's masque against masquing, his plea for temperance in a form traditionally used for extravagant display, appropriated the convention against which the masque at Ludlow Castle exerts its force. The chariot of Sabrina – the deity who resolves all enchantments, goddess of chastity, of the River Severn – rises out of the fresh stream adorned with gems, for Sabrina is the daughter of a king. She is summoned by a song and she appears singing in reply. That she may represent the ancient British church, sprinkling sacred and baptismal drops, is suggested by the prayer for her prosperity with which the episode concludes – a prayer which no goddess should need. 'Sprung of old Anchises' line,' she rises from the waters and as she sinks back, the Lady herself rises from the enchanted chair, and the action moves forward.

Milton was writing after the attack of Prynne had made clear Puritan hostility to the masque, but this hostility was sporadic. When Cromwell came to full power he himself commissioned a masque from James Shirley for the entertainment of the French ambassador, and for the wedding of his daughter Mary, Andrew Marvell composed a pair of songs in the tradition of the masque-pastoral, where the lady appears first by proxy in duet as a goddess, Cynthia, then in a more equal match, celebrated by the common people, as Marina, bride of 'the Northern Shepherd's son'.

A number of Marvell's poems were set to music – 'A Dialogue between Thyrsis and Dorinda' by John Gamble and by Matthew Locke, and also by William Lawes, who modified it (see Legouis' Commentary in *Poems*, p. 248). Lawes was killed when Marvell was but twenty-three, so that the poem is placed among the works of his youth. Carew, who was twenty-seven years older than Marvell, died when Marvell was only nineteen, but the poems were printed the same year (1640). Marvell was eight years later to write commendatory verses for Lovelace's *Lucasta*. The elegies on Lord Hastings (who died 24 June 1649) and the son of the great lord of earlier masquing, Francis Villiers (killed 7 July 1648) employ the imagery of a 'great Turnament' followed by a masque in which the gods are revealed by the drawing of a 'veil' (or 'traverse'):[9]

> Onely they drooping *Hymenaeus* note
> Who for sad *Purple*, tears his *Saffron*-coat
> And trails his *Torches* th'row the Starry Hall
> Reversed, at his *Darlings* Funeral

(ll. 43–6)

and by a 'serious imitation' of fight, which ends in the hero constructing a 'pyramid' of bodies for his sepulchre, so that his death really
sounds like some kind of martial game between Love and Death. It
was part of Marvell's wit to use the conventions of emblematic art in
new and startling contexts as, later, he was to use the ritual of the
masque for Puritanical sentiments.

Two pictorial companion pieces, 'The Unfortunate Lover' and
'The Gallery', are conceived in action as a series of transformation
scenes: the first opening with 'a masque of quarrelling elements', the
second presenting contrasting pairs of humours – Clora the mur-
deress, Clora as the dawn goddess; Clora as a witch, and Clora as
Venus. All these pictures furnish the lover's mind, his interior palace,
but his favourite is that of the simple shepherdess 'with which I first
was took'. In each poem the scenes depict energetic action; so too,
'The Picture of Little T.C. in a Prospect of Flowers' follows the lively
activities of the child, and looks forward to the even livelier activities
of her girlhood.

Carew could combine masque writing with lyric as two equally
acceptable forms of courtly exercise, for he was naturally in the
circuit of the court, son of Sir Matthew Carew, of the old Cornish
family, and cousin to Ralegh; his friend Aurelian Townshend came
from the gentry of Norfolk (the seat was at Dereham). Milton, son of
the City of London, could by use of paradox, exercise himself in the
masque form; but Marvell, son of a Yorkshire vicarage, and Milton's
junior by more than a decade, could not directly employ all that
vanished with the outbreak of civil war. He could, however, through
the force of its images transmute and use this obsolete political rite to
add depth and energy, to give to his lyric that special drive and
momentum which characterizes it, while within the poems the social
consequences of the breaking of old patterns produced tragic ironies.
The perplexed and troubled conscience, the divided loyalties of the
men who lived through so many changes of government in church
and state, could be reunited only by toil within 'the quick forge and
working house of thought'. Marvell's handful of lyrics produced as
prologue to a long and active political career, represent, in the most
concentrated form, this search for a new stability in a 'shattered
frame'.

The use of masque and pastoral as suppressed or as undersong can
be discerned in such lyrics as 'The Coronet', or the pastoral 'Dialogue
between Thyris and Dorinda', a poem of unexpected obscurity (it
was printed in the Folio between two political poems and, as we
noted above had wide success with a musical setting). The persona in
'The Coronet' (pp. 14–15), who openly rejects earthly for Christian
worship, also subsequently recognizes that even the second is cor-

rupted with worldliness. The argument of the poem moves through thesis and antithesis to synthesis. The first verse 'dismantles' the 'towers' that adorned the shepherdess's head, but within the new crown

> Alas I find the Serpent old
> That, twining in his speckled breast,
> About the flow'rs disguis'd does fold
> With wreaths of Fame and Interest.
>
> (ll. 13–16)

The serpent in Eden is fatal; but in terms of earthly wisdom the serpent in chaplet form was a symbol of eternity. As such, he appeared as the sceptre or emblem of that power in the final tableau of *Coelum Britannicum*:

> . . . the great Cloud began to breake open, out of which stroke beames of light; in the midst, suspended in the Ayre, sate Eternity on a Globe, his Garment was of a light blue, wrought all over with Stars of gold, and bearing in his hand a Serpent bent into a circle, with his taile in his mouth. (ll. 1075–80)
>
> (*Poems*, p. 182)

In the final verse, Marvell appeals to the Lord whom he had designed to honour, 'But thou, who only could's the Serpent tame . . .' either to pluck out the Serpent, or trample on both him and the poet's offering, so that the 'broken frame' may 'crown thy Feet, that could not crown thy Head'. Chapman and Donne had appropriated the coronet to pious uses, but this renunciation ends with a new image that might well have featured in the galleries of the Most Catholic Majesty.

The 'Dialogue between Thyrsis and Dorinda' (pp. 19–21) begins with praise of an Elysium where the lovers may, after death, 'pass Eternity away':

> Oh, ther's, neither hope nor fear
> There's no Wolf, no Fox, nor Bear.
> . . . .
> No Oat-pipe's needfull, there thine Ears
> May feast with Musick of the Spheres.
>
> (ll. 21–2, 25–6)

That shepherd's paradise, which Henrietta Maria had brought down to earth, had been sadly recognized by the great Elizabethan pastoralist, Drayton, in his latest work, *The Muses Elysium* (1630) as only a 'paradise within':

> That faire Felicia which was but of late,
> Earth's Paradise, that never had her peere,
> Stands now in that most lamentable state

. . . .
The little infant on the mothers lap
for want of fire shall be so sore distrest,
That while it draws the lank and empty pap,
The tender lips shall freeze unto the breast;
The quaking cattle which their warmstall want . . .
The hungry crows shall with their caryon feast.

('The Tenth Nymphall' ll. 65–7, 93–7.)[10]

The last and greatest crime is that of the men who fell all the trees till
the land 'stands disrob'd of all her rich attire', so that any wanting
timber to build are constrained to dig caves in the ground. Drayton,
now an old man, presents himself as the satyr who has strayed over
the mountains into the Muses' country; this piteous renunciation of
all that he had sung as a pastoralist must itself be put in pastoral
terms, as the welcoming shepherds promise him vengeance:

Here live in blisse, till thou shalt see those slaves
Who thus set vertue and desert at nought;
Some sacrific'd upon their grandsires graves,
And some like beasts in markets sold and bought
. . . .
Until those base Felicians thou shalt heare,
By that vile nation captived again,
That many a glorious age their captives were.

('The Tenth Nymphall' ll. 137–40, 146–8)

Marvell then had precedent for the ironic use of pastoral; the
Elysium that Thyrsis and Dorinda seek is very like Drayton's:

There, sheep are full
Of sweetest grass and softest wooll
. . . .
Shepherds there, bear equal sway,
And every Nimph's a Queen of *May*

(ll. 31–2, 37–8)

They depart to drink wine mingled with poppy, 'so shall we smooth-
ly pass away in sleep'.

This apparent sanction of suicide gives an accurate if mordant
view of successful court pastoralism, at the same time, of course, as it
suggests (if the religious interpretation is favoured) a 'life beyond the
grave'. For at all events, this is not the life of middle earth. The
implicit rejection of pastoral and the serene realms of the masquers'
Arcadia gives sharpness to this lyric, and it makes it, like *Lycidas*, an
indictment of the 'blind mouths'. The soothing, too innocent set of
questions and answers suggests (in their tone and movement) an
unconvincing ignorance. Of course, those who can never resist the
pun on 'die' will take another meaning, but this lyric, to my mind,

carries a political as well as a personal dimension; its Bower of Bliss no longer offers the harmless play of Arcadia.

'An Horatian Ode' may be placed between Cromwell's return from Ireland and his departure for Scotland, that is, between May and July 1650. In the opening lines, Caesar's crossing of the Rubicon is recalled in a reference to Lucan; but Cromwell urges his 'active Star' to a more than Caesarean birth, in violence beyond that of the Unfortunate Lover. He cut his way through his own party (he was soon to supersede Fairfax as Commander-in-Chief), went burning through the air

> And *Caesar*'s head at last
> Did through his Laurels blast.
>
> (ll. 23–4)

This triumph, however, is also a 'ruin'; and the royal actor on his tragic scaffold still carried a 'helpless right'.

Here Marvell was accurately reflecting the ironies of the moment when Charles stepped out from under the great painted ceiling of the Banqueting Hall, with its apotheosis of James I. He was beheaded at the door of his own theatre; his world of fragile images had been smashed by Cromwell's 'Trust in God and keep your powder dry'.

The building that has been begun is Capitoline, but the two rivals for the chief part in this tragic masque have discerned divided roles. It has been observed that 'there are two Cromwells in the poem, the scourge of God and the leader of His chosen people'.[11] The Royalists themselves had derived the king's right from ancient conquest till the war went against them; Cromwell tried to persuade Charles that trial by battle registered the judgment of God.[12]

The strength and anguish of the images breaks through the calm frame of Horatian verse. It has been remarked that if the poem shows poise and urbanity, it is the poise and urbanity of a man on the rack. The degree of shock which the execution sent through all England can still be traced in the poems written at Nun Appleton, where Marvell resided for two years from early in 1651 to early in 1653 in company with Fairfax, the man of conscience who would not lead an expedition against the Scots, from which the poet soon emerged resolved to spend his time in the public cause. Nun Appleton was for Marvell what, centuries later, Coole Park became for Yeats.

In celebrating Nun Appleton, Marvell drew upon the Horatian tradition of the country house poem,[13] to which Jonson had contributed in 'To Penshurst', his poem to Sir R. Wroth, Carew in his poems on Saxham and Wrest, Herrick in his panegyric to Sir Lewis Pemberton.[14] In all these, the modest, useful centre of hospitality is contrasted with more ostentatious buildings. Nun Appleton House was finished only in 1649, but it was a traditional place, except indeed for its elaborate garden. Marvell is able therefore to praise Fairfax in terms of his modesty, his sobriety, and his preference for good human relationships:

> A stately *Frontispiece of Poor*
> Adorns without the open Door;
> Nor less the Rooms within commends
> Daily new *Furniture of Friends.*
>
> (9.65–8)

At a time when most architecture was designed for ostentation more than use, this house which had been designed so that 'things greater are in less contain'd' expands to admit the greatness of the Lord General,

> But where he comes the swelling Hall
> Stirs, and the *Square* grows *Spherical*;
>
> (7.50–1)

Alteration of scale, like that of the masque, enlarges the central figure; Marvell is giving to Fairfax the kind of praise that the masquers gave to royalty, but he is paradoxically giving it in praise of an abdication of power. An ancestor had burst through the walls of another house of retirement, a nunnery, to claim his bride; Fairfax has built in the gardens a mimic fort with five bastions, but 'as aiming one for every sense'. His endeavour, like that in the struggle between the resolved soul and created pleasure, mounts by humility.

The playful development of floral salutes and parades may recall the pastoral world of Henrietta Maria as Chloris[15] or the gallantries of Lovelace's *Amarantha, a Pastoral* where the flowers salute the heroine in her country retreat with equal alacrity (but where the struggles of the Civil War are reduced to romantic monstrosities, mere bugaboos). Here the jests are poignant; even then Fairfax, had he not chosen retirement, 'might have made our Gardens spring/ Fresh as his own and flourishing'. But Paradise is now a waste land. Though Fairfax cultivates the trees of his own fields and groves, the desolate Felicia of Drayton had become still more desolate.

Moving on from the house to the garden and thence to the meadows, Marvell himself undergoes a kind of transformation or alteration of perspective, which reflects the larger social transformations of 'the Garden of the World'. This he describes in terms of the changing scenes in a masque. 'Marvell is looking not at things but images.'[16] Now men grow small, and grasshoppers huge; now the flowers seem fathoms deep in a sea of grass.

Fairfax's tenants are mowing the hay; after which they dance, set up haycocks, turn out the cattle to graze, and finally, as the meadows are flooded, the cattle, already diminished to the size of fleas in the huge expanse, but moving like constellations, become transformed with everything else, and we enter a world where glow-worms could be comets.[17] All this is described in symbols of warfare, and of masque.

> No Scene that turns with Engines strange
> Does oftener then these Meadows change.
>
> (49.385–6)

The scenes that turned were Inigo Jones's invention, first seen in *The Masque of Queens* (1609).

Changing scenes are revealed by a 'Traverse' or stage curtain, first used in public theatres, but (as shutters) introduced for *The Masque of Oberon* (1611). That this is what is meant, is made plain in stanza 56:

> This Scene again withdrawing brings
> A new and empty Face of things;
> A levell'd space as smooth and plain
> As Clothes for *Lilly* stretcht to stain.

The great painter Lely and the painted scene recall Davenant in 'the painted world' of *Gondibert* presenting the six days of Creation – Davenant, author of the last masque, and chief transmitter of scenic art to the next age. Davenant's *Gondibert*, an epic often compared by him, in his celebrated preface, to a palace, was perhaps the subject of parody here; but its huge extent brings a flickering between pygmy and giant scales, a 'blink' by means of which appalling events can be surveyed, calmly.

Here the only 'massacre' is that of the small birds hidden in the long grass, yet the words which Marvell uses are brutally accurate.[18] Women tossing the hay 'represent the pillaging', the revolting aftermath of battle. Yet somehow it has become a matter for fancy. The last fancy is that a second Flood is obliterating all Creation.

The poet finally retreats to the wood itself, the 'Ark', and in those depths meets new transformations, for he seems to have entered a fifth element

> Dark all without it knits; within
> It opens passable and thin;
>
> (64.505–6)

The effect of these changes is not unlike that which Eliot recorded at the outbreak of another war:

> As, in a theatre,
> The lights are extinguished, for the scene to be changed

With a hollow rumble of wings, with a movement of darkness on
darkness,
And we know that the hills and the trees, the distant panorama
And the bold imposing façade are all being rolled away –

('East Coker'. III)[19]

while 'they all go into the dark' – the captains, merchant bankers,
eminent men of letters . . .'
The wood is not only dark, but strange; prophecies consume all
history; all learning can be discovered in its 'light Mosaic'; and
suddenly Marvell too has passed through the looking glass, and
appears in full masquing costume, curiously embroidered:

> And see how Chance's better *wit*
> Could with a Mask my studies hit!
> The Oak-Leaves me embroyder all, . . .
> Under this *antick Cope* I move
> Like some great *Prelate of the Grove*,

(74.585–92)

Prelates, like abbesses, are not serious figures here (though the
Archbishop of York's Cawood Castle lay within sight). Reading in
'Nature's Mystick Book', the poet becomes mentally calmed, and the
excitement which had heated his brow and sent ideas spinning
abates. Indeed, the lavish recall of Marvell's wide reading almost
suggests the lavish bejewelling of the last masques, were it not so well
compounded. Neo-Platonism and contemporaries like Benlowes,
Cleveland, St Amant, Davenant, have each supplied Marvell's
imagination with ingredients; the flight of the mind, working at top
speed, is too quick for each to be identified. The poet, utterly secure
from the world's 'shot', can 'gaul its horseman all the day'; can even
plead to be imprisoned and chained in the wood, 'that I may never
leave.this place'. The magic wood tempts as the cloister might tempt.
With evening he emerges only to fish, a solitary sport indeed in a
place that makes Thessalian Tempe obsolete.[20] In the final scene, his
child pupil, running past, with her beauty charms the whole world
into harmony and stillness. Representative of study and of the future,
she rescues the poet from an indulgence which, like that of Thyrsis
and Dorinda, threatens to become too passive. She is compared with
a comet – how different from earlier alarming comets! – and she
portends action.
    At an earlier entrance to the realm of eternity, in Carew's masque,
a chorus of Druids, prelates of the grove, had seen their darkened
sphere lightened by the starry look of the Queen Henrietta Maria

> . . . let thy Divine
> Aspects (Bright Deity) with faire

> And Halcyon beames becalme the aire.
> > (Third Song ll. 1027–9, *Poems*, p. 181)

Now Mary Fairfax is also the halcyon, and with her appearance the theatre's 'shuts' begin to close in. The masque is ended; as strange looking fishermen carry off their upturned coracles, these offer an image of the whole darkening hemisphere above.

> So when the Shadows laid asleep
> From underneath these Banks do creep
> And on the River as it flows
> With *Eben Shuts* being to close,
> The modest *Halcyon* comes in sight,
> Flying between the Day and Night . . .
> > (84.665–7)

Resolutely the poet enters the house, to say his farewell, as he turns towards the world, turns from Fairfax to Cromwell, that fiercer star.

> 'Tis not what once it was, the *World*,
> But a rule heap together hurl'd;
> All negligently overthrown,
> Gulfes, Deserts, Precipices, Stone.
> > (96.761–4)

But at Nun Appleton, in the 'square' stanzas of his own architecture, he has learnt to re-edify from the work of Fairfax.[21]

> Your lesser *World* contains the same.
> But in more decent Order tame;
> You *Heaven's Center, Nature's Lap*,
> And *Paradice's only Map*.
> > (96.765–8)

In the rural retreat, memory of the courtly revels and of the civil war can be harmonized, if only momentarily. The fantasy of garden and meadows (antimasque) is succeeded by the gorgeousness of the woods and by the final transformation, the three stages of a masque. The bewildering shift of images that created the tensions of 'An Horatian Ode' are dissolved. The building of a house, here, as in 'Music's Empire' is the work of the poet and his lyre, of Amphion or Orpheus, not of an architect.[22] It seems that at this time of supreme difficulty the accompanying power of music had in fact helped the verbalizing of what seemed to elude even the poet's power to conceive in words; by the time Marvell was celebrating *The First Anniversary of the Government under O.C.*, (pp. 108–19), written for December 1654 and published anonymously next year, the musical builder of the new state had become Cromwell himself:

> While indefatigable Cromwell hyes,
> And cuts his way still nearer to the Skyes,
> Learning a Musique in the Region clear,
> To tune this lower to that higher Sphere.

(ll. 45–8)

This is essentially a masque in which Cromwell plays the chief part (ll. 49–66, 100–3). He made himself less by ruling:

> For to be *Cromwell* was a greater thing
> Than aught below, or yet above a King:

(ll. 225–6)

whilst his enemies confess he seems a king 'And yet the same to be a King does scorn' (l. 388). This is a ritual not of power but of moderation.

The poem on the death of Cromwell is more royalist in style; but after the Restoration, Marvell set to work recreating revived Stuart myths, for his last piece of masque writing is the ironic description of the Dutch fleet sailing up the Medway (*Last Instructions to a Painter*, ll. 523–6, 535–50) followed by a storm (ll. 551–60).

Marvell's poetic energy transformed a convention for the celebration of stability and assurance – although as Stephen Orgel has observed, it was usually invoked in times of conflict if not of actual war. The rapid changes of scene from grave to gay, from land to sea to the heavens which Shirley's description of 1631 made plain[23] might indeed in outline suggest the central sequence of *Upon Appleton House*, except that since the whole aim of the masque is an unquestioning state of rapturous social identification, Marvell's use of it to explore, test, and probe the inner conflicts of his solitude represents at the very least, after the masque's destruction, the introjection of this courtly rite. Damon the Mower recalls Death; he is a strangely unhappy figure.[24] It was just the impossibility of any court masque which distanced the dancing of the hey almost as fully as the revels of 'East Coker':

> In that open field
> If you do not come too close, if you do not come too close,
> On a summer midnight, you can hear the music
> Of the weak pipe and the little drum,
> And see them dancing round the bonfire
> The association of man and woman
> In daunsinge, signifying matrimonie –
> . . . .
> Rustically solemn or in rustic laughter
> Lifting heavy feet in clumsy shoes,
> Earth feet, loam feet, lifted in country mirth
> Mirth of those long since under the earth
> Nourishing the corn.[25]

In the words of Eliot, Marvell's wit 'involves probably a recognition, implicit in the expression of every experience, of other kinds of experience which are possible'. In withdrawing to the garden, his modest and impersonal virtue allows him to enter both a larger and a smaller world, where the floral dial supplies the cosmic emblem – the sun working alike on flowers and bees. Marvell's power of packing the universe into a little space depends on his capacity to pour new poetic wine into old wineskins. In the end he achieved poetry without even the support of music or other 'languages', yet also without any lurking desire to make his verses public. It is astonishing that such a piece as 'On the Victory Obtained by Blake' should not have been printed, yet but for an accident, as it seems, all the poems would have remained unknown. So far are they from the claims to sacramental power which underlay the ritual of the Caroline masque. They were the solace of a jealously guarded privacy.

Marvell had run down the scale of creation. He might become a forest bird, but equally might become a vegetable:

> Turn me but, and you shall see
> I was but an inverted Tree.
>
> (71.567–8)

Unlike other pastoralists, he does not locate Eden in the past, still less, however, in the present. It lies perhaps with the colonists in the Bermudas – or more securely within a green thought in a green shade. Poetry offered the shield of Perseus in which the unendurable and unthinkable might be transformed:

> How safe, methinks, and strong behind
> These Trees I have incamp'd my Mind.
>
> (76.601–2)

Poetry turns retreat into measured advance, dominance, triumph; not by the social ritual of the old masque – too often an instrument for self-delusion – but by the 'esemplastic power' of solitary meditation.

Notes

1 Some public functions of the national theatre were taken over by newsletters. Players had been 'the abstracts and brief chronicles of the time', even to the extent of staging recent murders and other crimes. As Professor D. M. McKenzie pointed out in his recent Sandars Lectures at Cambridge (1976), Ben Jonson returned to the stage after ten years' absence in 1626 to castigate in *The Staple of News* the league of seven

London publishers who formed a syndicate for such letters, led by Nathaniel Butter (known to Shakespeareans as publisher of the Quarto of *King Lear*). For Jonson, the critical commentary of the playwright was a truer index of the times than scraps of gossip.

2 The best known description of this aspect of the masque comes in one of Shirley's plays, *Love's Cruelty*, II. i. 'A masque prepared and music to charm Orpheus himself into a stone ... a scene to take your eyes with wonder, now to see a forest wave and the pride of summer brought into a walking wood; in the instant, as if the sea had swallowed the earth, to see the waves capering above tall ships, Arion upon a rock playing to the dolphin, the Tritons calling upon the sea nymphs to dance before you.' This is followed by a storm, that by a heavenly transformation scene, with angels, stars and the music of the spheres 'that you would wish to be drowned indeed in such a happiness'.

3 Rhodes Dunlap, ed., *The Poems of Thomas Carew with his Masque Coelum Britannicum* (Oxford, Oxford University Press, 1949), p. 77. Hereafter, references to Carew appear in the text with page numbers given in parentheses.

4 The works of Roy Strong and Stephen Orgel on Ben Jonson and Inigo Jones, and on the masque in general, have established this predominance; I have myself attempted to show its social implications in *The Living Monument* (Cambridge, Cambridge University Press, 1976).

5 Nabbes's masque is reprinted in *A Book of Masques* presented to Allardyce Nicoll (Cambridge, Cambridge University Press, 1967). Marvell was also indebted to Nabbes's *Microcosmos* for a 'masque of quarrelling elements' (see *The Poems and Letters of Andrew Marvell*, ed. H. M. Margoliouth (2 vols., Oxford, Clarendon Press, 1927), I, p. 255, notes to 'The Unfortunate Lover').

6 From Aurelian Townshend, *Albion's Triumph* (1631) in *Poems*, ed. E. K. Chambers (Oxford, Oxford University Press, 1912), p. 77.

7 This was *Salmacida Spolia* by Davenant, 1640; also reprinted in *A Book of Masques* (see n. 5 above). A reconstruction of all the social implications of the occasion has been provided by C. V. Wedgwood. 'The Last Masque', in *Truth and Opinion: Historical Essays* (London, Macmillan, 1960).

8 This masque is based on Bruno's *Spaccio de la Bestia Trionfante*, which dates from 1584; Townshend's *Tempe Restored* is similarly based on the Valois *Ballet Comique de la Reyne* of the same period.

9 It is notable that Marvell begins his poetic career with two elegies for dead youths, and that death obtrudes into his pastoral with the figure of the Mower ('Death, thou art a mower too'), and of course into his most famous love poem 'To his Coy Mistress'.

10 Quoted from John Buxton, ed., *Poems of Michael Drayton* (London, Routledge & Kegan Paul, 1953), 1,283–84, and below, 285.

11 John M. Wallace, *Destiny his Choice: The Loyalism of Andrew Marvell* (Cambridge, Cambridge University Press, 1968), p. 70.

12 *Ibid.* p. 28.

13 See George Hibbard, 'The Country House Poem in the Seventeenth

Century', *Journal of the Warburg and Courtauld Institutes*, 19 (1956), 156–74.

14 To which might be added *The Hock Cart* addressed by Herrick to Mildmay Fane, Earl of Westmorland and Fairfax's kinsman, with its reminder 'Feed him ye must whose food fills you' addressed to the labourers. (See Raymond Williams, *The Country and the City* (London, Chatto and Windus, 1973), p. 33 for an analysis of pastoralism.)

15   'Who hath not heard of Chloris and her bower
            Fair Iris' act, employed by Juno's power
            To guard the Spring and prosper every flower
            Whom jealousy and hell thought to devour? . . .
            Chloris the Queen of the Flowers.'

                                        (Ben Jonson, *Chloridia*, 1631)

The village May Queen was seated in a bower where she remained to preside over the May Day sports.

16 Wallace, *Destiny his Choice*, p. 253. Anne Berthoff, *The Resolved Soul: A Study of Marvell's Major Poems* (Princeton, Princeton University Press, 1970), pp. 171–97, deals with this part of the poem as 'The Masque of Nature' but is not really concerned with the form of the original masques.

17 See 'The Mower to the Glo-worms' (*Poems*, p. 47):

            'Ye Country Comets, that portend
            No War, nor Princes' funeral,
            Shining unto no higher end
            Then to pressage the Grasses fall.

18 'Massacre' – one recalls the battle cry 'Jesus – and no quarter!'

19 Quoted from T. S. Eliot, *Four Quartets* (New York, Harcourt Brace, 1943), p. 14.

20 *Tempe Restored* (1632), one of Townshend's masques for Henrietta Maria. Miss Scoular has identified his posture with emblem pictures of a river god. See her *Natural Magic: Studies in the Presentation of Nature in English Poetry from Spenser to Marvell* (Oxford, Oxford University Press, 1965).

21 John Wallace believes that 'the very stanza form itself is an image of Fairfacian virtue' because it embodies the form described by Puttenham in the *Arte of English Poesie* of 'the square or quadrangle equilater' (eight octosyllabic lines). Puttenham writes that 'The square [is] for his inconcussable steadiness likened to the earth', so that Aristotle terms a constant-minded man 'a square man' (*Destiny His Choice*, pp. 237–8).

22 'Loyalism was created from Chaos, in those moments of desperation when the only conceivable action is the performance of daily routine,' Wallace, p. 41.

23 See n. 2 above. The vast quantity of literary reflection packed into Marvell's poem has also been mentioned.

24 Since mowing is essentially temporary harvest work, Marvell may imply that Damon is no true rustic; he could not, like a shepherd, follow this occupation all the year, and at harvest time everyone must help get in the crop.

25 Eliot, *Four Quartets*, pp. 11–12.

Shakespeare and the
Performer's Art

V

Marlowe's *Doctor Faustus* and the Eldritch tradition

Doctor Faustus, most concentrated of Elizabethan tragedies before *Macbeth*, also ranges widely and is composed from the union of several older traditions. Hardin Craig has called it a perfectly generalized morality (*English Religious Drama of the Middle Ages*, 1955, p. 386). The bond by which Faustus gives himself to Lucifer is valid because it is made in the presence and against the miraculous intervention of God, the Judge in whose court the agreement is registered. *Doctor Faustus* is a tragedy of responsibility and choice, though not till the final scene does the full realization of his action come to the doomed magician when, like Everyman, but with such a different anticipation, he is called to his reckoning. Set against these tragic issues, much of the conjuring which fills the middle of the play may seem now irrelevant and tasteless. Perhaps it would become more explicable, if not more acceptable, were it seen as a development of what I shall call the eldritch tradition. Eldritch diabolism, while both comic and horrific, is amoral and does not involve personal choice or the notion of personal responsibility. The cackle of ghoulish laughter is essential to winter's tales of sprites and goblins, phantoms and illusions. Country mumming was and still is designed in the comic-horrific mood, whether this is displayed in the blackened faces of Plough Monday men, or the huge wicker monster of the Padstow Hobby; but in the early sixteenth century William Dunbar, a court poet, could exploit the same area of feeling. Of Dunbar, C. S. Lewis has written:

> In him more than in any other, the comic overlaps with the demoniac and the terrifying. He also is of the 'eldritch' school; the wild whoop of his noisiest laughter has, and is meant to have, something sinister in it . . . in 'The Dance of the Seven Deadly Sins' . . . these 'sweir bumbard belly huddrouns' and these highlanders whose clatter deaves the devil himself are intended to make us laugh. But notice, on the other hand, that we are

laughing at torture. The grotesque figures skip through fire, jag each other with knives, and are constantly spewing out molten gold with which they are constantly refilled 'up to the thrott'. (*English Literature in the Sixteenth Century*, 1954, pp. 94–5)

Compared with an earlier grave treatment of the Seven Deadly Sins, such as that in 'A Disputation between a Good Man and the Devil' (*Minor Poems of the Vernon MS*, EETS, 1892, pp. 329–54), the eldritch quality which Dunbar shares with *Doctor Faustus* involves the reader or spectator much more intimately, and is therefore by nature more dramatic in its appeal.

In his 'Visitation of St Francis' ('How Dumbar wes desyrd to be ane Freir'), the Scottish poet provided another illustration to *Doctor Faustus*. Seeing Mephistophilis for the first time in his own form, Faustus commands him to

> Go, and return an old Franciscan Friar,
> That holy shape becomes a devil best.
>
> (I.iii.25–6)[1]

In Dunbar's poem, the poet, being visited in a dream by St Francis and offered a friar's habit, declares that sanctity is more often found among bishops; that he has already worn the friar's habit and did not find it led to holiness.

> Als lang as I did beir the freiris style,
> In me, God wait, wes mony wrink and wyle;
> In me wes falset with every wight to flatter,
> Quilk mycht be flemit with na haly watter;
> I wes ay reddy all men to begyle.

> This freir that did Sanct Francis thair appeir,
> Ane fiend he wes in liknes of ane freir:
> He vaneist away with stynk and fyrie smowk;
> With him me thocht all the hous end he towk,
> And I awoik as wy that wes in weir.

Dunbar expressed the eldritch in savage energetic movement; and in *Doctor Faustus* the clowns' patter supplies a verbal equivalent to the galvanic frenzy of the Seven Deadly Sins of Dunbar. They 'bounce at the gate' and rush into the Duke's presence with merely comic bustle, but in the scene between Wagner and the Clown, images of hell-fire and the torn flesh of the victims are evoked by the backchat:

> *Wagner* . . . The villain's out of service, and so hungry that I know he would give his soul to the devil, for a shoulder of mutton, though it were blood-raw.
> *Clown.* Not so, neither; I had need to have it well roasted, and good sauce to it, if I pay so dear, I can tell you. (I. iv. 8–12)

Faustus's own tricks vary from those of the common conjurer to those of the eldritch 'shape-changer'; his transformations, though devoid of the moral significance which burns in the scenes of choice, combine the comic and the horrific, being designed to raise at once a shudder and a guffaw.

Benvolio and the knights who cut off Faustus's head, only to find that, 'Zounds, the devil's alive again', are deceived by an old trick, popular at Christmas feasts. Perhaps this very trick is behind the most eldritch of all monsters, the Green Knight of the fourteenth-century romance, who after a beheading picks up his head and rides away. For at the end of the poem the Green Knight confesses he was sent to Arthur's hall by the enchantress Morgan le Fay to terrify Guinevere. This final revelation that his magic shape was due to conjuring at once reduces its fearsomeness, placing it on a different supernatural footing. The beginning of the poem is altered by this disclosure at the end.[2] When such figures appeared at real medieval feasts, they would be as gigantic as the Green Knight, because the player's whole body would be encased in a false trunk, its shoulders appearing at the level of his eyebrows, with the false head fixed on top.

Conversely, the early jests about false heads and false legs which Faustus sheds so lightly gain a terrible retrospective irony when in the last scene the Scholars find his mangled remains – and it may be that the stage properties were identical.

Second Scholar.   O help us heaven! see here are Faustus' limbs
                    All torn asunder by the hand of death.
Third Scholar.   The devils whom Faustus served have torn him thus.

                                        (V. iii. 7–9)

A voluntary act of this sort was reputed to have saved a Pope who had sold himself to the Devil but who, unlike Faustus, contrived to evade the bargain:

Silvinus, ye pope, dede homage to ye devyl to come to hyg astate. ffirst he was a munke, whan he spak wyth ye feend, & dede hym homage. Yanne, ye feend dede helpe hym up, to be an erchebyssechop, & afterwards to be pope. Yanne he askyd ye feend, how longe he schulde lyve? Ye feend seyde, tyl he dyde synge a messe in ierusalem. (*Jacob's Well*, Chapter 4, EEETS, 1900, pp. 31–2)

Singing mass one day, Silvinus heard a great din of fiends and found that the name of the church was Jerusalem. But after shriving himself, he hacked off the limbs with which he had worshipped the Devil and had his body laid in a cart drawn by wild beasts, to be buried wherever they should take him. They bore the corpse to the church of St John Lateran, where he was buried.

And in signe yat he hath mercy of god for his penaunce, git, fro yat tyme hyderward agen ye tyme bat ony pope schal dye, his bonys in ye grave make dyn, and swetyn out oyle in signe of mercy.

For those who faithfully believed in hell-fire and the physical torture of the damned, this story would carry an eldritch mirth it no longer possesses. The Devil had cheated with the same pun that was later to cozen King Henry IV, but he had been cheated in his turn.

Other medieval poems bring horrific jesting very close to pure terror. Such is *The Aunters of Arthur*, with its yelling ghost rising from the Cumberland tarn, or the Auchinleck version of *St Patrick's Purgatory*, where the devils jest with unnerving irony, extending their menace in playful threats; similar grotesquerie is found in St Brendan's voyage. Gargoyles and the grotesques carved on capitals and misericords exemplify the same tradition. Grand, dignified, and melancholy devils belong to the sixteenth century rather than to earlier times; Mephistophilis is of this new order. Perhaps the conception of a deliberate rejection of God could be seriously entertained within a religious context only when a degree of general scepticism was well established.

In Marlowe's day, eldritch mirth is most frequently found combined with antipapal stories, with scurrilities and fabliaux in the popular jest-books of the common press. These play boisterously with notions of hell-fire, combining obscene tales with parody of holy water, sacred relics, and other rejected objects of veneration from the old faith. As though some lingering fear of summary vengeance forbade such mockery except under the protecting form of jests, there is a defensive refusal to risk a straight penalty by straight challenge.

One of these works, *Beware the Cat* (1570), attributed to no less a personage than William Baldwin, author of *The Mirror for Magistrates*, tells how witches in Ireland send to market fine red swine who, when led to the water, turn, like Faustus's horse, into wisps of hay. This book is full of magic shape-changes effected by the witches' familiars, the cats.

Tarlton's Newes out of Purgatorie (1590), presented by Robin Goodfellow, comes a degree nearer to the stage; it shows the famous clown – a baiter of papists and of precisians in his time – returning to witness for the existence of Purgatory, 'pale and wan'. The writer attempts to conjure him: 'Depart from me, Satan, the resemblance of whomsoever thou dost carry.'

At this, pitching his staff down on the end, and crossing one leg over the other, he answered thus: Why, you whorson dunce, think you to set Dick Tarlton *non plus* with your aphorisms? . . . Oh, there is a Calvinist; what, do you make Heaven and Hell *contraria immediata*? . . . yes, yes, my good brother, there is *quoddam tertium*. (ed. J. O. Halliwell, 1844, pp. 55–6)

He urges that men of old would never have paid so much for dirges and trentals for no gain; and writes further:

if any upstart Protestant deny, if thou hast no place of scripture ready to confirm it, say as Pythagoras' scholars did, *ipse dixit*, and to all bon companions it shall stand for a principle. (*ibid.* p. 57)

In *Tarlton's Newes* this championing of a papal doctrine is combined with extreme scurrility, as in the tale of Friar Onion, who pretended to be the Angel Gabriel in order to have his will of a woman. (The story is from Boccaccio, *Il Decamerone*, 4.2, though the name of Friar Onion is from 6.10.) The reckless jesting which was associated with Marlowe has its counterpart in the recklessness of Tarlton and other early clowns, and so contributed to the force of the comic scenes in *Doctor Faustus*; Wagner's assumption of the voice of a precisian is very like that of Tarlton in the jestbook.

Another work of similar kind, though like *Beware the Cat* directed especially against the Irish, was Barnaby Rich's *Greene's Newes from Heaven and Hell* (1593).[3] The ghost of Robert Greene, excluded from Heaven for writing about coneycatchers and from Hell for disclosing their tricks, comes to recite his adventures and ends up as 'the maddest goblin that ever walked in the moonshine'. There is a tragic undertone to this ribald work, for Rich was vainly seeking redress against a powerful enemy, Adam Loftus, Archbishop of Dublin, and his complaints are slipped in between churl's tales of a henpecked bricklayer who goes to Hell to avoid his wife, and of the ghost of a miller whose lecherous plans had recoiled upon himself and made him agent to his own cuckolding; he was now transformed into

a most deformed creature, with a monstrous pair of horns, growing from the upper part of his forehead, the tips whereof turned round into his eyes, and growing there again into his head, had made him stark blind, that he had no manner of sight. (ed. R. B. McKerrow, 1911, p. 44)

This eldritch monster, as terrifying as the fiend which Edgar describes at Dover Cliff in *King Lear*, is not perhaps more horrible than some of the cardboard monsters used on the stage for shows of detraction and scorn. These were often of a 'religious' intention. One such was given at court on Twelfth Night in the first year of Elizabeth's reign, where cardinals, abbots, and bishops were presented in monstrous animal forms; later, according to Lyly, Martin Marprelate was brought on the public stage with 'a cock's comb, an ape's face, a wolf's belly, cat's claws &c' (*Pappe with an Hatchet,*

1589; see E. K. Chambers, *The Elizabethan Stage*, 1923, 4.232).

So Mephistophilis transforms the Clowns into an ape and a dog, and this scene (III.3) follows immediately upon the scene of Pope-baiting. The grotesque hobgoblin pranks played by Faustus upon the Horse-courser and the Ostler are of the kind recounted in jestbooks, where they are connected with antipapal stories, and it seems very likely that, in the popular theatres, the Clowns' afterpieces were largely composed of such matter.[4] By bringing these jests and the Devil's fireworks within the compass of the play, something was achieved for Marlowe's contemporaries, if not for audiences of a later day; this was possible because the strength of the comic-horrific mood gave to these jests a macabre quality they no longer possess. There was something dangerous in the Clown's role; he was apt to be treated with sudden unexpected violence as when in *Titus Andronicus* he is condemned to death and goes off with a wry jest: 'I have brought up my neck to a fair end.'

By repute Marlowe died unrepentant and shared the fate of his own hero, as all the orthodox were convinced; but Robert Greene, another jester with holy things, lived to write his repentance in the very accents of *Doctor Faustus*. He began his reckless career with:

> Hell (quoth I) what talk you of hell to me? I know, if I once come there I shall have the company of better men than myself, I shall also meet with some mad knaves there, and so long as I shall not sit alone, my care is the less. (*Repentance of Robert Greene*, 1592; Bodley Head Quarto, 1923, p. 11. Cf. *Doctor Faustus*, I. iii. 58–60, II. i. 125–33)

And he ended with:

> Oh, I feel a hell already in my conscience, the number of my sins do muster before my eyes, the poor men's plaints that I have wronged cries out in mine ears and saith, Robin Greene, thou art damned; nay, the justice of heaven tells me I cannot be saved ... I am taught by the scriptures to pray; but to whom shall I pray? To him that I have blasphemed? ... Oh that my last gasp were come, that I might be with Judas and Cain, for their place is better than mine ... (*ibid.* p. 14)

Greene's Vision gives an even clearer echo of Faustus's opening speech at its own opening:

> I know Stipendium peccati mors, O then shall I fly from thy presence? (*Works*, ed. A. B. Grosart, 1881–3, 12.205)

These works may have been contributed to the Greene legend by other writers; he remained a popular figure, often coupled with Tarlton (who was given also some edifying ballads of repentance). Greene was alternately presented as a mad merry rogue, chronicler of coneycatchers, or as a tragic repentant blasphemer – the two sides of Greene's legend match the two sides of Faustus's story.

In the tragedy, however, implicit reconciliation of these two opposite states is attempted through different levels for the conjuring, which leads continuously from horseplay up to tragedy. This is not an argument for unity of composition, for it seems clear that Marlowe had a collaborator and also that the text was modified in transmission. It is a plea for unity of conception. The naive attitude which produced the jestbooks was incorporated in *Doctor Faustus* because the boldness of his intellectual challenge demanded this protective or compensatory relief. In real life any situation of unusual danger will often call out the impulse to ridicule or laughter. The 'savage comic humour' which T. S. Eliot felt in Marlowe has a historic basis in the eldritch tradition, here and in parts of *The Jew of Malta*. Today these are relatively inaccessible; they can be recovered best, perhaps, from the fooling in the tragedies of Shakespeare, especially of course in *King Lear*; but Shakespeare is so much subtler than Marlowe that the comparison does not greatly help. It is rather by comparison with literature of an earlier time, such as the works of Dunbar, that it may be possible to estimate the weight of the eldritch tradition in *Doctor Faustus*.

It is the comprehensiveness of the play that prevents it from being fitted into any of the earlier 'kinds'. What remains in it of the morality has been generalized, not only by the daring of Faustus's challenge and the pity and fear of his last hour, but also by the balance supplied in the figures of Mephistophilis, the Scholars, the Old Man, and even the Clowns.

Faustus's daring is embedded in familiar protective jest; the ingredients of this play were popular, however the transformation of the whole made them into something new.

Not only the scope, but ultimately, as I believe, the dignity of the play is increased by combining the intellectual aspiration and heroic dreams of the great scholar with the comic ghoulishness of the folk; by combining the fine and sensitive mind lured to self-destruction with the gross simplicity that has not yet reached the level of making a moral choice, whose terror is fitly represented by roaring property dragons and devils with fireworks. Faustus himself appeared in full canonicals; and perhaps, in view of the many tales about the visible appearance of the devil in this play (see Chambers, *The Elizabethan Stage*, 3.423–4), the cross was felt a necessary protection for the chief actor.

> The gull gets on a surplis
>   With a crosse upon his breast,
> Like Allen playing Faustus,
>   In that manner he was drest.
>   (S. Rowland, *Knave of Clubs*, 1609, p. 29)

Notes

1 I have used the parallel-text edition of *Doctor Faustus* by W. W. Greg (Oxford, Clarendon Press, 1950); quotations are from his accompanying *Tragical History of the Life and Death of Doctor Faustus: A Conjectural Reconstruction* (Oxford, Clarendon Press, 1950).

2 I would see the end of *Sir Gawain and the Green Knight* as a comical transformation, dissolving some of the horror of the beginning; it becomes more of a traditional Christmas game, or at least that possibility is raised. For the traditional views, see Albert B. Friedman, 'Morgan le Fay in Sir Gawain and the Green Knight', *Speculum*, 35 (1960), 260–74.

3 Pamphlets about wandering spirits, whether by Robin Goodfellow or depicting him, carry on the same tradition as Dunbar's 'Ballad of Kind Kittok', where the goodwife rides to Heaven on a snail in company with a newt, slips in when Peter is not looking, and slips out again for 'the aill of hevin wes sour'.

4 As late as 1681 such monstrous animals were used in antipapal processions, carried out on the anniversary of Queen Elizabeth's accession, 17 November, and culminating in the burning of the Pope opposite the statue of Queen Elizabeth at Temple Bar; see Sheila Williams, *Journal of the Warburg and Courtauld Institutes*, 21 (1958), 104–18.

VI

Shakespeare's primitive art*

Spectacle is that part of tragedy which has least connection with the art of poetry, as Aristotle believed: but, when the text of plays – even of Shakespeare's plays – provides only raw material for John Barton and other theatre directors, it might be thought 'So much the worse for poetry'.

Today Bali rather than Athens supplies dramatic models, and the cult of primitive theatre is so strong, that it may have been suspected I come to praise Shakespeare as a barbaric contemporary, after the fashion of Jan Kott – to enrol him in the theatre of cruelty. On the contrary, taking a conventionally historic view, I shall try to recover traces of the archaic spectacular tradition from which Shakespeare first started and to which, in the richly transmuted form of his final plays, he returned. I hope to identify the scenic proverb, the elements of that unspoken language which derives from the primal stage arts of gesture, costume, grouping, pantomime; to reveal the influence of those inexplicable dumb shows, which, although he rejected them, Shakespeare never forgot.

In doing this, it may be possible to uncover also something of his creative process. As his poetic imagination subdued itself to what it worked in, the visual and scenic basis of his art became absorbed into his poetry. An actor before he was playwright, Shakespeare carried always with him the memories of his repertory. It has been convincingly shown by Dr Edward Armstrong that Shakespeare's memories, as they sank below the level of consciousness, formed themselves into 'image clusters' or associative groups. Image clusters would have had visual and scenic counterparts, but since 'memory is an *imaginative* reconstruction',[1] what Shakespeare recalled from the stage, more especially when it need not have been conscious recall, was converted by that act 'into something rich and strange'.

*The annual Shakespeare lecture of the British Academy, 1965.

I would begin by distinguishing two traditions of spectacle in his inheritance, which might be termed the high road and the low road to drama proper. There are the lofty icons or tableaux of coronation, triumph, great marriages or funerals; and, at the other extreme, tumblers and jesters, comic quick-change artists, such as the poor tatterdemalion dwarf that William Dunbar introduced running through his parts at the Market Cross of Edinburgh (in 'The Manere of Crying of Ane Playe'). Both extremes met in the ring of Burbage's Theatre, London's 'game place' or 'playing place'; but Marlowe and Shakespeare began by taking the high road and rejecting 'such conceits as clownage keeps in play'. Marlowe's lofty first creation, Tamburlaine, is descended from the King of the Moors, who rode in many civic processions, followed by his train, and gorgeously attired in red satin and silver paper; the spectacle is transmuted into heroic poetry,[2] by which it has been preserved for posterity. The originals are long forgotten.

Marlowe's doctrine of power and glory was very largely a doctrine of sovereignty and he made use of another image by which it was forcibly brought home to the simple. Every parish church in the land contained a copy of Foxe's *Book of Martyrs* and the edition of 1580 has for frontispiece a crowned king mounting to his throne by trampling on a prostrate foe, whose triple crown is falling from him. The king is Henry VIII. The footstool is the Pope. Tamburlaine trampling on Bajazet repeats the image.

For many people the royal image assuaged a deep privation they felt in the loss of those older images that had been familiar for so long, whose simple wonder-working mechanisms the reformers had triumphantly torn out. Opponents of the stage were apt to charge the common players with what seems to us the very incongruous sin of idolatry, because they perceived a line of descent from the older icons to the new. One such sour cleric, writing in 1587 *A Mirror of Monsters*,[3] describes a marriage procession of Pride, Lord of the Theatre, and Lechery, Lady of Worldlings, which passed through the streets to the Chapel of Adultery at Hollow-well (that is, Burbage's Theatre in Holywell Street in the old grounds of a Benedictine nunnery). It was presided over by a magic winged image of a holy child, made of alabaster and painted in life-like colours. The Child Cupid carried emblems of torch and dart, and could nod the head in a magic fashion, which excited wonder as he was set up in a niche in the Parlour of Payne, where the North Wind assisted the miracle. The cleric adds to this infernal revelry a troop of monsters sent from Satan.

A grand wedding tableau also concludes *Tamburlaine*, Part I, where the royal virgin Zenocrate is crowned by a trinity of kings.

This, though doubtless without overt intent, recalls the sacred icon of a humbler Virgin crowned by a loftier Trinity; and the depth of conflict resolved in this play is suggested by its unconscious combination of Catholic and Reformed iconography.

In Marlovian style Shakespeare develops *Titus Andronicus* as a series of tableaux. The well-known contemporary illustration of the opening scene, by Henry Peacham, shows the Blackamoor flourishing a drawn sword over Tamora's doomed sons. In spite of the fact that he is himself a captive at this point, I think Aaron might have momentarily assumed the pose of a black-visaged headsman, to produce a tableau that must have been common enough in martyrology. The magician, the king, the blackamoor, the weeping queen, had long been familiar, so that imaginative roles of Shakespeare and of Marlowe are but half-emerged from a penumbra which surrounds and enlarges them beyond the dimensions of individual parts, to the sacred and archaic originals from which they derive.

The most powerful icon of *Titus Andronicus* is the silent figure of Lavinia mutilated. The first of her family to meet her unconsciously evokes the image of the green and the withered tree, one commonly used in festive procession to symbolize a flourishing and fading commonwealth; when she is next compared with a conduit running red wine, the shock of the conflicting festive image inflates the horror. She becomes herself, in metamorphosis, a stony silent image of violence and outrage:

> What stern ungentle hands
> Hath lopp'd, and hew'd, and made thy body bare
> Of her two branches – those sweet ornaments
> Whose circling shadows kings have sought to sleep in? . . .
> Alas, a crimson river of warm blood,
> Like to a bubbling fountain stirr'd with wind,
> Doth rise and fall between thy rosed lips . . .
> And notwithstanding all this loss of blood –
> As from a conduit with three issuing spouts –
> Yet do thy cheeks look red as Titan's face,
> Blushing to be encounter'd with a cloud.   (II. iv. 16–32)

The heraldic conventions of its images and the extreme violence of its plot[4] make *Titus Andronicus* unique among Shakespeare's works. In his English histories, I would like to think that he borrowed a tableau from that Coventry play given by the townsmen before Queen Elizabeth at Kenilworth in July 1575, when Shakespeare, a boy of 11, was living not far away. An old Hocktide contest between men and women had become associated with the memory of a battle between English and Danes, in which, after initial victories, the Danes were led captive by English women; this was combined with a drill display by the town's muster men. The image of this play may have been revived in *Henry VI* when Joan la Pucelle or Margaret of Anjou triumphed over English warriors; but since 'remembering is an imaginative reconstruction', the image has been reversed, and the foreign women triumph over Englishmen.

Londoners would not have recognized this image, since they did not know the original, but by the time he wrote the second part of *Henry IV*, Shakespeare felt sufficiently a Londoner to mock their local show. The London archery band was led by a small group of the élite, known as Prince Arthur's Knights, who marched annually in procession, each with his name from Arthurian story, and bearing his arms emblazoned. Justice Shallow, in recalling the exploits of his youth, claims to have played the part of the jester, Dagonet; but his memory prompts him rather to enact another part, that of a crafts-master whom he had admired.

> I remember at Mile End Green, when I lay at Clement's Inn – I was then Sir Dagonet in Arthur's show – there was a little quiver fellow, and 'a would manage you his piece thus; and 'a would about and about, and come you in, and come you in. 'Rah, tah, tah!' would 'a say; 'Bounce!' would 'a say; and away again would 'a go, and again would 'a come. I shall ne'er see such a fellow.   (*2 Henry IV*, III. ii. 271–8)

This is not very far from the open parody of Beaumont's *The Knight of the Burning Pestle*, when Ralph the bold Grocer-Errant reaches the culmination of his glory by playing the May Lord on a conduit head, and then leads out the musters to Mile End Green.

The high tradition of early tragedy had been established by Marlowe and mediated through the majestic presence of Edward Alleyn the tragedian. Alleyn was, however, a master of more than one style – of all the 'activities of youth, activities of age' that were found among strolling players, where he had learnt his trade. One of his star performances, the title role in Greene's *Orlando Furioso*, offers a display of virtuosity such as Dunbar's dwarf suggests. His own copy of the part, preserved at Dulwich, shows how gaily Alleyn could point it up. As he turned from lover to madman and back to warrior, Orlando must have raised both a shudder and guffaw. He tears a shepherd limb from limb (offstage) and enters bearing a leg on his shoulder; he fights a battle with spits and dripping pans (a familiar comic turn); his action and speech are constantly changing, and different rhetorical styles must have been put into play, as Alleyn, like a practised juggler whirling a set of clubs, spun up one after another his brightly coloured lines.

A single actor could hold an audience with such rapid transitions (the Admiral's Men later developed a group of plays for the quick-change artist) and the greatest actors prided themselves on 'Protean' mutability. 'Medley' plays rose from the mixed activities of the theatre. Burbage's playhouse could accommodate a monster, an antic, a grotesque dragon made of brown paper that 'would fright the ladies that they would shriek'. In medieval times such an irruption would have been termed a marvel; today, it would be a happening. The 'medley' evoked a mingled feeling of fright and triumph, gasps and laughter; but it was a professional show, as the older romantic adventures were not. There is much more professional distinction than at first appears between a shambling romance like *Sir Clyomon and Sir Clamydes*, which is older than the Theatre, and a medley like *The Cobbler's Prophecy*, written by Wilson in the late eighties. In his *Apology for Poetry* Sidney's description of a romance implies that the stage was set out with a group of symbolic objects, which, protected by the heavens, attracted the players into a variety of settings. The garden, the shipwreck, the cave with its fire-breathing monster, and the battlefield, must have made up a most elaborate play. Thanks to modern studies, we are now familiar with the visual aspects of the city gates, the tree, the cave, the ship, the arbour of the medieval and Tudor stages; these provided a gift for the artist's imagination to which only a Melanie Klein could hope to do justice.

Such symbolic objects were used also by Wilson and others in the medley plays, and in Shakespeare's early theatre. Studied coldly on the page, the medleys may appear to offer sheer nonsense, for their effect depends on what a modern French writer has termed 'the theatre's magic relation to reality and danger'. The magician with his wonderful shows (a type of the playwright) was a central figure, together with a pair of lovers, a clown, a speaker of riddles and prophecies, one or more of the classical gods and goddesses, and some fireworks. In Wilson's play one of the 'pavilions' was set on fire; in another, a juggler appeared to whisk away the serious title board 'Speculum' and to substitute 'Wily Beguiled'.

Medleys evolved their own set of sequences when they were the property of a famous troupe like the Queen's Men, and eventually must have delighted the audience only by an unpredictable mixture of predictable items, that belong together because they have been seen together before.[5]

In *The Old Wives' Tale* George Peele raised the romance to a similar professional level by setting it in the framework of a story about three actors who have lost their way in a wood. Antic, Frolic, Fantastic, the servants of a lord, whose names proclaim their quality, take refuge in a cottage, where the old wife's tale comes to life; but the audience are released from the confines of time and space and move freely between a magician's study, a well, a hillock with magic flames upon it, and crossroads in a wood. There is no need for a plot; the princess 'white as snow and red as blood', her two brothers, the wicked enchanter, the wandering knight, are as familiar as the set of emblematic objects among which they move. Gaps in the action are taken for granted. There are twenty-four parts (many silent) in this brief play, designed for a company of about ten.

Shakespeare began by turning his back upon medley and romance, to write classical plays like *Titus Andronicus* and *The Comedy of Errors*. The fecundity of the early staging was transferred to his vocabulary, where he poured out crowded images, mingled, as Dr Johnson was to observe, with endless variety of proportion and innumerable varieties of combination. The conflict of incompatible and paradoxical images which surges through his comedy derives indirectly from the physical crowding of the old stages, and therefore was readily acceptable to his audience. Ben Jonson thought that Shakespeare was carried away by his own facility – 'His wit was in his power; would the rule of it had been so too.' Charles Lamb noted that 'Before one idea has burst its shell, another has hatched and clamours for disclosure'. Primitive art, repudiated as spectacle, is transformed by Shakespeare into a characteristic mode of imaginative working, where the dumb language of shows combines with higher, more articulate, forms. Greene, railing on Shakespeare as an 'upstart Crow', was putting him in the shape of an Antic, the lowest and most scurrilous type of dumb player; but as author ('Johannes Factotum') Greene suggests he has turned the actor's versatility into writing, with the 'ease' and 'facility' that his friends were later to praise. He sees the connection between Shakespeare's two activities, the second an extension of the first.

Shakespeare has left at least three accounts of this process: Richard II's soliloquy in Pomfret Castle, Duke Theseus on the poet's eye, and the fifty-third Sonnet, all (as I would think) written somewhere about his thirtieth year, in 1594.

Alone in a prison cell, the uncrowned Richard peoples his little world with a teeming succession of diversified forms, which come nearer to the comic actors' multiple roles than to the playwright's art. [And Burbage, it should be remembered, was an even more Protean actor than Alleyn.]

> Thus play I in one person many people,
> And none contented. Sometimes am I King;
> Then treasons make me wish myself a beggar,
> And so I am. Then crushing penury
> Persuades me I was better when a king,

Then am I king'd again; and by and by
Think that I am unking'd by Bolingbroke,
And straight am nothing. (V. v. 31–8)

Richard tries to hammer out his inner conflict to a set pattern; but
a charm of music hushes his restless activity of mind and returns him
to the hard immures of his prison. This suddenly begets an image or
icon of the tragic mode.

I wasted time, and now doth time waste me;
For now hath time made me his numb'ring clock. (V. v. 49–50)

The prisoner develops the image of a clock at length, his finger
becoming the hand, his face the dial (from which he is wiping the
tears), and his groans the bell; while the gay motion of organic life is
transferred in his imagination to the coronation of his supplanter. He
sees himself as a wooden 'Jack o' the clock' such as provided a simple
foolery for onlookers by its movement.[6]

Recalled again to his surroundings, he hears from a poor groom of
the stable of the usurper's triumph, and 'in the quick forge and
working house of thought' transforms himself in his degradation as
Bottom was transformed, by the ass's head.

I was not made a horse;
And yet I bear a burden like an ass,
Spurr'd, gall'd and tir'd by jauncing Bolingbroke. (V. v. 92–4)

A popular game with the Coventry men and others – mounted men
on one another's shoulders for comic mock-tournaments.

The nature of our general perception of the world, and of our own
body, is so primitive and deep-seated a foundation of our identity
that we cannot imagine how these basic levels of perception may
change from age to age. But from Shakespeare's work it may be
gathered how the icon's immobility and the medley's ever-changing
succession of 'streamy associations' became integrated in full poetic
drama, the fusion of poetry and spectacle, of inner and outer worlds.
This remains primitive art only in the sense that our perception of
the world is itself analogous to a work of art – 'a complex ordering
of attitude and belief achieved a stage earlier than discursive
statement'.[8] It utilizes but is emphatically not the same as that mental
process (conducted largely through visual symbols) which we meet in
dreams – primitive thinking, as one psychologist terms it.[9] Plays are
'such stuff as dreams are made on' – they are not dreams.

The capacity for pre-conscious and intuitive ordering found in
both Marlowe and Shakespeare is characteristic of drama, where

preverbal and verbal languages combine in one total statement. As Duke Theseus observes, the 'seething brain' of the poet apprehends more than cool reason ever comprehends, giving to things unknown, to airy nothing a *shape* (which was the technical name for an actor's costume) a *habitation* (or 'locus' on the stage) and a *name* (which the early actors wore pinned to their chests on a scroll). *A Midsummer Night's Dream* is full of the magic of the early stage; Professor Coghill has recently pointed out some links with the play of magic and quick changes of identity, *John a Kent and John a Cumber*.

The Sonnets, which I take to have been written about the same time, open with a strong and familiar icon. A beautiful youth, embodiment of spring, is urged to marry and produce an heir. The choice of topic has caused some surprise, and C. S. Lewis went so far as to inquire: 'What man in the whole world, except a father in law or potential father in law cares whether any other man gets married?'[10]

But *was* the theme so very unusual? Was there not at least one great person, in whose excellence the red and white rose united, who for some thirty-five years had been constantly exhorted not to let beauty's flower fade unpropagated? Any poet approaching a new patron would find the royal model readily adaptable, since every noble household reproduced in miniature the patterns of royal service. Beginning to learn his courtier's alphabet, Shakespeare naturally fell to his copy book. That great icon of springtime beauty which Spenser had once delineated in his April Eclogue remained the fixed form for praises of the Queen, in her public capacity, though she was now sixty years old: Sir John Davies produced in 1596 *Astraea*, his enamelled acrostics, in which she magically controls the seasons, like Titania and Oberon.

> Earth now is green and heaven is blue,
> Lively spring, that makes all new,
> Jolly spring, doth enter;
> Sweet young sunbeams do subdue
> Angry, aged winter.
>
> Blasts are mild and seas are calm,
> Every meadows flows with balm,
> The earth wears all her riches.
> Harmonious birds sing such a charm,
> As ear and heart bewitches.
>
> Reserve, sweet spring, this nymph of ours,
> Eternal garlands of thy flowers,
> Green garlands never wasting;
> In her shall last our youth's fair spring,
> Now and for ever flourishing,
> As long as heaven is lasting.

In her private person Elizabeth might typify 'angry, aged Winter': but not as Astraea. Shakespeare's youth is more vulnerable than this changeless image; 'the world's fair ornament', he dwells where 'men as plants increase' and beauties must 'die as fast as they see others grow'. His beauty must therefore be transmitted to his heir (and this was also his duty as heir of a great family); yet the poet too, as father-creator, can dream that in his verse 'I engraft you new'. The play of fancy deepens, the royal icon gives way to a multitude of images, as the beloved is seen to sum up 'all those friends which I thought buried'. Now 'their images I loved, I view in thee', till ultimately the whole world becomes reflected in this one being and so integrated in the poet's mind. The beauty of the beloved, like that of God, is seen everywhere, and he sums up the loveliness of past and present, of both the sexes, of all the seasons, of history and poetry. In the fifty-third sonnet, Shakespeare's Adonis and Marlowe's Helen attend on the beloved, who combines the loftiness of a Platonic ideal with the Protean 'shadows' and 'shapes' of the actors' art.[11] Here is the swarming profusion of the medley – gods, shepherds, lovers, magicians with their attendant spirits – completely harmonized and introjected by a complex poetic image:

> What is your substance, whereof are you made,
> That millions of strange shadows on you tend?
> Since every one hath, every one, one shade,
> And you, but one, can every shadow lend.
> Describe Adonis, and the counterfeit
> Is poorly imitated after you;
> On Helen's cheek all art of beauty set,
> And you in Grecian tires are painted new.
> Speak of the spring and foison of the year:
> The one doth shadow of your beauty show,
> The other as your bounty doth appear,
> And you in every blessed shape we know.
> > In all external grace you have some part,
> > But you like none, none you, for constant heart.

Eventually, in Sonnet 104, Shakespeare denies that Time moves for his beloved, and in the last poem of all, the lovely boy, an emblem of eternal youth, stands charming the glass of old Father Time, stilling in its clockwise motion the onward sweep of Chronos' 'sickle hour'.

It is no part of my present argument to trace the development of Shakespeare's art after the stage of full integration represented by *Richard II*. From 1594 his career was bound up with the Lord Chamberlain's Men; stability and cohesion came to his theatre. It was true of the whole age, but especially of Shakespeare, that he united the cosmic with the human image, most powerfully in his great tragedies.

If I may quote a poet of our own day:

> Sorrow is deep and vast – we travel on
> As far as pain can penetrate, to the end
> Of power and possibility; to find
> The contours of the world, with heaven align'd
> Upon infinity; the shape of man!
>
> Kathleen Raine, 'Sorrow' (from *Living in Time*)

In *Hamlet* Shakespeare refashioned an old tragedy, where the original Hamlet may have offered the same kind of Protean jesting as Orlando Furioso, the comic madman. By transforming and incorporating such a role, Shakespeare regained imaginative access to a great fund of energy, and the character is his most complex creation. Yet there is a void at the centre of Hamlet the man – the unfocused, unplumbed grief, the 'pang without a name, void, dark and drear' which all his complex introspection leaves a mystery, an eloquent silence. And there is a ghost at the centre of *Hamlet* the play; the chthonic King is the only true ruler. Echoes of Marlowe cling to the part of the Ghost; for example, the story of his murder recalls a trick of the devilish Lightborn, murderer of Edward II:

> Whilst one is asleep to take a quill
> And blow a little powder in his ears,
> Or open his mouth and pour quicksilver down.
>
> (ll. 2366–8)

The great icon which unites the two Hamlets, father and son, is also Marlovian in style; it emerges with the arrival of the actors at Elsinore, in the First Player's speech of the death of Priam. The apparition of Pyrrhus, avenger of his father Achilles, upon Priam (with whom, as the murderer of Hector, Priam has pleaded for his son) is a figure of strange but arrested power. As he finishes the description of Pyrrhus, Hamlet hands over to the first Player, who recounts how the very wind of Pyrrhus' sword felled Priam, but at that moment the crash of the falling towers amid 'the nightmare of smoke and screams and ruin'[12] arrested his action. Pyrrhus stands in tableau, flourishing his sword, a mechanical figure of destruction in his black armour smeared with blood, a kind of iron man.

Like Tamburlaine, or like Aaron in *Titus Andronicus*, he remains larger than life:

> So, as a painted tyrant, Pyrrhus stood
> And like a neutral to his will and matter,
> Did nothing.
>
> (II. ii. 474–6)

and there was silence for a space, till the burning towers crashed thunderously again, and the blade fell.

After meeting this icon, Hamlet in a great burst of self-directed rage recognizes the embodiment of what he had before encountered in the Ghost, issuing its archaic but absolute command, Revenge! It is a compulsion, it is a *must*, laid upon a man by an archaic part of himself, a decayed part reactivated by his father's death. The compelling power of that part of ourself which we do not desire to meet can return only in such images. Yet the tempest of Hamlet's passion evokes in him the notion of the play-within-the-play, by which he catches the conscience of King Claudius, even as he himself has been caught. All this depends on the 'theatre's magic relation to reality and danger'; for Hamlet remembers how guilty creatures sitting at a play have been forced by what they saw to recount their crimes. After the play has indeed caught its victim, we see Hamlet stand with drawn sword flourishing over the kneeling figure of the praying Claudius, in exactly the same posture as that of Pyrrhus over Priam. The icon is re-enacted in the prayer scene; but Hamlet does not let his sword fall. He puts it up with the thought of yet more horrid and complete revenge, which shall damn Claudius both body and soul.

Shakespeare here appeals to the most primitive and terrifying aspects of theatrical participation; the sequel to this act is the second and final appearance of the Ghost.

When Shakespeare came to the writing of his final plays, popular art was dying in the countryside. Robin Hood and the hobby horse were everywhere put down; the court was evolving a new Italianate form of masque, and a new theatre. Shakespeare reactivated his own early memories and transformed into scenic terms for the new stage the medleys of twenty-five years before – 'tales, tempests and such drolleries' as Ben Jonson scornfully termed them. The utmost reaches of his imagination evoked the scenic emblems of Shakespeare's youth – the cave, the living statue, the ship – and some of the ancient roles – the may queen, the monster, and the magician – using them to explore an interior world where fine and delicate sensibilities alternated with 'imaginations foul as Vulcan's stithy'.

Pericles, first of these plays, is presented by the ancient poet Gower, who here performs the kind of Induction that old Madge, Frolic, and Fantastic had given in *The Old Wives' Tale*. But he is a Ghost.

> To sing a song that old was sung,
> From ashes ancient Gower is come . . .
> It hath been sung at festivals,
> On ember-eves and holy-ales;

> And lords and ladies in their lives
> Have read it for restoratives.   (Prologue, 1–8)

Much of the moral action is in dumb show, and much of the writing
is absurd. Like the hero of the old romance, Sir Clamydes, the
wandering knight Pericles is shipwrecked on a foreign coast and wins
its princess for bride in spectacular tournament. His father-in-law
plays fast and loose with the unknown prince and his own daughter
in a style which burlesques the old quick changes:

> Will you, not having my consent,
> Bestow your love and your affections
> Upon a stranger, who, for aught I know
> May be, nor can I think the contrary,
> As great in blood as I myself?
> Therefore, hear you, mistress: either frame
> Your will to mine – and you, sir, hear you –
> Either be ruled by me, or I will make you . . .
> Man and wife.   (II. v. 75–83)

This clownish jocularity is exercised in a play which seems to exist
only as matrix for the great tableau and icon, the discovery scene of
the last act. When Marina's sacred charm of music has reanimated
the frozen image of Grief that is Pericles, then a figure no longer of
cosmic dimensions, but subject to cosmic influences, has been recalled from dereliction so extreme that it could have been embodied
only in traditional forms, not originally carrying the personal stamp
that Shakespeare here bestows upon them. In returning to these
archaic forms Shakespeare breathed new life into them and recovered a 'radical innocence'.[13] The basis is so simple and the shaping
spirit of imagination so concentrated that there is in *Pericles*, so to
speak, more gap than play. This is no longer, as in the original old
wives' tales, a gap in narrative, but a gap in realization. Shakespeare
has gone so deep that he has momentarily lost his unifying power, so
splendidly displayed in the Roman plays. The single icon emerges,
surrounded by old-fashioned romance in debris, and by the macabre
comedy of the brothel scenes. Shakespeare even needed to lean on the
work of an inferior collaborator.

   Cymbeline carries echoes of several medley plays, in particular of
Sir Clyamon and Sir Clamydes and *The Rare Triumphs of Love and
Fortune*.[14] From Jupiter to Cloten, the roles repeat earlier counterparts; Imogen's later adventures as Fidele have their counterpart in
those of Fidelia and Neronis. In 1957, at Stratford, the stage was
arranged in a simultaneous setting, Tudor-fashion, so that the
emblems of castle, bedchamber, cave, and wood in surrealist fantasy
appeared together, 'throwing over the whole production a sinister

veil of faery, so that it resembled a Grimm fable transmuted by the Cocteau of *La Belle et la Bête*'.[15]

The costumes, disguises, tokens, tricks of this play, the medley of Roman, British, and medieval themes, turn all to dream and fairy tale; by this means the sensitive core of tenderness, anguish, and vital playfulness that Imogen embodies can come into being. Imogen is a heroine who would be at home in the high romance of Sidney's *Arcadia*, with Philoclea, her sister in affliction. She is one who makes an art of living, from cookery to leave-taking of her banished husband, devising 'pretty things to say' even for that moment of separation, after which, as she tells her father,

> I am senseless of your wrath; a touch more rare
> Subdues all pangs, all fears.   (I. i. 135–6)

When she reads Posthumus' accusation, Pisanio comments:

> What shall I need to draw my sword? The paper
> Hath cut her throat already.   (III. iv. 30–1)

These are wedded lovers, and the poisoned imagination of Posthumus sinks far below Sidney's world of romance, to the level of Iago and of the brothel scenes in *Pericles*. Yet in spite of his words, Posthumus' actions suggest that he believed in Imogen's innocence all the time; the letter which summons her to Milford on the dangerous journey from her home would have had no effect on one who had really forgotten him completely, and given away 'the manacle of love', the bracelet which was his last token. When he himself appears in real gyves, Posthumus has spontaneously repented; and a vision of his dead father and two brothers mysteriously links with the next scene, in which Imogen also meets again her father and her two long-lost brothers. Thus the union of the wedded lovers is shown to exist at a level beyond that of overt statement.

The fairy tale gives underlying support to the impossibilities of this play. To reach the totally unfamiliar, it is necessary to cling to the familiar; from moment to moment this new kind of medley convinces, although the princess so wounded by the accusation of Posthumus could not have assumed the role of Fidele, and lived to be struck down once again. It is a kind of posthumous life for *her*, she is playing a part; the grotesque symbolism of Cloten's dead figure in her husband's garments is impossible and hideous, but perhaps also a kind of black comedy of actors' 'shapes'. The magic drinks, changes of identity, and visionary spectacles of the last part of the play no longer carry any relation to reality and danger; they are the means by which Shakespeare can leave gaps in his work. They also seem to function by some associative process in the release of energy from below; the primitive art assists or accompanies or is a necessary concomitant of new, difficult poetry for which the play reaches out.

The original of the next play, *A Winter's Tale*, belongs to the same period as the medleys and was a narrative of Shakespeare's old enemy and detractor, Robert Greene. The old tale ended tragically and was named *Pandosto or the Triumph of Time*. Construction through gaps in the story is emphasized by the appearance of Time as Chorus, who separates the two halves of Shakespeare's play: but the action is clearer, and firmer, the poet has regained his mastery of plot. In the first half, Leontes is overwhelmed by that poisoned level of the imagination which Posthumus had shown, and which had been displayed in the brothel scenes of *Pericles*. Leontes' jealousy invades him suddenly and spontaneously at the moment when he *sees* his wife and his friend in playful familiar talk together. The image speaks to him of what might be. All this is imaginatively realized, but then the marvels begin. They are the work of Apollo, a much more effective deity than Diana in *Pericles* or Jupiter in *Cymbeline*. First comes an oracular message, then the death of Mamilius, and finally the icon of Hermione as she appears in Antigonus' dream. The significance of this dream was pointed out by Anne Righter in a paper read last year at the International Conference at Stratford. As the instrument of Leontes' vengeance, Antigonus is accursed, and the vision of the Queen comes to warn him of this fate. Although she appears 'in pure white robes, Like very sanctity', her eyes 'become two spouts'; she is portentously like Lavinia. Antigonus falsely accepts this as an omen that the babe is indeed a bastard; no sooner has he laid it on the earth than thunder is heard, and the sounds of a hunt. It is the god Apollo, descending in storm, Apollo the Hunter, who chases the guilty man as Prospero and Ariel hunt the guilty with dogs in *The Tempest*. Antigonus himself becomes the quarry, and the 'Marvel' of the bear, at once grotesque and horrifying, would raise the old mixture of fright and laughter in the audience – especially if a real bear were let loose among them.

By contrast, in the last scene, the high magic of the holy statue that comes to life is Christian in its forms. The icon of Hermione is kept in a chapel 'holy, apart' as Paulina tells the penitent king. Perdita kneels before it with the pretty proviso:

> Give me leave,
> And do not say 'tis superstition that
> I kneel, and then implore her blessing. Lady,
> Dear Queen, that ended when I but began,
> Give me that hand of yours to kiss.   (V. iii. 42–6)

The coldness of the stone has chid his own coldness in Leontes, but Paulina tells him

It is requir'd
You do awake your faith.   (V. iii. 94–5)

The magic is powerful, the charm is musical; the figure is transub-
stantiated back to flesh and blood, and Leontes puts all in three
words: 'Oh, she's warm.'

Although a statue which comes to life is not unknown to earlier
plays, or to later ones for that matter,[16] this single scene offers the
deepest integration of spectacle and poetry in the last plays; and for
the audience, who have been given no more than hints and guesses
that Hermione may be living, the final descent is a most powerful
coup de théâtre, made eloquent by silence and music wedded to
poetry.

In this, it is a wonderful advance on the descent of Jupiter,
spectacularly the highlight of the whole play *Cymbeline* but poetically a gap and a void. Hermione has replaced the gods in this scene; the
triumph is that of a divine humanity. Was there here some unconscious recall of a Catholic image of the mother, mingled with the
semi-divine Elizabeth, Virgin Queen but nursing mother of her
people (as she termed herself to Parliament), wedded to her kingdom,
whose reign was already assuming legendary greatness as the weakness of her successor appeared?

In its spontaneous-seeming, yet perfectly disciplined, form, *The
Tempest* represents the final triumph of art, an art based on imagination perfectly attuned to the stage. Spectacular but not naïve, classical in form, poetic but no longer with the poetry of the gaps, it presents
a close, delicate wholeness:

> A condition of complete simplicity
> Costing not less than everything.

The Tempest is a play of high magic throughout, although its
ruling intelligence is human and fallible. Prospero's magic is
Pythagorean, based on that 'monstrous imagination' that Bacon was
to reject:

> that the world was one entire perfect living creature; insomuch as
> Apollonius of Tyana, a Pythagorean prophet, affirmed that the ebbing and
> flowing of the sea was the respiration of the world, drawing in water as
> breath and putting it forth again . . . They went on, and inferred that if the
> world was a living creature, it had a soul, and spirit, calling it spiritus
> mundi.   (*Sylva Sylvarum*, century x)

White magic, by 'giving a fit touch to the spirit of the world', can
make it respond. Prospero is at first subject to the stars and courts an
auspicious influence; whereas the monstrous Sycorax had worked
black magic by the manipulation of physical charms on the sublun-

ary level. She was able to exert physical compulsion on the higher
spheres, even those beyond the moon – for so I read the crux

> That could control the moon, . . .
> And deal in her command without her power.
>
> (V. i. 270–1)

To the guilty Alonzo the whole world speaks with one voice:

> O, 'tis monstrous, monstrous!
> Methought the billows spoke and told me of it;
> The winds did sing it to me; and the thunder,
> That deep and dreadful organ pipe, pronounced
> The name of Prosper.   (III. iii. 95–9)

It is from the spirit Ariel that Prospero himself learns to feel
sympathy with Alonzo, returning from his stony remoteness to that
quick freshness of feeling with which his own child responds.

> Oh, the cry did knock
> Against my very heart.   (I. ii. 8–9)

Ariel's strange shapes, which include that very old-fashioned one of a
coat of invisibility, sometimes reflect the inner states of those he
works on. Dozens of strange shadows attend on him, and not every
one of them is a blessed shape; for the men of sin he plays the Harpy,
for the lovers a bounteous Ceres; when he comes to the clowns 'like
the picture of Nobody', he plays old tricks from the repertory of
earlier spirits,[17] and piping a merry catch, leads them into a horse-
pond. His imprisonment, told by Prospero, recalls a potent device of
the early stage; in *The Fairy Pastoral*, William Percy described
exactly how the Hollow Tree was constructed. The clowns are
clowns of the old type, and to them Caliban is but a fairground
monster, to be shown to gaping crowds. He is confined by Prospero
in a rock, another familiar scenic device. The old emblems of the ship
and the cave are used, and a special 'quaint device' for the banquet
that vanishes, leaving a bare table, which is carried out by spirits.
Pure shows, like the dance of harvesters, unite the Jacobean masque
with the revels of *The Old Wives' Tale*, where there is also a
harvesters' dance.

Prospero's physical needs are served by Sycorax's son till, by way
of ordeal, Prince Ferdinand takes his place as logman. Caliban
accuses Prospero of usurping his island, and Prospero later accuses
Ferdinand of this design, thus visiting the sin of the father upon his
child. The murderous conspiracy of the false princes and the grosser
rebellion of the clowns are alike frustrated by Prospero (whose art of
government had certainly improved in exile) and the theme of
usurpation dissolves in a lovers' jest, in the final tableau where

Miranda and Ferdinand are revealed playing with ivory kings and queens at chess.

> *Miranda.* Sweet lord, you play me false.
> *Ferdinand.* No, my dearest love,
>   I would not for the world.
> *Miranda.* Yes, for a score of kingdoms you should wrangle,
>   And I would call't fair play.   (V. i. 171–5)

Alonzo greets this restoration of the son he had lost as 'a most high miracle', but the disclosure has not the startling quality of that in *The Winter's Tale*, and Gonzalo's quiet comment points the distinction:

> I have *inly* wept.   (V. i. 200)

Finally, the whole dramatic action is dissolved by a series of transformations. For what is the magician but, as always in the old plays, a stage manager of shows, with his wand and his magic inscribed 'book' – what is this but a sublimated Master of the Revels? What the fellowship of the bottle with their stolen frippery and their game of kings and subjects, but a reductive mockery of the poorest players in the service? Pointing to the royal badge of Naples on the sleeves of Trinculo the fool and 'King Stephano', Prospero asks,

> Mark but the badges of these men, my lords,
> Then say if they be true.   (V. i. 267–8)

A man wearing King James's badge spoke the lines.

Finally, with no more dignity than a fashionable hat and rapier will confer, yet as one who dares more than Dr Faustus did – to make every third thought his grave – the old man appeals in his epilogue to the theatre's magic relation of reality and danger in a prayer of primal simplicity:

> As you from crimes would pardon'd be,
> Let your indulgence set me free.   (Epilogue 19–20)

The final plays represent an interior conflict, resolved in association with revived memories of a more primitive stage, and asserted with ever clarifying force.[19] It would be dangerous to speculate further than this. We may note the prevalent themes of death and rebirth, petrification and release; the common element of false accusation, banishment, and usurpation; the relations of fathers and children; the combination of extreme purity and scurrility. Do these suggest some possible conflicts of an ageing man? Prospero's farewell to Art, though not actually Shakespeare's last word (things do not work out quite so tidily as that) may represent an inner acceptance, that only at great price could be put into speech, and after many attempts; but here, as always, the Actor-Poet found, for his familiar ritual, the fitting words.

Notes

1 E. A. Armstrong, *Shakespeare's Imagination* (London, Lindsay Drummond, 1946), p. 122, quoting Sir Frederick Bartlett.

2 See J. P. Brockbank, *Dr Faustus* (London, Edward Arnold, 1962), pp. 23–4. The following paragraphs develop from chapter 3 of my book *English Dramatic Form* (London, Chatto & Windus, 1965).

3 William Rankins, *A Mirrour of Monsters*, 1587, sigs. C.1–C.2. The image of Cupid and the presence of Venus seem to point to the infernal Venus of Robert Wilson's play, *The Cobbler's Prophecy*, and her adultery with 'Contempt', which is celebrated by a masque of animal forms led by Folly.

4 See Eugene Waith, 'The Metamorphosis of Violence in *Titus Andronicus*', *Shakespeare Survey*, 10 (1957), 39–49.

5 Among such plays are *The Cobbler's Prophecy, The Rare Triumphs of Love and Fortune, John a Kent and John a Cumber*; perhaps *Friar Bacon and Friar Bungay* and *The Woman in the Moon* might be considered variants on this form.

6 The famous figures of the pageant in the clock of St Mark's, Venice, are the best-known examples; but a crowd will gather today to watch the figures in what was Fortnum and Mason's clock in Piccadilly. It is interesting to compare Marvell's satire on kings:

> 'Image like, an useless time they tell
> And with vain sceptre, strike the hourly bell.'
> (The First Anniversary', ll. 41–2)

7 The term is Edward Armstrong's; *Shakespeare's Imagination*, ch. 13.

8 D. W. Harding, *Experience into Words* (London, Chatto & Windus, 1963), p. 182.

9 J. A. Hadfield, *Dreams and Nightmares* (London, Penguin Books, 1954), ch. 6.

10 C. S. Lewis, *English Literature in the Sixteenth Century* (Oxford, Clarendon Press, 1954), p. 503.

11 According to Stephen Gosson, a 'shadow' is a minor actor; compare Macbeth's 'Life's but a walking shadow', and Puck's 'If we shadows have offended'.

12 The phrase is Harry Levin's.

13 'All hatred driven hence,/The soul recovers radical innocence/And learns at last that it is self-delighting,/Self-appeasing, self-affrighting.' Yeats, 'A Prayer for my Daughter' from *Michael Robartes and the Dancer*.

14 See *Cymbeline*, ed. J. C. Maxwell, New Cambridge Shakespeare (Cambridge, Cambridge University Press, 1960), pp. xxii–xxvii.

15 *Ibid.* p. xl (quoting Kenneth Tynan).

16 A statue on a grave comes to life in *The Trial of Chivalry*; and pictures in Massinger's *The City Madam*. There is a portentous set of statues in Middleton's *A Game of Chess*, but these are idols of the Black, i.e. Spanish party.

17 For instance, Shrimp of *John a Kent* and Robin Goodfellow of *Wily Beguiled*.

18 A. M. Nagler, *Shakespeare's Stage* (New Haven, Yale University Press, 1958), p. 100, discusses this trick; in medieval terms a 'secret'.

19 That there was perhaps a general movement in this direction does not modify the nature of Shakespeare's achievement, for he was the only actor-playwright with personal knowledge of the earlier stage. For a useful summary of the common stage practice, see Dieter Mehl, *The Elizabethan Dumb Show* (London, Methuen, 1965), ch. 2.

VII

Dramatic role as social image:
a study of *The Taming of the Shrew*

I

Since the approach to Shakespeare's plays through poetic imagery rather than character was first propounded, about thirty years ago, the unwary have seen it as an alternative method to the approach through character and story. The antithesis is, of course mistaken, since dramatic characters are only another, though the most complex, form of image, projections of the poet's inner vision, interpreted by the actors and re-formed within the minds of spectators, in accordance with those inward images which shape and dominate the deeper levels of thought and feeling in every one.[1]

This 'internal society' is made up of images first imprinted in early childhood, which though differently charged with love or hate, and differently arranged, are basically the same in all men. The more truly representative an artist's work the more completely can it offer to the artist and the spectator an opportunity to harmonize the conflicts of their 'inner society' by projection upon the persons imaged. Art thus becomes a species of abreaction, with a directly therapeutic function. No one need resort to those fanciful clinical reductions with which certain psychiatrists have attempted to explain the tragic characters of Shakespeare,[2] since this is a process which applies equally to the 'normal' and healthy; indeed the production and appreciation of art may be taken in itself as a sign of health.

It has always proved difficult to extract from the comedies any structure of images other than images of man; and some of these are well-known stage types, which might seem at first sight to be too stiff and rigid to supply the delicate and complicated adjustment required for individuals, each differing from the other. In real life, to see persons as merely fulfilling one or two roles, as merely a lawyer, a priest, a mother, a Jew, even as merely a man or a woman is to see them as something less than images of God; for practical purposes this may be necessary. The distinction between acquaintances and friends may be measured by the greater variety and flexibility of roles in which we meet our friends. Assigning and taking of roles is in fact the basis of social as distinct from inward life; in comedy, characters tend to be presented socially, in terms of roles, which, as in the case of classical comedy or the *commedia dell'arte*, are fairly stereotyped. Recipes for depicting clowns, young lovers, pantaloons, boastful cowards are necessary as the social basis for drama; the images must be current coin, negotiable in the common market, but the artist will always select, recombine, and break up the ingredients of the familiar roles.[3] He may in addition, by means of those subsidiary images through which one character in a play describes another (imagery that is, of the kind usually opposed to character-drawing) suggest attitudes and approaches for the audience which may run contrary to or modify the main presentation of the role; such images indeed constitute minor alternative roles for the character in question. Other images may not be verbalized but presented only in mime. Thus the constant grouping and regrouping of roles for any dramatic figure may be varied by different spectators or actors (who will notice those which suit themselves and ignore those which do not). So many men, so many Shylocks, Falstaffs, Rosalinds, Katharines.

To accept liberty of interpretation yet accept also community of experience is perhaps an act of faith, yet of rational faith. In looking at the role as image, it is necessary to remember always the nature of Shakespeare's theatre and audience, as providing not the last word in interpretation, but the first. He was addressing a crowd socially heterogeneous, mostly masculine, who required a delicate adjustment of native popular traditional art with the socially more esteemed classical and foreign models.

In his earlier plays these different needs are met by different groups, serious lovers, comic clowns; as his art developed, he succeeded in blending the roles more subtly and freshly.

II

The Taming of The Shrew repays examination from this point of view. It is an early comedy (before 1594),[4] with a main plot based on the popular dramatic role of the Shrew, but highly original in treatment, and a subplot drawn from an Italian model, Ariosto, as adapted in Gascoigne's *Supposes*; both deftly worked together and strengthened by an Induction organically related to the main theme. In *The Taming of A Shrew* mediocrity shows what could be done to destroy the inner fabric of the vision while preserving the outlines of the story.

The wooing of Katherine takes up rather less than half the play, and her part is quite surprisingly short; although she is on the stage a good deal, she spends most of the time listening to Petruchio. The play is his; this is its novelty. Traditionally the shrew triumphed; hers was the oldest and indeed the only native comic role for women. If overcome, she submitted either to high theological argument or to a taste of the stick. Here, by the wooing in Act II, the wedding in Act III and the 'taming school' in Act IV, each of which has its own style, Petruchio overpowers his shrew with her own weapons – imperiousness, wildness, inconsistency and the withholding of the necessities of life – combined with strong demonstrations of his natural authority. Petruchio does not use the stick, and Katherine in her final speech does not console herself with theology. To understand Shakespeare's skill in adaptation, the traditional image of the shrew, as she had developed from Chaucer's time, must be recalled.

Shrews might be expected to be especially common in England, that 'Hell of horses, purgatory of servants and paradise of women', but stories of shrews belong to the general medieval tradition of bourgeois satire, as well as to folk tales. Jean de Meung's portrait of 'La Veille', Eustace Deschamps' *Miroir de Mariage*, *Les Quinze Joyes de Mariage* and the *Sottie* have their English equivalents in Chaucer, the Miracles and the interlude. The Wyf of Bath is the great example of the shrew triumphant; in the Miracle plays Noah's wife evolves from simple boozing and brawling to a notable housewife, from a formula to a simple dramatic role. The gossips' league which appears in the plays is given a courtly setting in Dunbar's poem, 'Twa Mariit Wemen and the Wedo'.

Two short plays on shrews from the early Tudor stage are *Johan Johan* (1533/4) and *Tom Tyler and his Wife* (c. 1561). In both these plays, the pusillanimous husband is the centre of the picture. Tib, wife of Johan Johan, deceives her husband with the parish priest; his tremendous opening speech, in which he proclaims his intention of beating her, and beating her horribly, directs the audience's attention firmly to his abject but boastful state. Only at the end does a three-cornered fight develop. The remarkable miracles with which Sir Jhan the priest edifies the supper party, his smooth graciousness give him an odious mastery over poor Johan Johan who, deprived of his eagerly expected pie (like Katherine of the beef) and sent away from table is so poor-spirited a wretch that his sudden onslaught most unexpectedly relieves all the pent-up hatred of priestly hypocrisy which is the serious, though covert, intention of Heywood's farce.

Tom Tyler is another such meek-hearted husband; misled by Desire, the Vice, he has married with Strife. She, with her gossips Sturdy and Tipple, forms a drinking party, but chases Tom back to his work when he ventures to seek a pot of beer. His valiant friend Tom Taylor puts on the Tyler's coat, and undertakes the correction of Strife; but after he has beaten her into submission, Tom Tyler foolishly confesses the trick and gets a worse drubbing than ever. Two sage parsons, Destiny and Patience, introduce and wind up the gay little frolic, in which the rival conspiracy of men to combat the gossips' league, though at first unsuccessful, is able with the church's help finally to tame a shrew. Flat morality is in sharp contrast to lively fun; the two artisans alone are characterized as people, and this helps to concentrate the sympathy on them. They are wage earners, whose wives do not share their work as country wives must do, but are free to gad about with no supervision and to spend their husband's earnings. The valiant Taylor is contrasted with the hulking inoffensiveness of the Tyler, and both with Strife, who is much less of a morality figure than the rest, being one of those 'sklendre wyves' 'egre as a tygre yond in Inde' whom Chaucer had celebrated, a true daughter of the Vice. She exploits her husband as drudge and provider:

> What a husband have I, as light as a flye?
> I leap and I skip, I carry the whip,
> And I bear the bell; If he please me not well,
> I will take him by the pole, by cocks precious soul.
> I will make him to toil, while I laugh and smile,
> I will fare of the best, I will sit and take rest . . .
> I will teach him to know the way to Dunmoe.
> At board and at bed I will crack the knave's head,
> If he look but awry, or cast a sheep's eye;
> So shall I be sure to keep him in ure,
> To serve like a knave and live like a slave.[5]

All the moralizing is subject to parody, including that of Patience, who leads the final song and dance, and, after the fighting, justifies submission all round, with a perhaps unintended hit at a very exalted personage:

> Which God preserve our noble queen.
> From perilous chance that has been seen,
> And send her subjects grace, say I,
> To serve her highness patiently.

Tom Tyler is close in spirit to the ballad and the jig; in 'The Wife Wrapt in a Wether's Skin' (Child, 277) a timid husband finds a surer method of punishment by proxy; his wife is too highborn to spin, wash, or work, so Robin wraps her in a wether's skin, and since he may not beat her because of her great kindred, he beats the wether's skin till he has tamed his wife. In a longer, more savage version, the wife is beaten till she swoons and then wrapped in the salted hide of Morell, an old horse. This seems to be a magic charm: she is to stay in the salt hide for ever if she does not submit. The jest ends with a party at which the wife shows her obedience, and the conclusion reads

> Finis quoth Mayster Charm her
> He that can charme a shrewde wyfe,
>   Better than this
> Let him come to me and fetch ten pound
>   And a golden purse.
>   (Hazlitt, *Early Popular Poetry*, iv, 179)

Tom Taylor and Tom Tyler, at the height of their triumph, likewise rejoice in a song which puts a wife among the higher domestic animals:

> Blame not Thomas if Tom be sick,
> His mare doth prance, his mare doth kick,
> She snorts and holds her head so high,
> Go tie the Mare, Tomboy, tie the Mare, tie.

The two plays differ in their appeal, though they are alike in theme. *Johan Johan* has shown anticlerical colouring; *Tom Tyler* in spite of its moral framework is the more frivolous. They are alike in stressing the husband's part, and in the similarity of name that links him with the tamer, who seems therefore like another self. Johan Johan has been server to Sir Jhan the priest and Tipple observes of Tom Tyler 'Belike he hath learned in a new school'.

III

The theme of the School for Henpecked Husbands was one of those taken up by Shakespeare. Although he used many features of the older tradition, his play has the advantages both of novelty and familiarity. It is unnecessary to postulate a lost source play unless Shakespeare is held to be constitutionally incapable of inventing a plot; for there is no sound external evidence for it.

Petruchio, keeper of the taming school in which the 'tutors' Hortensio and Lucentio are his immediate pupils (IV. ii. 54–8) and Christopher Sly a more remote one, owes his victory to his eloquence and his natural vigour. He enters full of enthusiasm to see the world and enjoy his inheritance, blown by

> Such wind as scatters young men through the world
> To seek their fortunes farther than at home,
> Where small experience grows.   (I. ii. 48–50)

and the first two dozen lines show his readiness to let his fists walk about a man's ears. Shrews commonly marry old men, or their social inferiors; Petruchio undertakes his 'labour of Hercules' in the spirit of an explorer, and the challenge of his America, his Newfoundland, exhilarates him. When she breaks his friend's head, he asserts with a significant oath:

> Now, by the world, it is a lusty wench,
> I love her ten times more than e'er I did.
> O, how I long to have some chat with her!   (II.i.159–61)

His demonstrations of physical exuberance, wit and bawdry are provocative courting plumage, of Mercutio's style in wooing rather than Romeo's. The wedding night has as climax his sudden bout of unclerkly asceticism. 'Come, I will bring thee to thy bridal chamber' he exclaims, and the servants, stealing back, observe:

> He kills her in her own humour.
> Where is he?
> In her chamber. Making a sermon of continency to her,
> And rails, and swears, and rates, that she, poor soul,
> Knows not which way to stand, to look, to speak.   (IV. i. 164–9)

For contrast, there are no less than four old men. Katherine is the first shrew to be given a father, the first to be shewn as maid and bride; she is not seen merely in relation to a husband. The savage and hysterical attack on her sister is counterbalanced by the comic description of her bash at her tutor. She is unteachable; the point is explosively made.

At the beginning both characters are shewn at their least attractive. Kate's first speech is vulgar, thick-sown with proverbs; she threatens to 'comb' her suitors' 'noddles' with a three-legged stool and they in turn defie her roundly:

> From all such devils, Good Lord deliver us.   (I. i. 66)

'This fiend of hell', 'the devil's dam', 'Is any man so very a fool as to be married to hell?' The image persists through the first scene, with the charitable alternatives that she is 'stark mad' or that she should be 'carted' like a whore. It is all very violent and in a 'low' style. Petruchio is introduced in a low comedy turn with his servant, and with a great flourish proclaims his intention to marry for money – a wife as hideous and old as the hag of the Wife of Bath's Tale if need be (I. ii. 69). Money is always to the fore in tales about shrews, and Katherine's father, by offering his younger daughter to the highest bidder, effectively shews that he prizes it; Petruchio after all takes little trouble to secure the best offer, but takes the first good one that comes. When at the end, he bets on Katherine's duty – a very safe bet, and a large one –

> I'll venture so much of my hawk or hound,
> But twenty times so much upon my wife.   (V. ii. 71–2)

Baptista backs Bianca, but at the end sportingly comes forward with a second dowry for Katherine 'for she is changed as she had never been'. The 'old Italian fox' lives like a lord; but money helps to set the shrew where she belongs, within the merchant class. When Henry V woos another Kate, he thinks in terms of fair French towns, though he too finds that the role of a bumpkin has its value in a whirlwind courtship.

Petruchio gets a plain description of Katherine's accepted role; she is 'renowned in Padua for her scolding tongue'; but his tongue is equally renowned among his own servants (I. ii. 106–15). Natural exuberance is matched in him by variety and colour of speech; he has every rhetorical weapon at command, from the high-flown terms of his address to Vincentio to the fluent cursing which he bestows upon servants and tradespeople. The basis is bluntness, 'russet yeas and honest kersey noes', and when he uses the high style it is a spirit of mockery, in contrast with the learned eloquence, in the opening scene, of Lucentio, the student.

The short scene between his resolution to woo, and the wooing scene itself shows Katherine beating Bianca and Bianca subtly retaliating under the guise of sweet compliance:

> If you affect him, sister, here I swear
> I'll plead for you myself, but you shall have him.   (II. i. 14–15)

Katherine frankly wants a husband, and abuses her father for preferring Bianca.

She is met by her wooer with a teasing shower of contradictory epithets: 'plain . . . bonny . . . sometimes curst . . . prettiest Kate in Christendom . . .' that ends according to a plan already confided to the audience by Petruchio:

> Hearing thy mildness praised in every town . . .
> Myself am mov'd to woo thee for my wife.   (II. i. 190,193)

Kate's wits are waked, and a quick crossfire of repartee leads to the traditional slap. If however the audience expect a fight they do not get it; Petruchio, in his role of Hercules, simply holds his Protean enemy fast, and indulges his humour of finding everything agreeable, provoking her with oratorical flourishes to another wit combat and then issuing his absolute fiat.

> For by this light, whereby I see thy beauty,
> Thy beauty that doth make me like thee well,
> Thou must be married to no man but me;
> For I am he am born to tame you, Kate.   (II. i. 265–8)

Katherine furiously tells her father that he has offered to wed her to a lunatic. She repeats it, as later she stands waiting for her bridegroom; he is a 'frantic fool' maliciously jesting with 'poor Katherine' as she tearfully calls herself, so that she may be mocked by the world:

> 'Lo there is mad Petruchio's wife,
> If it would please him come and marry her'.   (III. ii. 19–20)

It is in fact as a madman that Petruchio appears in the end. He has assumed the part she assigned him, the traditional fate of a shrew's husband, as the Abbess had lengthily explained to Adriana in the *Comedy of Errors* (V. i. 68–86). The most important passages about the wedding are given in description; the broken-down horse, who is anatomized at much greater length than his rider, with Petruchio's wild attire, prepare the listener for the church scene in which the bridegroom swears, hits out and plays the part of a madman who is also possessed. The likeness of the pair only brings out Petruchio's pre-eminence.

> He's a devil, a devil, a very fiend
> —Why, she's a devil, a devil, the devil's dam.
> —Tut, she's a lamb, a dove, a fool to him . . .
> Such a mad marriage never was before. (III. ii. 151–3,178)

Though at one point it is suggested that 'he hath some meaning in his mad attire', no one seems to disagree when Bianca sums up at the exit of the pair, 'Being mad herself, she's madly mated'. The central point, the knot of the play, is here.

Petruchio has already invited the audience to stand with him; he confides his plan just before the wooing starts (II. i. 167–79). He will ignore Kate's forward behaviour and describe it instead as if it were what it ideally should be. He will assume a virtue for her if she has it not; maintain before her the image of perfection which he is trying to create; or (if the audience are prepared to be so subtle) will pierce below the surface of Kate's angry, thwarted, provocative abuse to the desire to be mastered and cherished which her conduct unconsciously betrays.

This mastery he asserts immediately after the wedding, with an unequivocal statement of his legal rights, and a mimic marriage by capture.

> I will be master of what is mine own—
> She is my goods, my chattels, she is my house,
> My household stuff, my field, my barn,
> My horse, my ox, my ass, my anything . . .   (III. ii. 225–8)

In the next scene, after the full horrors of the journey – again given to one of the clowns for embellished description – Kate does not fail to address him respectfully as 'husband'.

Having drawn his ideal in wooing, he now holds up a mirror to her worser self, and gives her a travesty-performance of her own behaviour. She had beaten Hortensio; he beats his men. She had tied up Bianca; he hurries her breathlessly about. All is done, as he explains to the audience in the central soliloquy which is the grand exposition of his strategy, to 'curb her mad and headstrong humour'.

He is not preparing the audience for what is to happen, but directing them how to take it. The image he uses is that of manning a falcon.[6]

> My falcon now is sharp and passing empty,
> And till she stoop, she must not be full-gorg'd,
> For then she never looks upon her lure.
> Another way I have to man my haggard,
> To make her come, and know her keeper's call:
> That is, to watch her, as we watch these kites,
> That bate and beat, and will not be obedient . . .
> (IV. i. 174–80)

Kate is not to be wrapt in a wether's skin; a more subtle form of the animal tamer's art is called for, but it is animal taming none the less. Only it allows Petruchio to maintain a pretence which may be taken as rather more than a subterfuge:

> Ay, and amid this hurly I intend
> That all is done in reverend care of her . . .
> This is the way to kill a wife with kindness. (IV. i. 183–4, 192)

He concludes with a triumphant and direct appeal to the audience (both Sly and the Globe spectators) to identify themselves with him:

> He that knows better how to tame a shrew,
> Now let him speak; 'tis charity to shew.   (IV. i. 194–5)

The full torrent of his eloquence is finally loosed in the tailor's scene, not without some occasional plain hints to Kate ('When you are gentle, you shall have one too', if she wants a gentlewoman's cap). All the usual desires of the shrew, clothes, feasts, company, lovemaking, are dangled before her only to be snatched away. She is shewn what it means to be Petruchio's household stuff; finally she capitulates and enters his private universe, in which 'it shall be what o'clock I say it is', in which Petruchio decides whether the sun or the moon is shining in the sky.

But this universe turns into the public one without warning; at the end of the act it is Kate whom he accuses of madness, when, obediently following his eloquent lead, she greets Vincentio in high style as

> Young budding virgin, fair and fresh and sweet.   (IV. v. 36)

She meekly apologizes for 'my mad mistaking'.

Petruchio's last demand is a mere flouting of decorum; he wants a kiss in the public street. He gets it, with one un-called-for endearment that shows how far Hortensio's

> Petruchio, go thy ways, the field is won   (IV. v. 23)

falls short of the fullness of victory. The shrew's role is transformed, and the charming young woman whom Petruchio imagined, he has now, like Pygmalion, obtained in the flesh.

Katherine has never been in league with society, like older shrews, but always at odds with it. Henceforth her relations to others, as she shows in Act V, are to be through Petruchio. Very early in the play he had based his confidence of taming her on his knowledge of a man's world:

> Think you a little din can daunt mine ears?
> Have I not in my time heard lions roar?
> Have I not heard the sea, puff'd up with winds?   (I. ii. 196–8)

Have I not above all, he concludes, been in battle!

On the same ground Katherine bases her final plea for obedience. Her grand oration does not invoke the rather muddled theology which winds up *The Taming of A Shrew*, but recalls man's social claims as breadwinner, protector and temporal lord (those claims which Tom Tyler's wife so shamelessly ignored). A man

> commits his body
> To painful labour, both by sea and land,
> To watch the night in storms, the day in cold,
> While thou liest warm at home, secure and safe.(V. ii. 148–51)

Women are incapable of man's work; their minds should be as soft as their bodies. Kate's plea is in the high style, directly opposed to the 'low' style of her first speeches; but it has little more weight than the sermon of Patience in *Tom Tyler*. It is the lovers' battle that the audience is really invited to enjoy – the raillery which conceals attraction, the 'war' of wits which allows love and hate open play, in the fashion of Berowne and Rosalind, Benedick and Beatrice. Kate, though overmatched, remains the lusty wench Petruchio had sought;

even at the end, she demonstrates her powers by haling the other recalcitrant wives before their husbands. She is not simply transformed into the image of Bianca, who at the opening had displayed such readiness to strip off her finery at Kate's bidding, as Kate now does at Petruchio's. Bianca takes Kate's likeness more completely; for with her violent retort to the bridegroom's plaint, 'The more fool you, for laying on my duty', the younger sister clearly assumes the scold. The third bride, being a widow already, has a tone of easy practised insolence; it is she who flings back the old taunt of shrewishness, Kate's original role, of which in the last couplet she is divested for ever.

—Now go thy ways; thou hast tam'd a curst shrew.
—Tis a wonder, by your leave she will be tam'd so.(V. ii. 188–9)

IV

Three later examples of the shrew in Elizabethan drama may be considered to show how the part developed. Dekker and Middleton's *The Honest Whore* (1604) and Fletcher's *The Woman's Prize or the Tamer Tamed* (?1604/1610) both depict a shrew who voluntarily relinquishes her role and submits to her husband. In *The Honest Whore* the subplot shows Candido the patient man, a linen draper, subjected to a series of very rough tests by his wife, who has a woman's longing to provoke him. He refuses to be provoked, and when finally, having committed him to Bedlam, she repents and gets him out again, he turns the tables by assuring her that she was the madder of the two, that he has cured her humour by submitting to it; concluding with a set speech in praise of patience. In Part II, he is shewn married to a second wife; here he is instigated by a courtier to be severe with her and even threaten her with the yard measure, whereupon she instantly capitulates and delivers an oration against the sovereignty of women. The tricks which the patient man endures, very like those described in the Elizabethan translation of *Les Quinze Joyes de Mariage*, add up to a series of merry jests. Simple fun turning to simple didacticism is well within the popular sympathies of a city audience: toughness is represented by the prentices who attempt to defend Candido against his wife and her accomplices.

In *The Woman's Prize*, a sequel to Shakespeare's play, Fletcher shews Petruchio in his old age. He has come to London and for second wife taken an Englishwoman, who, under the leadership of 'Colonel Bianca', barricadoes herself on her wedding night and starts a campaign against husbands. The mock-battle is exactly calculated for a courtly audience's humour; but in the last three acts, wiles

succeed defiance. By a series of tricks which include pretending that
her husband has caught the plague and so shutting him up and
depriving him of all his goods, pretending to run mad herself, and
finally, when he shams dead, preaching a sermon to the 'corpse' on
his unmanliness, Maria sufficiently shows the mettle of her pasture.
As Petruchio finally observes:

> Well, little England, when I see a husband
> Of any nation stern or jealous,
> I'll wish him but a woman of thy breeding.

Both plays depend on gulling the husband by a series of fantastic
tricks; yet Maria, no less than Candido's wife, having conquered,
suddenly submits and vows herself her husband's servant. The chief
mood being that of farce, a milder age seemed to require this happy
ending.

Maria at one point recalls Petruchio's main speech from the older
play and praises the wild bird, the haggard.

> Hang these tame hearted eyasses, that no sooner
> See the lure out, and hear their husband's hollow,
> But cry like kites upon 'em; the free haggard
> (Which is that woman that hath wing and knows it,
> Spirit and plume) will make an hundred checks,
> To show her freedom, sail in ev'ry air,
> And look out ev'ry pleasure, not regarding
> Lure nor quarry till her pitch command
> What she desires; making her founder'd keeper
> Be glad to fling out trains, and golden ones,
> To take her down again.

The tanner's wife who leads the regiment of country women, invokes
a still older play, when she swears that Maria shall march off with
terms of victory.

> She shall, Tom Tiler's,
> And brave ones too. My hood shall make a hearse cloth.
> And I'll lie under it like Joan O'Gaunt,
> Ere I go less; my distaff stuck up by me,
> For the eternal trophy of my conquests,
> And loud Fame at my head, with two main bottles
> Shall fill to all the world, the glorious fall
> Of old Don Gillian.

The gossips' league is here revived; but Petruchio still insists that his
first wife was 'a fury to this filly'. There is a feeling of the audience
being asked to play old parts and strike the old attitudes; the romp is
somehow a little too self-conscious; there is too much burlesque in
the farce.

Jonson, the most masculine of Elizabethan comic dramatists, does not give weight to any woman's part. He himself was married to 'a shrew, but honest'. His sketches of female violence culminate in *The Silent Woman* (1609) which dissolves and distributes the role of the shrew among a number of characters, and places it in a wider general context of social satire. Low comedy is provided by Mistress Otter, the rich shopkeeping termagant who has married a broken-down captain: she gives her husband a beating in the good old-fashioned style, to the accompaniment of drums and trumpets and she draws up articles of obedience for him before she marries him. The Ladies Collegiate are a foundation of courtly dames, resembling the cabals of Restoration comedy or even the *School for Scandal*:

> that live from their husbands; and give entertainment to all the wits and braveries of the time, as they call them; cry down, or cry up, what they like or dislike in a brain or a fashion, with most masculine or rather hermaphroditical authority.

Epicoene, the Silent Woman, whose marriage to Morose transforms her, as it transformed Bianca, from modesty to a scold, is discovered at the end, to be no more a woman than was Sly's lady-wife, and so Morose is freed; all the other shrews remain triumphant. In the course of the play, Truewit, the connoisseur of women, delivers a tremendous Character of an Ill Wife to Morose, and an equally lengthy oration on how to court a woman to his nephew: Morose also catechizes his future wife on her longing for chattering, courtship and fine clothes. The social follies of a whole troupe of gulls and fops counterbalance those of the Collegiate Ladies, and all join in brutal torment of Morose. Poor Captain Otter, who among his boon companions pretends to despise and rule his tyrant 'princess', has a humour of drinking toasts from the three cups he calls his bear, his bull and his horse; Morose's humour of silence shows itself not only in his choice of a wife but in the fantastic arrangement of his household, which in its way, is as odd as Petruchio's; every character is an eccentric, an original variant upon a familiar stage type. In Jonson's play the theme of the shrew has become only one role in a society where the tension lies in the whole action, not in parts: in which roles are fixed, sharply defined, Theophrastian. Unity of action and of tone, control of a consistently ironic point of view hold them together. There are two standards of what constitutes right social behaviour: that of the fops and the Ladies Collegiate and that of the wits, Dauphine and his friends; but there is no free play of sympathy. Satire offers the audience a direct and assured moral judgment, the pleasure of siding with authority: it offers also the covert satisfaction of surveying the baseness which is to be judged,

Jonson stands to Shakespeare in this respect as Dunbar stands to Chaucer. The audience are invited throughout to identify themselves with the point of view of the wits, which is detached, amused, ironic and merciless. The whole plot turns on Dauphine's stratagem of 'marrying' his uncle to a boy; but life and vivacity is stronger in the parts of the chief victim and of the fools and gulls than in that of the cool young cavalier who plays with his victim, velvety as the Lord with Christopher Sly, but does not confide either to the spectators or to his friends what he is about. The loudest horseplay and the nearest approach to the old comic tradition is Captain Otter's drinking scene, where he boasts in the manner of Johan Johan:.

> Wife! buz! titivilitium! there's no such thing in nature. I confess, gentle-men, I have a cook, a laundress, a house drudge that serves my necessary turns and goes under that title; but he's an ass that will be so uxurious to tie his affections to one circle.

Immediately Mistress Otter enters and falls upon him; but even this is by the malicious contrivance of Truewit. Similar grand roles are assumed by the two gulls who claim to have enjoyed Epicoene's favours; by the Ladies Collegiate who claim freedom for a life of gallantry, but are tricked by Dauphine into competing for his attentions and betraying each other to him treacherously; and of course by Epicoene, whose disguise is maintained to the end. Disguise turns Otter and the Barber into a lawyer and a divine, to the ridicule of both professions. Money is, as usual, the basis of the intrigue; Dauphine extracts a settlement from Morose.

Jonson's 'humours' were said to be drawn from the life, and in the Prologue he gives a warning against 'particular sleights of application'; this suggests not only that the social images he created were based upon eccentric individuals (as the character of Morose is said to be) but that the audience's impulse to reject these roles and fasten them on to somebody else is very strongly aroused. Morose, the hero victim, is the dark antithesis to his nephew; a wit himself, in spite of his defeat he possesses a power, a massiveness of character, that the young men do not show. The main conflict lies between two men, representatives of Crabbed Age and Youth; although all the conscious identification is with Youth, yet it is in his saturnine foe that the deeper, more Shakespearean complexity of character is to be found. All the characters are static, inflexible, all equally interconnected in a web of purely external relationships: in Morose alone some reflexion of an 'inner society', troubled and rejected, may be discerned.

Notes

1 For a brief and lucid discussion, see John Rickman, *Selected Contributions to Psychoanalysis* (London, Hogarth Press, 1957), p. 159.
2 See Kenneth Muir, 'Some Freudian Interpretations of Shakespeare', *Proceedings of the Leeds Philosophical Society*, VII, part 1 (July 1952), 43–52.
3 See Bernard Hart, *The Psychology of Insanity*, 5th ed. (Cambridge, Cambridge University Press, 1957), pp. 115–16.
4 The date of publication of *The Taming of A Shrew*, which I take to be derivative from Shakespeare.
5 This does not prevent her complaining of his unmanliness in striking a woman.
6 Taming a falcon by keeping it without food or sleep brings about a strong sense of conflict described by the modern falconer T. H. White.

VIII

'King Henry IV'*

There was once a summer school at the other Stratford where, in two successive hours, a first speaker said that anyone who doubted the unity of the great continuous ten-act play was disqualified to understand Shakespeare; while a second said that anyone who thought 2 *Henry IV* more than a feeble 'encore' must be illiterate. The link that I would see is that of adaptability, the imaginative ability to create a part and to play it. In Part 1, this playful, heroic, or sometimes merely crafty capacity distinguishes each of the main characters. In Part 2, the role-taking (to use familiar jargon) is subtle, Machiavellian and by no means subjected to plain ethical judgments of right and wrong. In dismissing Falstaff, Henry V appears both kingly *and* treacherous – because his two roles can no longer be played by the same man; the King cannot be true to the reveller of Eastcheap. In the play as a whole, the width of reference and ambiguity of response shows Shakespeare's full maturity. 'The solution to the problem of life is seen in the vanishing of this problem', said the philosopher Wittgenstein; and Machiavelli's contribution to political thought consisted in dropping theories of political government and observing the facts of behaviour, in all their awkward complexity. 'We are much beholden to Machiavel', said Bacon, 'who openly and unfeignedly declares . . . what men do, and not what they ought to do'. A famous book on princely education, Elyot's *Book of the Governor*, had aimed in the early sixteenth century at producing a traditionally good, well-equipped and high-principled ruler. Machiavelli perceived the emergence of secular sovereignty; and the rest of the world was horrified at what he saw. It had already arrived when Warwick the Kingmaker, in Henry VI's reign, putting pressure on the Vatican to back his policy, manoeuvred in a way any modern student of

*A lecture given at the summer school at Stratford, Ontario, 1966.

politics would readily define; but the next century still had no words for it. Behaviour was ahead of statement; for it is the artist that first catches the implications of behaviour. 2 *Henry IV* came out shortly after the first edition of Bacon's essays; these men, however different their minds, were observing the same phenomenon. Shakespeare gave it imaginative form, Bacon gave it definition.

As an actor, Shakespeare was gifted with a special insight into the quick-change aspects of political life; Protean variety, which was the outstanding quality of Elizabethan acting, elicits exactly what the new politics demanded of the ruler. Many have noted that Richard III is a natural actor in his wooing of Anne, his scenes with Clarence, with Edward. However, he is drawn as conventionally wicked; for 'men should be what they seem'. In *Henry IV* Shakespeare is questioning the popular frame of assumptions more radically; yet he had to avoid shocking his audience.

The uncertainties, the troubles, the doubtful roles, the lack of any suitable heir – these issues were calculated to touch powerfully the feelings and engage the interest of any audience in the late 1590s. And the glorious resolution of all doubts in the triumphant coronation of Henry V was exactly what the country was momentarily to feel when James I peaceably succeeded in 1603. Alas! James was no Plantagenet – but instead of leading his people to war against France, he at least united them with Scotland.

Shakespeare was not writing a political treatise or constructing an allegory, but he was playing variations on a live political issue; in these plays the whole of society enters into the conflict. The colourless citizens of *Richard III*, the symbolic gardeners, Welsh tribesmen, the groom of the stable who appear in *Richard II* play minor roles. But here the life of London, and Gloucestershire, and the north is fully drawn into the play; while Shakespeare presents, in ever varying forms, a generous and yet sceptical questioning of that traditional principle which his earlier plays assume. This is political drama in a far profounder way than its dynastic interests would suggest, for the psychology of political life is here developed; the most successful man is he who can adapt himself most flexibly while retaining a clear sense of direction and purpose. This was exactly what the apparently changeable but really determined Elizabeth had done. Unlike her successor, she did not theorize; but she was a superb practitioner.

The Queen *was* the government; so throughout her reign the question of what would happen if she died untimely had troubled her subjects. A disputed succession meant the possibility of civil war – the ultimate worst thing for the sixteenth century (as perhaps it still is). This was a topic which no writer would dare directly to treat on the stage, for the consequences would have been extremely serious;

but in the mirror of history it had been reflected ever since the young lawyers in 1561 put on *Gorboduc* – a play written by one of the Queen's gravest counsellors. This play enjoyed a great and continuing success; it is about the wickedness of dividing a kingdom – as Hotspur and the conspirators propose to do. Other plays dealt with similar subjects – *Horestes, Locrine, The Misfortunes of Arthur.* These are now little more than names in a textbook; but then they were the means by which the warnings and counsels of her subjects might be tendered to the Queen herself. They were played before her; when later still in 1601 Essex and his friends wanted to raise the city of London, they put on the old play of *Richard II.*[1] We see this use of history today in such plays as Brecht's *Galileo*, Eliot's *Murder in the Cathedral*, Sartre's *Lucifer and the Lord.*

Within *Henry IV*, each character plays several roles, and the leading characters often substitute for each other. Falstaff is the father of Hal's wit, the King father of his chivalry; Harry Monmouth is the son of Henry's loins, but Harry Hotspur the son of his wishes.[2]

Falstaff plays any and every part. His imagination devises ever-fresh fancies for himself and his followers, which are taken up and discarded as fast as they are conceived. He describes Hal and himself as thieves, in gorgeously poetic terms; he next promotes himself to judge – but is ready to turn hangman; he then becomes melancholy and repents. In the heat of exploit Falstaff is a 'young man' that 'must live', and the victim of Hal's love charm; in the next scene he is 'poor old Jack'. Having justified himself for robbery on the grounds of a vocation for it, he raises a tempest of rage when his pocket is picked, and takes the opportunity to repudiate all his debts. Playing the knight of chivalry, he asks Hal to bestride him if he is down, and boasts that his deeds surpass Turk Gregory's. He rises in fact from his mummer's sham death to claim the spoils of victory.

Against Falstaff's instinctive mobility, Hal's role-taking looks deliberate. He early casts himself for the role of Percy, playing it in a mixture of admiration and irony; in his revels, he plays the part of Prodigal Prince, with Falstaff as his father; and then, assuming the King, deposes and banishes Falstaff as later he will do in earnest. But he can play the potboy in a leather apron, equally well. The fantasy life of Eastcheap (even the robbery is a jest), playing at capital crime, at exhortation, at soldiering, is sharply dismissed by the Prince, even while he enjoys it. It is Idleness – according to Puritan opponents, the capital sin of all players. Idleness and Vanity are keywords in Part 1; both were favourite terms of abuse for the players, but Shakespeare draws their sting. It is in the comedy of Gadshill, sweeping along through the first two acts, that the grand genial theme of Robbery is stated. Thief . . . hangman . . . gallows . . .: the sinister possibilities are suggested only to be brushed aside, for the thieves are in company with 'nobility and tranquility, burgomasters and great oneyers'. In the older plays, it is the King's own money which is taken. Later the note is graver; the rebels carve up the commonwealth and use her as their booty; the King himself is confessedly one who stole the diadem and put it in his pocket; the tussle with Hotspur over the prisoners is an attempt at Gadshill measures. According to Holinshed, Hotspur said of Mortimer, 'Behold the heir of the realm is robbed of his right, and yet the robber with his own will not redeem him.'

Falstaff of Gadshill is succeeded by Captain Falstaff, robbing under royal warrant by his misuse of the King's press. At Shrewsbury the Prince robs Hotspur of all his honours, and finally, most shameless of all, Falstaff robs the Prince of the glory of killing Percy, and staggers off, a porter of the 'luggage' that once was the fiery Hotspur. The Prince, with an indifference more telling than contempt, offers to 'gild' what he at the same time labels as a 'lie'.

Falstaff's chief weapon is neither his sword nor his bottle of sack, but his jests; his power to defend the indefensible springs partly from nimble wits and partly from that innocent and unstudied shamelessness which breeds lies gross, open and palpable as the fantasies of childhood. Somewhere in Falstaff lurks the small boy who boasts that he has just killed a lion. Only by degrees does he penetrate from his Castle of Misrule, the Boar's Head Tavern, to the world of heroic action in which Percy moves; only in Part 2 to the world of judgment, organization, political theory which surrounds the King. He is an Actor, not in the calculating fashion of Richard III, but with the instinctive, ductile mobility of a jester who takes up any position you throw him, and holds it.

Henry IV, as in the play of *Richard II*, stands for the life of judgment against that of the fantasy and imagination; it is his superior skill in deploying his forces that defeats the dash and fire of Hotspur.

Percy's scornful mimicry of the popinjay lord reveals that he, like Hal and Falstaff, lives in the life of the imagination. To think of a plot is enough for him; he can feed on his motto *Esperance*; mappery and closet-war are quite alien to him. Yet when he meets the more primitive imagination of Glendower with its cressets and fiery shapes, its prophecies out of the common lore, Hotspur baits Glendower mercilessly. Glendower is Hotspur's Falstaff.

Before Shakespeare wrote, Hotspur was already a potent name in such common lore. Every member of the audience would have known that old ballad of Douglas and Percy by which Sir Philip Sidney had confessed himself stirred more than with the sound of the trumpet. Hotspur's contempt for balladmongers is ill-deserved; for they were to keep his fame alive. In *The Battle of Otterburn* a single combat, such as the Prince offers at Shrewsbury, is offered by Douglas to Percy, and the conqueror salutes his gallant foe, as the Prince, laying his royal favours on the mangled face, salutes the dead Hotspur. In the ballad, it is Percy himself who

> leaned on his brand
> And saw the Douglas dee:
> He took the dead man by the hand,
> Saying, Woe is me for thee;
>
> To have saved thy life, I would have parted with
> My lands for years three;
> For a better man, of heart, nor of hand
> Was not in all the north country.

The resurrection of Douglas to join the conspirators in this play adds greatly to their potency. Hotspur could so easily have won at Shrewsbury; the battle against odds is a true foretaste of Agincourt – the little troop with its Welsh and Scots contingent, led by one man's courage. Harry learns his role at Agincourt from Hotspur's at Shrewsbury.

Harry Monmouth, the changeling prince, born in the enchanted west, publicly takes up the role of chivalrous knight in Vernon's splendid description of his mounting his horse; and Hotspur cries:

> Come, let me taste my horse,
> Who is to bear me like a thunderbolt
> Against the bosom of the Prince of Wales.   (IV. i. 119–21)

The essence of chivalry is the mounted charge: knights must have horses – and rivals to encounter. The images are cosmic, grand. As Harry says 'Two stars keep not their motion in one sphere'. The image of the rising sun dispelling clouds, which the Prince uses in his opening soliloquy, is inevitably parodied by Falstaff: 'Shall the blessed sun of heaven prove a micher and eat blackberries? a question not to be ask'd. Shall the son of England prove a thief and take purses? a question to be ask'd' (II. iv. 394–7).

Harry of Monmouth and Hal of Eastcheap are different roles for the same young man, who had learnt manysidedness among the pots of ale, where Hotspur contemptuously places him. The opening soliloquy shows the Prince as a passionless manipulator of events, whereas Hotspur is carried away by rage, ardour or mockery. In his presence, calculation fails; his uncle Worcester, the supreme Machiavel, gives up schooling him and at the last dupes him. (In his source, Shakespeare could have found that Worcester had in fact

N/B

been tutor to Hal; a suitable appointment, had he cared to develop it.)

Hal's many parts, however, do not cohere as naturally as do Falstaff's. In Falstaff the contradictions spring from a great natural vitality; they are the fruit of abundance; in his presence, jests alone are plotted. The Prince is nimbly versatile, witty in a biting style and noble in a restrained one; irony and control are his modes, as lustiness and shamelessness are Falstaff's. In wit they are evenly matched; but Hal dispenses patronage, and a follower can never be quite a friend. The mixture of apparent intimacy and real insecurity which Falstaff develops at the Boar's Head is like that attained by players with such noble patrons as Southampton or Pembroke; and the real Boar's Head Tavern was one of the players' winter houses. Falstaff harps constantly on Hal's position as heir apparent, and though he may dare to call him 'cuckoo' and ask, 'Help me to my horse, good king's son', there is behind the Prince's retort, 'What, shall I be your ostler?' something of the sting that appears in 'I know you all', with its later, more dramatic sequel, 'I know thee not, old man'.

Falstaff's gross body, his constant and clamorous needs, for sack, for wenches, for a hand to his horse (the Prince can vault into the saddle), makes him helpless at times with the helplessness of the flesh and of old age, which raises its voice in the shrill reproaches of the long-suffering Mistress Quickly. Falstaff needs his wits to live; Hal needs his only to jest, and is an extraordinarily ascetic Rioter. In the old plays of the Prodigal Son, an addiction to harlots always characterized the Rioter. In Part 1 Falstaff represents misrule and good cheer rather than riotous life. Dover Wilson noted the many images of food which are applied to him – the most frequent is 'butter'; he 'lards the earth' and is 'as vigilant as a cat to take cream'. Though gross, these images are rich, nourishing, festive.

It is because he inhabits such a mountain of flesh that his wit 'strikes fiery off'. He uses his bulk as a shield to turn reproaches into a jest, and in his extraordinary union of the child, the animal and the criminal, never pursues any single aim, so that all his disabilities serve only to illustrate his freedom. The dexterity with which he extricates himself from danger is a quick and natural response; when he hacks his sword or attempts to cozen, he is always exposed. His confidence in himself is deep, animal, instinctive; in this, he resembles Hotspur. They represent the nobility of instinct, a feckless, unthrifty splendour of living which is unknown to the prudent court. Coarseness and violence, the stench of the battlefield and the smell of the stable, cling to Hotspur, who would have his Kate swear like a mosstrooper, and leave modest oaths to citizens' wives. The praise of instinct which

Falstaff bestows on himself has some truth in it. He swears commonly and most properly by himself, for out of himself a whole world of living roles is created for himself and others to play.

Henry IV has only one role to play – that of the King. He has shown courage, and a disregard for conventional restraint and for all the sacred taboos in assuming the crown; as L. C. Knights has observed, he remains the embodiment of the guilt that is inseparable from getting and keeping power. His vision of a united England sets him above his enemies; but against his deep repentance, and that of the Prince in face of his father's 'dear and deep rebuke', is set the mock repentance of Falstaff, couched in the canting whine of the sectaries. Falstaff thus protects himself against the uncou' guid by stealing their thunder.

Interplay of character, exchange of roles, melting of mood into mood, and free range combine to give Part 1 its 'divine fluidity'. All is lucent, untrammelled in the consequence. The consequences are presented in Part 2.

II

Here the characters are sharper, clearer, more definite; they do not blend but contrast. Instead of lambent interplay, division or fusion of roles is provided, with clear separation of man and office. There is more oration and less action; the action belongs to the common people, while the King utters his great soliloquies and Falstaff talks directly to the audience on the virtues of sherris sack.

The embodiment of some of the leading themes appears in the Prologue Rumour, and I was sorry that this Prologue was cut in your production. Morally, Rumour embodies the Lie; socially, she represents 'rotten Opinion' or Seeming; politically, the unstable and troublesome times. The rebels are first shown a false image of victory, then a false peace which is prelude to a new conspiracy, and finally a false show of war, when the true grief lies in the King's death. She addresses the audience as her 'household'; it is a slightly malicious opening jest.

The last abortive rebellion of Henry IV's reign is led by the two symbolic figures of Mowbray and York; Mowbray, the son of Bolingbroke's first public challenger, and York, the prince of the church who echoes Rumour on the 'still discordant wavering multitude':

> The commonwealth is sick of their own choice; . . .
> An habitation giddy and unsure
> Hath he that buildeth on the vulgar heart.   (I. iii. 87,89–90)

A religious rising in the north was the only rebellion of Elizabeth's reign: as a boy of five, Shakespeare might have seen the levies marching up against the Catholic earls, the Nevilles and Percies. Perhaps some of his London audience had marched too.

To his King's anxious calculations of his enemies' strength, Warwick, who is Shakespeare's countryman and speaks always with the voice of Truth, replies:

> Rumour doth double, like the voice and echo,
> The numbers of the feared.   (III. i. 97–8)

Like voice and echo, opposed rulers of church and state recall the deposition and death of Richard II, the Archbishop dwelling on the treachery of the multitude who then denounced and would now worship him, Henry dwelling on the treachery of Northumberland, once Richard's friend, then his, and now his sworn foe.

The connection between ecclesiastical and temporal rule is debated when the armies meet. Lancaster says the Archbishop is misusing his position as God's deputy to take up arms against God's temporal substitute, the anointed King.

> You have ta'en up,
> Under the counterfeited zeal of God,
> The subjects of his substitute, my father,
> And both against the peace of heaven and him
> Have here up-swarm'd them.   (IV. ii. 26–30)

But the treachery of John of Lancaster's ruse is hardly excused by his neat explanation that wrongs will be redressed, while traitors will suffer; and a final blasphemy is not lacking:

> Strike up our drums, pursue the scatter'd stray:
> God, and not we, hath safely fought today.   (IV. ii. 120–1)

Comment is provided in the last scene of this act by Henry himself:

> God knows, my son,
> By what by-paths, and indirect crook'd ways
> I met this crown.   (IV. iv. 184–5)

No one, least of all Bolingbroke, denies the guilt of usurpation or the conflicts it brings. Treachery in the political sphere replaces the mock robberies of Part 1; the presiding Genius is not Valour, but Wit, not Chivalry but Statecraft. God send us His peace, but not the Duke of Lancaster's, the commons might exclaim.

The lament of Hotspur's widow is immediately followed by the appearance of Falstaff's whore; it is one of the telling silent strokes. Doll hangs on Falstaff's neck and tells him whether she sees him again there is nobody cares. The life of the play resides in these common parts, the roles of his followers who do not think of Hal as their future governor. He himself plays the prentice's part: this was a shrewd touch to endear him to all the prentices in Shakespeare's original audience – an important playgoing group. The action of Falstaff's own followers is largely parody. Pistol presents a great parody of the imaginative life; he outgoes even Falstaff's soaring inventions, a wild impossible creature who talks in scraps of play-speech, and feeds on his own mad imagination. If the ghost of Hotspur walks in Part 2, he is named Pistol. It has been said that we always fundamentally talk about ourselves, or aspects of ourselves; so, if Falstaff represents something of Shakespeare's own assessment of himself, may not Pistol be a player's nightmare? A parody of Ned Alleyn's rant, perhaps, but also an embodiment of Shakespeare's deepest fear – a wild tatterdemalion spouter of crazy verses, hopelessly mistaken in all he says and does, thrown off even by Falstaff. Pistol embodies the life of dream, of playmaking at its most distorted and absurd. It is fitting that he brings the deceptive good news of Hal's succession to Falstaff. When the King wakens from his dream of Eastcheap mirth, both Falstaff and Pistol are jailed. Pistol roaring his defiant Spanish tag as he is carried off, in cruel parody of Hotspur's motto, *Esperance*: 'Si fortuna me tormenta, spero me contenta.'

The great mythological popular scene of the stolen crown is haunted not by an explicit recollection of Richard II, but an echo of his fate, the sad ceremony by which Bolingbroke unkings himself. Giving shape to his imaginary fears, Henry mockingly hails his son by the new title which for all the audience evoked the 'star of England', victor of Agincourt.

> Harry the Fifth is crown'd! Up, vanity:
> Down, royal state! . . .
> O my poor kingdom, sick with civil blows.
>
> (IV. iv. 120–1,134)

Behind the dying king, the anxious father peers out, as death bores through his castle wall. The man fenced in by office, the body fretted by care, bequeath themselves to dust. Bolingbroke admits that even his expiatory crusade had not been without its prudential aspect; he had known only a 'supposed Peace', but he prays for 'true peace' at home in his own son's time. And pat to the catastrophe comes the old prophecy's fulfilment – he is to die in Jerusalem, if not quite the Jerusalem his rather stumbling piety expected.

The transmission of office, the demise of the crown as distinct from the death of Henry Bolingbroke, involves Prince Henry in the last death-pangs of his old self. In his brief appearance before the King's last sickness, the Prince is shown with Poins, who, unlike Falstaff, is bluntly honest. The Prince must mock his own greatness, gird at Poins, but half confide in him. Hal of Eastcheap has no right to weep for a father's sickness, and is well aware of it. He takes up the prentice's part and surveys from this vantage Falstaff's descent 'from a god to a bull'. The encounter is momentary: there is a revival momentarily of the old manner ('Why, thou globe of sinful continents') a recollection of Gadshill; and a carefully casual goodbye, whose finality was beautifully suggested in the playing: 'Falstaff, good night'. This is the Prince at his most sensitive, subtle and inconsistent. When he finally takes up the poisoned gold of the crown and receives absolution from his natural father, he becomes warmly and simply a tearful son in the closet; but in public, wearing the 'new and gorgeous garment, majesty', he stands as father to his brothers, son to the Lord Chief Justice, and to Falstaff an image of the Last Judgment itself (the Exhortation of the York Judgment Play might serve as parallel to the rejection speech).

In his fears Henry Bolingbroke had given a 'character' of his son, in which sharp changes of mood and irreversible decisions are the leading traits. A strong personality, when its deeps are broken up by an internal earthquake, shows a new and unrecognizable landscape. The 'noble change' so coolly predicted in Part 1 is painfully accomplished in Part 2. The Lord Chief Justice, like the Archbishop a symbol of office, represents the better side of the last reign, all that was true in its 'supposed Peace'. This is how he justified the jailing of the unreformed Prince:

> I then did use the person of your father
> The image of his power lay then in me.   (V. ii. 73–4)

He suggests that Henry should imagine a future son of his own spurning his own image; and the King allows the argument as 'bold, just and impartial'. He is no longer an individual, but a power whose image may by delegation reside in other bodies than his own, such as those of Judge or Prelate. The shadows of past and future kings melt away as the Sun of England mounts with measured confidence an uncontested throne.

Yet he sets himself under the law: 'You shall be as a father to my youth'. Henry, who had played so many parts, now accepts only one. Complete identification of man and office closes the visor of his golden armour upon him, and he becomes the centre of the group of brothers, an impersonal Lancastrian King. Henceforth he has an uncontrollable tendency to speak like a royal proclamation. However, in one jest dexterously combining religious reproof and a recollection of old times, Falstaff is symbolically buried:

Leave gormandizing; know the grave doth gape
For thee thrice wider than for other men.   (V. v. 54–5)

In a metaphor derived perhaps from the parable of the tares, the Archbishop of York had seen the fourth Henry's friends and foes growing so inextricably together that he might not pluck up the one without destroying the other. This is not Henry V's problem in weeding his garden now. Falstaff, and that old father antic the law, Justice Shallow, are swept off to prison by Henry's new father and his colder self, John of Lancaster, who, fresh from the beheading of an Archbishop, can hardly see Falstaff's banishment as anything but a 'fair proceeding'.[3] It is a highly conventional scene, the traditional judgment scene for a bitter or moralist comedy, so that even Doll and Mistress Quickly are swept into the net. Rumour is confounded, Seeming is cast off, and Order restored.

At the height of his second military triumph, the capture of Colville, Falstaff boasts, 'I have a whole school of tongues in this belly of mine, and not a tongue of them all speaks any word but my name'. This elaborate way of saying that 'Everyone that sees me, knows me', by its metaphor suddenly clothes Falstaff in the robe which Rumour had worn in the prologue. Within the play, he is her chief representative; as indeed he admits by implication in a self revealing comment on Shallow: 'Lord, lord, how subject we old men are to this vice of lying'.

The delights of the Boar's Head and of Gloucestershire, with their undertones of death and old age sounding through the revelry, like the coming of winter in a harvest play, depict the wide commonwealth, the unthinking multitude of common folk about whom Bolingbroke and the Archbishop have been so loftily eloquent. Among the least of the rout, a little tailor with the 'only man-sized voice in Gloucestershire', suddenly echoes one of Prince Harry's proverbs from Shrewsbury: 'We owe God a death'. Feeble, who outbuys a whole army of Pistols, serves to link the multitude and the throne, as in earlier comical histories such local heroes as George-a-Greene had done.

The audience feels no compulsion to take the side of law and order; indeed the tragic themes predominate in reading, but on the stage this is Falstaff's play. The imaginative life of the action lies less in the sick fancies, the recollections and foreshadowing of Bolingbroke than in the daydreams and old wives' tales of Mistress Quickly and Justice Shallow. Neither Hal nor Falstaff daff the world aside with quite the carelessness they had shown before. More wit and less fun, more dominance and less zest, more shrewdness and less banter belong to these two; humour and gaiety have split off into the life of common men and women. Falstaff's mistaken dream of greatness is shattered and he hears himself reduced to a shadow of the King's imagination; for Henry V stands where his father had stood, for the life of reason and judgment against the life of fantasy.

> I have long dreamt of such a kind of man,
> So surfeit-swell'd, so old, and so profane;
> But being awak'd, I do despise my dream.   (V. v. 50–3)

This was the formula by which the sovereign arose from a play – 'Think all is but a poet's dream', as Lyly had urged Elizabeth. But against the voice of reason and judgment may be set a feminine voice, which was to be heard again pronouncing Falstaff's epitaph:

> Well, fare thee well. I have known thee these twenty-nine years, come peascod-time; but an honester and truer-hearted man – well, fare thee well.   (II. iv. 369–71)

Truth resides officially with Henry V, yet in spite of his double triumph (honour, that 'word', has been snatched from Hotspur as if it were a boxer's belt, and now the lie and opinion are banished), Kate Percy and Mistress Quickly remain unconverted; while the incorrigible Pistol produces a line which is both a theological definition of Truth or Constancy and a parody of the motto of Queen Elizabeth herself: 'Semper idem: for obsque hoc nihil est'.

Henry sweeps all the nation behind him, except two women and a few fools. Such exceptions, however, are not to be despised in the world of Shakespeare's England. The uncertainty of the public view of Truth has been demonstrated. 'Thou art a blessed fellow', says Truth's champion, Prince Hal, to Poins, 'to think as every man thinks; never a man's thought in the world keeps the roadway better than thine'. There is no need for an unconditional identification with Falstaff; indeed there is no possibility of it; for the virtue of Shakespeare is to present many incompatibles not reconciled, but harmonized.

Notes

1 The deposition scene was left out of the first printed version.
2 'Hal' a more vulgar abbreviation may be used only in Eastcheap: 'Young Harry' is the familiar form at court. Compare Falstaff's description of himself, 'Jack Falstaff with my familiars, John with my brothers and sisters, and Sir John with all Europe'.
3 No one would dream of calling John of Lancaster 'Jack'.

IX

What Shakespeare did to Chaucer's *Troilus and Criseyde*

Troilus and Cressida, unlike most of Shakespeare's plays, was designed to be read as literature and not only for the boards. The Preface to the Quarto calls it a comedy as distinct from a mere play, serving as 'commentary' to 'all the actions of our lives', and appealing to judgment as well as pleasure. This advertisement, though neither of Shakespeare's nor his company's devising, was written by one who knew his public and aimed at catching the select few, with the warning that Shakespeare's plays would soon be difficult to get hold of. The key word is 'wit', but such wit as does not exclude labour; for the writer adds that the play deserves to be properly set forth, with commentary and notes, like the classics. Could he return to survey the endeavours of Campbell, Hillebrand, Baldwin and others, he might write himself down no minor prophet.

Among the marks of conscious labour and effort are the formal debates in camp and citadel, the complex and strange vocabulary, and the great variety of sources. The tone and flavour of the play, disturbing and ambiguous, controls and directs the response; and the 'conclusion of no conclusions' is in keeping with it. A bitter comedy for the Inns of Court men may have been what Shakespeare set out to write; but no work of his can be pigeonholed, and *Troilus and Cressida* bears less resemblance to the formula of Comical Satyre than does *Hamlet* to Revenge Tragedy.[1]

In the division of interest between the two plots, most of the 'commentary' is put into the story of the siege; the dramatic excitement and the main channel of sympathy lies in the love story. My concern is chiefly with the story of Troilus and the way in which by comparison with the original work of Chaucer, Shakespeare's governing intention is revealed. I shall be less occupied with the extent of the borrowing than with the nature of the handling and the temper of approach.

II

Behind the story of the siege, there has been discerned the work of Homer, in French or in Chapman's translation of *Seven Books of the Iliads*, Lydgate, Caxton, and possibly a drama or two. Behind the story of Troilus there is Chaucer, Henryson and a general popular tradition.

The sack of Troy was to the sixteenth century the highest secular symbol of disaster, the 'great crash'; it was what 1914 was to writers of the twenties and thirties, and as such it had already been used by Shakespeare in his most ostentatiously literary work, *The Rape of Lucrece*, where the 'augmentation' of Lucrece's woes in the tapestry of Troy makes it the emblem of betrayal. Soon after *Troilus and Cressida* was finished, the image rose again to Shakespeare's mind in the passion of the mobled queen, and Hamlet's passionate soliloquy upon it. Pyrrhus, the true son of Shakespeare's own Achilles, minces the limbs of Priam in a blind violence which otherwise in the play of *Hamlet* remains hidden – for murder and lust, combined in the person of Claudius, are masked in more than Sinon's cunning.

Such accounts of the siege as Shakespeare might have read in English were from the literary point of view neither stimulating nor shapely. He had either to quarry from the rambling narratives of Caxton or Lydgate,[2] or stumble through Chapman's text of Homer, which the contortions of syntax no less than the pidgin-Latin vocabulary made very nearly unreadable (these first seven books became much clearer in Chapman's final version). The influence of Chapman on the language of *Troilus and Cressida* is at its greatest in the debating scenes, where something near a scholar's rhetoric was required to sustain the height of argument. Years before, in *Love's Labour's Lost*, Shakespeare had laughed at scholars' terms; here in a limited way he returned to them; but combined with the 'conceited wooing of Pandarus Prince of Licia', with the satyrical snarling of Thersites, and with the speech of the lovers themselves, which ranges from high terms to barest simplicity.

Those concerned with the sources of *Troilus and Cressida* have devoted most space to the story of the siege. R. K. Presson, whose treatment is the latest and most lengthy,[3] gives only twenty-five pages out of one hundred and fifty-seven to Chaucer's poem, with which however he 'inclines to think' Shakespeare was familiar. In depicting the siege, Shakespeare had relied upon at least two and possibly three versions; he selected, recombined, and rearranged the ingredients with the utmost freedom. For the love story he went to the greatest poet accessible to him in English; and his treatment of Chaucer is at once consistent and paradoxical. The high and heroic romance is in every way deflated. If the whole play reflects Shakespeare's reactions towards some deep betrayal, with roots vast, ramifying and obscure, it is not likely that only by chance he took Chaucer for this more intimate and dramatic half of the story: a poetic ideal was being ironically distorted and defaced. That the author of *Romeo and Juliet* had learned from the author of *Troilus and Criseyde* would seem to be one of those possibilities not to be measured by the number of detectable parallels. A poet learns his trade not from books of rhetoric but from other poets; and the Wyf of Bath and Harry Bailly still remain the only peers of Angelica and Falstaff.

In refashioning this story, Shakespeare was doing to Chaucer what Chaucer had already done to Boccaccio; but he was not the first to produce what the rhetoricians would call a 'correction' of Chaucer's work. In Thynne's edition of 1532, Robert Henryson's *Testament of Cresseid* was printed as a sequel to Chaucer's poem, and it was even copied by a sixteenth-century writer into a fifteenth-century manuscript.[4] If he read it, Shakespeare made no direct use of this poem; indeed it was Rollins' thesis that Shakespeare reversed later developments of the story in ignoring the pitiable end of the heroine.[5] But the imagery of disease, so violently presented in Henryson in his picture of Cresseid the leper, was dissolved into the general language, where, joining with the tradition of comical satyre, it appeared in the language and person of Thersites (a figure very much enlarged from hints in the original story of the siege). Henryson's stern and elliptic statement of the punishment wrought by Time and Change – Saturn and the Moon – upon Cresseid's beauty carries the concentration of a Scots ballad and the solemn retributory weight of Scots piety, as in the brief epitaph carved upon her tomb of 'merbell gray'

> Lo, fair ladyis, Cresseid, of Troyis toun,
> Sumtyme countit the flour of Womanheid,
> Under this stane lait Lipper lyis deid.

To encounter such a harsh, incongruous if noble ending joined to the delicate intricacy of Chaucer must have been jarring and bewildering to a sensitive reader ignorant of the history of its composition. Such a sequel would violate rhetorical decorum if read as part of the original, but it might supply a hint to be improved upon. Henryson, while inflicting the full horrors of the spital house upon Cresseid, does not question the beauty of the love that was once between her and Troilus, and her dying remorse and lament belong to an unperplexing if bitter world, where truth is honoured even in the breach of it. Shakespeare's exploration of betrayal goes further than either Henryson's or Chaucer's. There is no physical destruction; only, 'if beauty have a soule this is not shee'.

III

Compression and inversion direct Shakespeare's use of Chaucer. The original narrative is an inward one; experience, not events form the ground of it.

> The double sorwe of Troilus to tellen . . .

Each of Chaucer's five books is represented by one or two scenes in Shakespeare, the division between Chaucer's books corresponding roughly to the division between Shakespeare's acts. Book I, the love woes of Troilus, is represented by I. i; Book II, the wooing of Criseyde, by I. ii (with the scene of Helen, III.i, as appendage – Helen and Paris appear in Chaucer's second book); Book III, the consummation of love, is represented by III. ii; Book IV, the parting, by IV. ii and IV. iv; Book V, the betrayal, by V. ii. Chaucer's story is leisurely and, especially in the wooing, he protracted events; throughout, as Shakespeare tells it,

> Injurious time now with a robbers hast,
> Cram's his ritch theev'ry up hee knowes not how.   (IV. iv. 41–2)

Yet the clear inversion of every idealistic feeling save those of Troilus is so relentless that a 'mirror image' emerges. As Shakespeare shows them, Pandarus and Cressid distort Chaucer's two subtlest creations, for neither, in their Chaucerian form, is to be found in *Il Filostrato* or any of the earlier accounts; it was precisely to the most original parts of Chaucer that Shakespeare turned for his bitterest refashioning.

Chaucer, in Book I, shows Troilus as absurd and unreasonable; both his lovers are 'tetchy' – especially, in Book II, Creseyde. The raging of the hero and the hesitancy of the lady remain none the less wholly sympathetic, whilst in Shakespeare the tetchiness is transferred to Pandarus, whose cheap display of power in his petulance to Troilus conceals the salesman's trick of pretending indifference to stimulate the customer. He next opens his attack on Cressid with the same comparison with Hector that Chaucer's Pandare also employs (Book II, ll. 170–207; cf. I. ii.50–95) but in Shakespeare by depreciation of the great hero, in Chaucer by admiring comparison. To whet Pandarus, Shakespeare's Cressid mockingly disdains Troilus, while Creseyde frankly acknowledges his prowess. For the delicate and subtle fencing with words between medieval knight and lady ('I shal felen what he meneth, ywis'), there is substituted a frank and brutal exchange, culminating in the open taunt 'You are a Bawde!' Cressid's soliloquy proclaims her simple creed, the art of the coquette raised to a rule of life, based on the assumption that what is to be looked for in man is simply 'lust in action'. Chaucer's Creseyde, on the contrary, will not admit to herself or to Pandare even the natural flattery which she feels at the prospect of a royal lover. She is a young widow, sensitive, loath to make any emotional commitment (Book II, ll. 750–6), but innocent enough to be deceived by Pandare's dramatic threat of a double suicide for himself and Troilus. Though on Pandarus' word, still a virgin ('How now, how now, how go maidenheads?') Shakespeare's Cressid is both wily and raw; unlike Chaucer's lady, she is unmoved by the sight of hacked arms and helm as the hero passes her on his return from battle; at the first interview she betrays her own arts completely to Troilus

Perchance my Lord I show more craft then love . . .   (III. ii. 49)

and, warm from her first encounter, generalizes glibly on her original theme;

> Prithee tarry, you men will never tarry,
> O foolish Cresseid, I might have still held of,
> And then you would have tarried.   (IV. ii. 15–17)

for Cressid, as Ulysses was shortly to observe, is a natural 'daughter of the game'.

Chaucer's lady, reading in her chamber, playing with her maidens, conducting her lawsuit under masculine tuition, is gracious and dignified; Pandare, though he does not disguise his ultimate hope that the lovers may be united, does not dare to press even for an interview. She is not ignorant of 'the right true end of love' but restrained by modesty and pride. Pandare sees ahead and is content to move slowly; she lives in the moment, as she is later bitterly to acknowledge (Book V, ll. 734–49) so that the delicately complex process of the wooing (which Chaucer admits to spinning out as long as possible, Book III, ll. 1195 ff.) allows her to dissolve her hesitancies only at the last possible moment, after three separate stages in the wooing have been depicted, and several years are supposed to have elapsed.

The wooing itself has acted as 'a spur to valiant and magnanimous deeds' and Chaucer's Troilus has become a more renowned fighter 'in hope to stonden in his lady grace' while Shakespeare's Troilus is enervated and drawn from the battle by his love. When the play opens, his protracted wooing is nearly over. The actual scene of Cressid's surrender (III. ii.) has several reminiscences of Chaucer. Troilus' rapture

I am giddy; expectation whirles me round . . .   (III. ii. 17)

though it leads him to fear 'sounding destruction' is not as acute as that of the medieval knight, who does actually fall in a swoon. At an earlier interview, Chaucer shows him feverish and overcome, for the physiology of wooing, as Chaucer understood it, though it leads to increased valour in war, involves deep disturbance and not unmanly tears (Book III, ll. 57–8, 78–84). All the gasping and palpitating is on the part of the knight, who like Shakespeare's Troilus, forgets his rehearsed speech; the lady remains inwardly calm enough to make even her final surrender with a laugh against herself, though by this time she too quakes like an aspen leaf (Book III, ll. 1210–1). The difference in tone between Shakespeare and Chaucer can be most easily gauged by a comparison of the song in praise of love which Antigone sings to Creseyde (Book II, ll. 827-75) with the bawdy verse that Pandare sings to Helen (III. i. 108–19). Shakespeare's destruction of the character of Pandarus is as thorough as that of Creseyde. In Shakespeare he gloats over what he does not see with obscene insistence, while in Chaucer he drily mocks, and comments to himself as he finally settles for a night before the fire. The greeting of Creseyde (or Cressid) next morning (Book III, ll. 1555–75 – cf. IV. ii. 24–34) contrasts very neatly the same jests as spoken in the 'high rhetoric' of courtesy and in the 'low rhetoric' of the stews.

While described on the title-page of the Quarto as 'Prince of Licia', Shakespeare's Pandarus calls Troilus simply his 'Lord' and would appear to be on much the same footing as is Parolles to Bertram or that later procurer, Webster's Flamineo, to Brachiano. Pandare in Chaucer is the Prince's comrade in arms, and his loyalty to both lovers is emphasized at the moment of initial success (Book III, ll. 239–343). Creseyde has just received Troilus 'to her service' and the ultimate outcome can hardly be doubted, though the lady's feelings must be observed. 'My dearest lord and brother', Pandar begins, 'I have become for your sake the kind of creature who brings men and women together. Take pity of her; I have betrayed her to you, but don't betray her to the world by boasting of her favours.' To which Troilus replies with fervent oaths, and indignant denial that Pandare's act of 'compaignie' should be classed as mercenary sale.

> Call it gentilesse,
> Compassioun and felawship and trist.   (Book III, ll. 402–3)

And he offers to get his own sister for Pandare as recompense – an offer which in Shakespeare is transferred to become part of Pandare's own assault upon his niece's feelings ('Had I a sister were a grace or a daughter a Goddesse, hee should take his choice'). Far from apologizing for his conduct, Shakespeare's Pandare identifies his role with that of the 'traders in the flesh'. At the end of the lovers' contract, in which they prophetically sketch their several fates and draw the moral, he bestows his name on 'all pitiful goers between to the world's end' and draws in the very spectators to the brothel.

> And cupid grant all tong-tide maidens here,
> Bed, chamber, Pandar to provide this geere. (III. ii. 206–7)

The device is repeated in the epilogue, where Pandarus prays to those members of his livery present in the audience to condole with him:

> As many as be here of *Pandars* hall,
> Your eyes halfe out, weepe out at Pandars fall . . .
> Brethren and sisters of the hold-door trade . . . (V. x. 46–50)

At the corresponding points in his story, Chaucer too directly addresses his hearers. After the bedchamber scene, he humbly appeals to all lovers to correct and improve his telling of the noble tale; and at the end, his formal address to his book, 'litel my tragedie', merges into another to the same 'yonge fresshe folkes, he or she' to forsake the love of man for the love of God; then comes the dedication to Gower and Strode, and finally the prayer to the Trinity which he took from Dante's *Paradiso*. The human tragedy, while subsumed into something greater, remains beautiful in itself.

> Thynketh al nys but a faire,
> This world, that passeth soone as floures faire.

Shakespeare chose to end with a reference to the celebrated brothels of the Bankside owned by the Bishop of Winchester. It completes his lacerative destruction of Chaucer's whole vision, which has already replaced the sensitive Creseyde, and the recklessly devoted, mockingly sympathetic Pandare, by a combine of amateur drab and professional agent.

The lengthy wooing and three years 'bliss' of Chaucer's lovers are condensed by Shakespeare into a single meeting and one night's enjoyment. Yet their secret is known to Paris and Aeneas; under pretence of arranging excuses for Troilus, Pandarus has dropt some broad hints. Troilus makes no attempt at concealment and assumes before Diomede the right to protect Cressid. She herself is the only one to take precautions, when she thrusts Troilus back into her chamber on the arrival of the Lords.

IV

With the exchange of Cressid for Antenor, Shakespeare draws his two plots together; the connection with Chaucer grows fainter. In Chaucer, Hector's noble instinct is to refuse the exchange – 'We usen here no woman for to selle'[6] – but he is overruled by the mob; while

Troilus, who is present at the council, does not speak for fear of compromising Creseyde. Later however both he and Pandare lament at length and propose to abduct Creseyde, who is herself the one to counsel moderation and to promise that she will steal or beg her way back to Troy. Shakespeare's Troilus stoically accepts the public decision in which he took no part: 'Is it so concluded?' and overrules Cressid, who is hysterically protesting; he promises to corrupt the Greeks' sentinels and make his way to her by night. Shakespeare's Troilus is altogether more disciplined and active; Cressid's lament recalls something of the original, though she does not go to the length of threatening suicide (Book IV, ll. 771–7, 813–9, 862–8; cf. IV. ii. 102–115).

Chaucer's Creseyde, handed over in silence by Troilus at the town's end, arrives at the Greek camp half-fainting and is received only by her father.

> She . . . stood forth muet, milde, and mansuete.   (Book V, ll. 194)

The slow dragging hours of her lover's vigil on the walls, the despair of Criseyde as she gazes at the towers of her home from the Grecian camp, the ruthless skill of Diomede prepare for the long-delayed end. The prisoner, caught in the war machine, is battered into subjection; she is in essentials the same as the Cressida of Walton's recent opera, and ends so broken that her final pitiful letter shows her incapable even of the consistent lie. Chaucer's lovers, after their parting, never meet again; Troilus, whose eagerness and trust had made him mistake every approaching figure for that of his love, whose obstinacy of belief had persisted against even the damning evidence of the letter, is finally convinced by the sight of his love-token upon Diomede's captured coat-armour. Pandarus, though his superior insight told him that Criseyde's return was not to be hoped, is as outraged by this proof of infidelity as Troilus himself. The 'doctrine' of the ending is set forth in the interpolated passage from Boethius which is put into the mouth of Troilus in Book IV (ll. 958–1078). It is Fate or Necessity which decrees the separation; but only after death can Troilus accept it. Shakespeare's Troilus gives to Cressid in the moment of parting the orthodox religious explanation; they are punished for idolatry;

> Cressid, I love thee in so strain'd a purity,
> That the blest Gods as angry with my fancy,
> More bright in zeale then the devotion which
> Cold lippes blow to their deities, take thee from me.   (IV. iv. 23–6)

Then, with utmost speed, comes the disaster. If the wooing was condensed, the betrayal is concentrated much further. While Chaucer dwells on the pangs of suspense, and of ebbing hope ('Hope is alwey lesse and lesse, Pandare!' cries Troilus), Shakespeare uses an extreme form of shock, of dramatic reversal and recognition. In the reception scene and the tent scene, by a blinding demonstration, first the spectators and later the hero are shown the quicksands of Cressid's faith.[7] The irony is pointed by Cressid's resumption of her old arts, in words that constantly echo earlier scenes.

> I prithee do not hold me to mine oath . . .   (V. ii. 26)
> Nay, but you part in anger . . .   (V. ii. 44)
> Come hither once again . . .   (V. ii. 49)

and, in reply to Diomede's 'Will you then?' perhaps the savagest line of the play;

> In faith I will lo, never trust me else.   (V. ii. 59)

After her maudlin tears over the pledge, in which she rises to verse at the thought of Troilus' 'memorial dainty kisses' to her glove, she veers again;

> Well, well, tis done, tis past; and yet it is not.
> I will not keep my word.   (V. ii. 97–8)

Ulysses, who reads her at a glance, watches half-incredulously the despair of Troilus: the gloating of Pandarus is replaced by that of Thersites; three different readings of the event are supplied by the three watchers.

In Chaucer the evasions, excuses and counter-accusations of Creseyde's final letter to Troilus display the collapse of desperate resistance; but what Shakespeare's Cressid here displays is spontaneous, strange, and yet horribly familiar. Shakespeare's Troilus, like Chaucer's, had had his fears (IV. iv. 79–85; cf. Book IV, ll. 1485–91), but the suddenness and completeness of this metamorphosis destroys more than the image of Cressid; it destroys his whole world. Chaos is come again. The principle of contradiction no longer applies; a thing may be itself and also something else.

> If there be rule in unitie it selfe
> This was not shee.   (V. ii. 139–40)

If beauty have a soul[8] – if the outward and inward ever correspond to each other – this is not she; the existence of truth, of the womanhood that was in 'our mothers', of sanctimony itself is questioned. Chaucer's hero accepts his fate as divinely ordained: Shakespeare's hero inhabits a world in which the natural sequence of events ('discourse of reason' as they are perceived) is utterly suspended. The varying and incompatible points of view represented by the three watchers are not further apart from the incompatible fighting within Troilus himself. From such a world the gods are altogether absent and, when at last they reappear in the last scene of all, they are hostile.

> Frowne on, you heavens, effect your rage with speed,
> Sit gods upon your thrones, and smile at Troy.   (V. x. 6–7)

For to Shakespeare, the agony of Troilus over Cressid's falsehood is distanced and given final perspective, not as in Chaucer by the hero's death and the enlarged world of the epilogue, but by its place in the greater story. Hector falls by the unchivalrous butchery of the Myrmidons; but Troilus himself is in no chivalrous mood by then. In Hector's death, which leaves him the champion of a doomed city, Troilus finds the 'moment of truth';[9] and the Folio text borrows a climax of Chaucer.

> March away;
> Hector is dead; there is no more to say.   (V. x. 21–2)

Namore to seye. No more indeed, but the final testament; which is not Cressid's but Pandar's, and spoken to the audience. This ending was perhaps among Shakespeare's second thoughts; yet it makes a very fitting contrast with the armed warrior of the Prologue. For the strength of this play lies in a vision not of the grandeur but the pettiness of evil; the squalor and meanness and triviality of betrayal, which here enjoy their hour.[10]

Notes

1 See O. J. Campbell, *Comicall Satyre and Shakespeare's 'Troilus and Cressida'* (San Marino, Huntington Library Publications, 1938). Peter Alexander, *Shakespeare's Life and Art* (London, J. Nisbet, 1939), mentions the Inns of Court.

2 The task of turning narrative romance into dramatic form is stressed as one of the chief dramatic problems of the Elizabethan playwright by Madeleine Doran, *Endeavors of Art* (Madison, University of Wisconsin Press, 1954), ch. 5.

3 Robert K. Presson, *Shakespeare's 'Troilus and Cressida' and the Legends of Troy* (Madison, University of Wisconsin Press, 1953).

4 LI, St John's College, Cambridge. M. R. James, *A Descriptive Catalogue of the Manuscripts in the Library of St John's College, Cambridge* (Cambridge, Cambridge University Press, 1913), p. 274. The 'explicit' at the end of the Chaucer would make clear that it *was* a sequel.

5 Hyder E. Rollins, 'The Troilus–Cressida story from Chaucer to Shakespeare', *PMLA*, XXXII (1917), 383–429.

6 Compare the refusal to chaffer for Helen in Shakespeare II. ii, and Paris' words to Diomede, IV. ii. 77–80.

7 In Henryson there is a sudden similar shock in the smiting of Cressid with leprosy; and later there is a poignant silent encounter of prince and lazar.

8 The various uses of the word *soul* in this scene are worth exploring.

9 The manner of Hector's death is taken from the accounts in Lydgate and Caxton of Troilus' own death.

10 Perhaps the final irony is provided by the writer of the preface to the Quarto who declares that Shakespeare's comedies (including this) 'seeme (for their height of pleasure) to be borne in that sea that brought forth Venus'.

X

The balance and the sword in *Measure for Measure*

Measure for Measure, performed at court before the king on St Stephen's night (26 December) 1604, marked the end of a climactic year for Shakespeare and his company. On 15 March, as the King's Men, they had marched in their royal livery from the Tower to Westminster, in coronation procession that took from eleven o'clock till five. Less than a month later on 9 April their theatre opened after a long closure for plague; during the whole of August with nine others, Shakespeare had been deputed to wait on the Spanish Ambassador, Don Juan Fernandez de Velasco, Constable of Castile; for peace with the old enemy, Spain, was sworn that month. They would savour thus a first taste of Spanish punctilio, and the religious household of a Spanish grandee, for none had been seen in England since the Armada years; the Constable brought a train of two hundred followers (see below, p. 168).

The company staged a courtly satire, starring a disguised duke which had been played by boys of the Chapel; entitled *The Malcontent*, it was the work of a young lawyer, John Marston. Three editions appeared in 1604.

Shakespeare's personal life had its difficulties; nine years later, a legal case in the Court of Requests showed that he lodged with a French family, near the royal court of justice at the Old Bailey. He was acting as go-between for the marriage of the daughter of this house, Marie Mountjoy, to a former apprentice; perhaps he knew that her mother was having an illicit love affair with a neighbouring tradesman. Possibly his younger brother Edmund lodged with him; for three years later in the neighbouring parish of St Giles, the burial of an illegitimate child fathered it on Edmund. In his country home at Stratford, his eldest daughter was undergoing some kind of religious crisis; for soon she was cited in the ecclesiastical court for staying away from Easter Communion.

So girls' dowries and girls' problems were on his mind, just as his company asked for a comedy; he threw together his memories of an old play, *Promos and Cassandra*, bits from his own earlier comedies, *All's Well that Ends Well* and *Much Ado About Nothing*, added a song of great beauty and pathos (he was also engaged on a tragedy in which a striking feature was to be 'the willow song'); then his imagination fired, and he found himself writing things that resembled passages from those very private poems, his Sonnets, which he never intended the world to hear.

* * *

The play itself was full of surprises. The man who proves not a judge but a blackmailer is given his infamous payment by his own betrothed in disguise; the executed criminal is not the young sinner Claudio, nor the old sinner Barnardine; the unknown Friar charged with conspiracy turns out to be the Duke; the judge then stands in the prisoner's place; the judge is being married, but sentenced also to death. The essence, as in a modern detective story, is surprise and speed. As the absent ruler returns to his city, praising his deputy, and promising new honours, Isabella raises her cry:

> Give me justice, justice, justice!   (V. i. 5)

The outward conduct of the Duke betrays the most elementary principle of justice, for he appoints Angelo, the accused man, judge in his own cause. Every law student who had crossed by Temple Stairs to the Globe Theatre would know that a judge or advocate is forbidden by oath to take any case in which he has the slightest personal interest; this is one of the principles of natural justice. And in disguise as the Friar, the Duke returns to accuse himself:

> The Duke's unjust
> Thus to retort your manifest appeal,
> And put your trial in the villain's mouth
> Which here you come to accuse.   (V. i. 293–301)

In Ben Jonson's *Sejanus*, which his company had staged, the same plea had rung out in the trial scene of Silius

> Is he my accuser,
> And must he be my judge?   (III. i. 199–200)

Shakespeare's London had seen Francis Bacon leading the prosecution against his former patron, the Earl of Essex, in 1601; it had also seen that very year, Essex's fellow prisoner, and Shakespeare's patron, Southanpton, released from the Tower where for two years he had lain under sentence of death. The deserved sentence was lifted, by the mercy of the new ruler, upon one whose dissolute youth had been a subject of lament in the sonnets. If some shadow of the Earl of Southampton's reprieve lies behind that of Claudio, this would of course have been a private matter for the playwright himself, for the 'justice' of *Measure for Measure* is not at all that of the law – of Astraea, the heavenly goddess with the balance and the sword, emblems of equity and of retribution. The Duke does not cease to judge his own cause; for when Lucio, the rake, is sentenced to marry Mistress Kate Keepdown, whose child he has fathered, rather than sentenced to death, he protests 'Marrying a punk, my lord, is pressing to death, whipping and hanging' – only to receive the retort from his former victim

Slandering a prince deserves it.   (V.i.522)

This ducal forerunner of Gilbert's farcical Mikado is determined to make the punishment fit the crime in his own way, but he becomes ever more Gilbertian and even less like a judge in bestowing the last award – to Isabella. It is the solution of *Trial By Jury*, Gilbert's first farce

> Barristers, and you, attorneys,
> Set out on your homeward journeys;
> Gentle, simple-minded Usher,
> Get you, if you like to Russia;
> Put your briefs upon the shelf,
> I will marry her myself!

Something like this farcical note (though not for the marriage) is supplied by Lucio, especially in the last scene. This autocrat, in disguise, had promised Isabella

> Grace of the Duke, revenges to your heart,
> And general honour.   (IV.iii.132–3)

He is now speaking as the fount of justice, the fount of honour, and (though he is in a Catholic country) the head of the church. It is only if the roles are confused that farce results.

A code of shame and honour, more efficacious and self-enforced than a code of crime and punishment, belongs particularly to sexual offences, and to slander. Claudio was paraded through the streets (this form of penance is found elsewhere in Shakespeare[1]) whereas the Duke had himself foreborne in person to press the laws he had left in abeyance lest this should bring slander upon him – as it does, though not in the way he had anticipated. He gave Angelo full scope

> So to enforce or qualify the laws
> As to your soul seems good . . .   (I.i.66–7)

which is to abrogate all statutory law in favour of equity. (It was in fact decreed under James that if law and equity were in conflict, equity should prevail.)

Angelo's open shaming is the object of the judgment scene. It is so complete that he does not wish to live; his pride, his very identity had been removed.

The repentant Juliet was prepared to 'take her shame with joy' (II.iii.30–36) and whilst the Friar told her her sin was the heavier, the Duke tells Claudio

She that you wrong'd, look you restore.   (V.i.123)

Confusion between ecclesiastical and civil law was nowhere stronger than in the matter of marriage and sexual offences. There has been much discussion about the validity of precontracts, such as Claudio and Angelo both admit, though the one was private and the other public; in such matters custom ruled, though the church had revised its canon law.

Whilst much of the law was ecclesiastical, the matter of dowries was of course within the civil law. Most noble marriages were regarded less as contracts between individuals than as the means of joining alliances, as part of a family power structure or an ambitious man's plan to rise. Thus, in 1601 John Donne had been thrown into prison for stealing a marriage with the niece of the Lord Keeper, his employer; and so had the priest who performed the ceremony.

The dowry of Juliet was the object of Claudio's concealment of the contract, whilst the forcible marriage of Angelo and Mariana was ordered with the object of giving her a dowry to wed a better husband – an idea taken over from the old play. In the earlier versions, of course, there was but the one feminine character, the sister (or in earliest forms the wife) of the condemned man, who really was killed.

By the magical double substitution of Mariana for Isabella and Ragozine for Claudio, Angelo's criminal intent is nullified; in her plea for mercy, Isabella eventually enters this fact, with the alternative pleas in the case of blackmail, a first offender; in the case of the judicial murder, that under the letter of the law, the penalty might be enforced.

The ruler's exercise of spiritual authority is as outrageous as his legal decisions. To assume a holy habit, and power of absolving sins which he did not possess, to hear confession (V. i. 524) and to betray secrets of the confessional given to himself (III. i. 165) and to others (IV. iii. 127) is so monstrous that a Spanish censor has simply cut the whole play out of the Folio in a copy at Valladolid.

Of course the Friar has been seen as a divine figure by some scholars – by others as a monster. Yet again he has been seen as a surrogate for King James, but this view has been vigorously rebutted.[2]

Whilst earlier humanist definitions of the Prince or Governor required him to practise the four cardinal virtues of fortitude, temperance, prudence and justice, the last was most essential. Clemency was also a great virtue in a prince but Machiavelli thought it better for a prince to be feared than loved, if he could not inspire both feelings; he also thought that offenders should either receive a free pardon or execution for crime against the state; and the Duke seems disinclined for anything resembling a middle way. He 'dresses' Angelo in his own love and lends him his terror; both attributes are given at the end of *Henry VIII* to the future Queen Elizabeth. 'She shall be lov'd and fear'd' for 'Peace, plenty, love, truth, terror' wait upon her (V. v. 48). The short rhymed verses in which the ruler defines his double office at the end of Act III, where the action veers towards comedy, resemble those used for the god Jupiter in *Cymbeline*; both may represent some aural memory from Shakespeare's youth of the octosyllabics used in the old craft mysteries for the speeches of divinity.

> He who the sword of heaven would bear
> Should be as holy as severe;
> Pattern in himself to know,
> Grace to stand; and virtue, go . . .   (III. i. 254–7)

With such a standard the earthly ruler is almost inhibited from action. Angelo takes a different and a more legalistic view: his office is not holy.

> I not deny
> The jury, passing on the prisoner's life,
> May in the sworn twelve have a thief or two
> Guiltier than him they try   (II. i. 18–21)

but he adds 'what open lies to justice, justice seizes' adding

> When I, that censure him, do so offend,
> Let mine own judgment pattern out my death,
> And nothing come in partial.   (II. i. 29–31)

Later he declares to Isabella that strict enforcement of the law is mercy –

> I show it most of all when I show justice;
> For then I pity those I do not know,
> Which a dismiss'd offence would after gall . . . (II. ii. 101–3)

In his disguise as a Friar, the Duke makes this point again at the end of the play

> Laws for all faults,
> But faults so countenanc'd that the strong statutes
> Stand like the forfeits in a barber's shop.
> As much in mock as mark.   (V. 1. 317–20)

which Escalus immediately pounces on as 'slander to the state'.

But the state in this play appears to mean the Duke, or his deputy; he has no council, only friends and followers. In comedy the ruler is often in this position, and acts quite arbitrarily (as do the Dukes in *As You Like It* and *Twelfth Night* and the French King in *All's Well That Ends Well*). In some comedies, where a judgment often concludes the play, the judge is himself absurd, the most ludicrous being the Governor in Chapman's bitter comedy *The Widow's Tears*. In particular the most disgraceful sins of prodigal young men were apt to be overlooked – as Heywood's *If you Know not me you know Nobody*, Dekker's *The Honest Whore* or the anonymous play, *The London Prodigal*, performed by Shakespeare's company this very year, and on the title page attributed to him!

It is the *mercy* of the law according to the Duke that decrees the law should be enforced against Angelo as it had been against Claudio:

> The very mercy of the law cries out
> Most audible, even from his proper tongue
> 'An Angelo for Claudio, death for death'.
> Haste still pays haste and leisure answers leisure;
> Like doth quit like, and measure still for measure.   (V. i. 405–9)

The trite form in which it is stated reduces this proverbial wisdom to triviality. It also however recalls the verse from St Matthew's gospel which points to the difference between judgment as the Duke finally sees it and as Angelo sees it.

> Judge not, that ye be not judged. For with what judgment ye judge ye shall be judged; and what measure ye mete, it shall be measured to you again. And why beholdest thou the mote that is in thy brother's eye but considerest not the beam that is in thine own eye. (7. 1–3)

It is not the business of the individual to sit in judgment, except upon himself. The subjective aspect of judgment is put lightly by Orlando against the ready condemnations of Jacques: 'I will chide no breather in the world but myself, against whom I know most faults' (*As You Like It*, III. ii. 262–4). Isabella seems to envisage the judgment of souls, when they are weighed in the scales of heaven, as she warns Angelo:

> We cannot weigh our brother with ourself   (II. i. 126)[3]

and it is not herself she is putting into the scales when she later decides against the monstrous ransom – 'More than our brother is our chastity' (II. iv. 184). For, as another woman had pleaded 'My chastity's the jewel of our house' (*All's Well That Ends Well*, IV. ii. 46) and since Isabella is later prepared publicly to confess to an unchastity she did not incur, it is not her public reputation that deters her; nor, considering the situation of Claudio and Juliet, is it merely the life of her brother and herself that is involved, but a possible innocent:

> I had rather my brother die by the law than my son should be unlawfully born. (III. i. 187–8)

she tells the Friar. Angelo himself feared the revenge of Claudio for dishonour done to his house, while trusting that a woman's fear of shame (IV. iv. 21–3) would prevent any disclosure by Isabella.

Isabella's relations with Angelo and with Claudio provide the emotional conflagration of the play, its active heart. The most powerful tie is the stable one of brother and sister. In *The Family, Sex and Marriage in England, 1500–1700*, Lawrence Stone has observed that the fraternal relation of brother and sister was often the most disinterested and strongest of all family ties.[4] As the eldest son inherited an estate, the younger brothers were usually at odds with him, and he, very often with his parents, who used their children as bargaining counters in the struggle for power; but brothers and sisters were not rivals in the power structure and such famous examples as the Countess of Pembroke and Sir Philip Sidney, Penelope Rich and the Earl of Essex, the Princess Elizabeth and Henry, Prince of Wales had an important effect on public life. At his trial for rebellion, Essex pleaded that he had been under Penelope's influence, while she asserted she had been more like a slave than a sister. When the Prince of Wales lay dying, he was to call repeatedly for his sister who, when kept from him for fear of infection, tried to make her way in disguise. Shakespeare had developed this relation both in Viola and Sebastian and in Ophelia and Laertes.

When Isabella hears her brother at first willing to face death

> If I must die,
> I will encounter darkness as a bride
> And hug it in mine arms.   (III. i. 84–6)

she recognizes a voice of their kinship, a voice from their father's grave; for she herself had used the very same metaphor in rebutting the suggestion of Angelo

> Were I under the terms of death,
> Th'impression of keen whips I'd wear as rubies,

> And strip myself to death as to a bed
> That longing have been sick for, ere I'd yield
> My body up to shame . . .   (II. iv. 100–4)

This is the familiar image of the martyrdom as a bridal, and Isabella's simile might be paralleled from Southwell or other devotionalists; but the sexual image has another context in the mind of Angelo.[5] The bleeding wretches laid upon hurdles, and drawn through the streets of London to their deaths, had been trained to imagine this as a glorious consummation. Claudio's mortuary preparation by the Friar with just such a religious exhortation – 'Be absolute for death' – only makes him more vulnerable when put to the test. Isabella, as has been seen, does not avoid the violent phrase, and she asks her brother

> Is't not a kind of incest, to take life
> From thine own sister's shame?   (III. i. 140–1)

Next, she is tempted to think him not her brother but a bastard. It is the same woman who on hearing of Angelo's final order for her brother's execution, which she believes to be carried out, cries 'O, I will to him and pluck out his eyes!' (IV. iii. 116). It is *this* woman who kneels as advocate for Angelo's defence.[6]

The retribution was to be exacted in a later play; another bastard was hear in *King Lear* (given two years later, St Stephen's day 1606 at court)

> The gods are just, and of our pleasant vices
> Make instruments to plague us:
> That dark and vicious place where thee he got
> Cost him his eyes.   (V. iii. 170–3)

* * *

The purpose of all the reversals and surprises here is to turn the sight inward upon the self. When the Duke, who 'above all other strifes, contended especially to know himself' (III. ii. 219–20) decided as Friar that 'craft against vice I must apply' it is to meet falsehood with falsehood. Isabella is very reluctant to speak falsehood at the seat of justice:

> To speak so indirectly I am loath;
> I would say the truth;   (IV. vi. 1–2)

whilst the Duke's use of 'very mercy' is far from verity – for Claudio, as he well knows, is not dead. The word 'very' is thoroughly mocked in the comic attempt to find out what was done to Elbow's wife – where it occurs fifty-seven times; truth is trivialized, but the extreme difficulty and uncertainty that attends a quest for truth in this sense is at least fully attested.

Truth lives within, and it is the Duke's purpose to turn Angelo's eyes within. Angelo has to learn the full lesson set by Isabella

> Go to your bosom,
> Knock there and ask your heart what it dòth know
> That's like my brother's fault.   (II. ii. 136–8)

These words achieve the opposite of their immediate purpose for they give Angelo the first prompting that something 'like my brother's fault' is indeed lodged within Angelo's heart. The well-trained young novice is applying the Lord's injunction 'Let him that is without sin cast the first stone' (John, 8. 7) as well as that prayer which is so often echoed by Shakespeare, as a personal utterance, in the last lines of Sonnet 120, in the last lines of the epilogue to *The Tempest*, 'Forgive us our sins as we forgive those that sin against us'. A mutuality of forgiveness means Desdemona forgiving her death, taking it upon herself, or Antony's generosity to the treacherous Enobarbus; such generosity is found again and again in the Sonnets

> Take all my loves, my love; yea, take them all   (Sonnet 40)
> For thy right, myself will bear all wrong   (Sonnet 88)

and finally in Prospero

> they being penitent,
> The sole drift of my purpose doth extend
> Not a frown further.   (V. i. 28–30)

The blunted sword, or sword of mercy, which in Spenser lay at the feet of Mercilla belongs to the world of external justice; the relationship in the Sonnets makes use only with playfulness of legal terms, and the aim of the Duke is rather regeneration or recreation.[7] The world reflects back upon each individual the image with which he confronts it; this psychological truism suggests that Angelo's neglect and contempt for a sexual object once attained is very easily converted to self-hatred when he is exposed. It is again a mood reflected in the sonnets (Sonnet 129).

   The purpose of a play being to touch each individual member of the audience, the fantastic events of a comedy do not have the context of a public world. Yet here, Mistress Overdone, Elbow and Pompey are familiar figures from London comedy, while Lucio, who at the beginning of the play organizes what action there is, becomes as it were another deputy for the Duke; first giving his own character to the absent ruler, then fathering his own aspersions upon the Duke himself, in his role of Friar. The symbiosis between these two, almost as close as that between King Lear and his fool, permits Lucio an intolerable series of interruptions in the final scene, which are like subversive Freudian comments upon the justice being meted out.

Claudio's shopsoiled Mercutio, a figure out of John Donne's satires of London life, Lucio is dismissed to prison when the blind and obdurate Barnardine is given into the custody of a friar for spiritual education.

Justice being left with her balance, but not her sword, the Duke finally offers a share of his power to Isabella. This is not a wooing, but a species of coronation; perhaps as Angelo might be physically stripped of the insignia of a judge and of a noble (he is the Duke's cousin, apparently his next of kin), so perhaps Isabel should receive the coronet or the sceptre that honours Truth. In this final scene a surprising number of characters are mute; Angelo says nothing at his reprieve, Claudio and Juliet, Isabel and Barnardine, receive their awards as part of that whole interior exploration of the larger self, the little realm of man, which each spectator, in the depths of his own being, would register, when the mendicant Friar, the Beggar, becomes arbiter sovereign.

The alternative roles of Friar and Duke do not create a character in depth; they are rather like the alternative aspects of the monarch which are by now familiar from the cult of Queen Elizabeth.[8] Hence this play has become a subject of prolonged critical debate; which was perhaps Shakespeare's intention, for to win an audience to debate is to involve them, and here the young lawyers who formed the most intelligent part of his audience would find as much material for argument as the legally minded Scottish king.

The double action, inward and outward, in this play, would be seen by Shakespeare's contemporaries as working like the Ptolemaic spheres, enclosed within each other, moving in contrary directions. The outer world reflects back upon man that aspect with which he confronts it, so that measure for measure is the law of relations between man and man, but the retributive powers of the world are complemented by diabolic or angelic impulses from within the heart of each man, so that Isabella calls out lust unknown to himself in Angelo, the Duke by apparently satisfying his desire calls out an impulse to murder. Mariana, whose earthly hopes had been destroyed by her brother's death, calls out in Isabella an impulse of compassion, which expresses itself in hard and legalistic terms. Thus the two spheres join in her final plea.

Notes

1 In 2 *Henry VI*, II. iv. the Duchess of Gloucester does open penance in a white sheet in the London streets. This form of shaming was still observed, and in 1616 Shakespeare's son-in-law Thomas Quiney was so

condemned for getting an illegitimate child, by the Ecclesiastical Court at Stratford; a penance subsequently commuted.

2 See Richard Levin 'The King James version of *Measure for Measure*', *New Readings versus Old Plays* (Chicago, University of Chicago Press, 1979).

3 Cf. III.ii.258–9, V. i. 113–5 for other uses.

4 (London, Weidenfeld & Nicolson, 1977), p. 115.

5 Cf. Peter Milward, *Shakespeare's Religious Background* (London, Sidgwick & Jackson, 1973), pp. 58, 78; and Harriett Hawkins in *Shakespeare Survey*, 31 (1978), 105–13.

6 One of the titles of the Virgin Mary is the Advocate for Souls.

7 Cf. Isabella's plea, II. ii. 77–9.

8 See Frances A. Yates, *Astraea* (London, Routledge & Kegan Paul, 1973), Part II. The two halves of the disguised ruler in *The Malcontent* similarly do not cohere to make a naturalist character: they are rather alternative approaches to the world of courtly vice and depravity.

XI

An interpretation of *Hamlet**

In this discussion of *Hamlet* I shall be concerned in the first place with
the subjective view of this play, that is, I shall consider the play from
Hamlet's own point of view, as the sympathetic reader or spectator
might see it. But in the second place, I shall consider it from the
objective point of view and look at the character of Hamlet from
the outside and see it as a study of a particular kind of person as
the detached observer might see it.

The view of *Hamlet* which I wish to begin with is that which could
reveal the scepticism, the self-questioning of a man ill-adjusted to his
world, built on the basis of a much simpler problem, the standard
dilemma of the revenger. Keats spoke of the quality that went to form
a man of achievement, especially in literature, and which
Shakespeare possessed so enormously. I mean negative capability,
that is, when a man is capable of being in uncertainties, mysteries,
doubts. It seems to me that recently in criticism of *Hamlet* this
capacity has been singled out as the peculiar strength of the play: the
ability to tolerate a state of interior conflict, to reserve an area of
mystery ('You would pluck out the heart of my mystery', Hamlet
accuses Rosencrantz and Guildenstern); to reject the pleasure that
comes of acting by rule and by rote.

This is not so in Shakespeare's other major tragedies. The darkness
of *Macbeth* never occludes a clarity that keeps alive in Macbeth
remorse and the knowledge of what he has done. 'Direness may
become familiar' to his slaughterous thoughts. But he still calls them
'slaughterous'. There is a residue of clear judgment, as of sheer
animal courage that remains with him to the end, and which leaves at

---

*This article was delivered as a lecture at the Faculty of Literature, Hiroshi-
ma University, on 30 April, 1964, to celebrate the fourth centenary of
Shakespeare's birth.

the last something of a man, some lineaments of nobility.

Lear and Othello alike, being wrought on, are perplexed in the extreme; but in both these plays, there are standing on either side of the protagonist his good and evil angels, and though the depths of destruction leave him helpless at the end to do more than turn in the direction of the good, yet this he does. Having made the wrong choice, he then, after traversing a great arc of experience, reverses that choice. The dilemma for the spectator in this case is, rather, 'Why should such things be?' But the defeat (which is the triumph) leaves the spectator assured that this mystery is beyond sorrow and joy. In a region of 'calm of mind', all passion is spent. It is not so altogether with *Hamlet*.

Hopkins, the Victorian poet, wrote to his fellow poet Bridges:

> You do not mean by mystery what I mean. A mystery to you is an interesting uncertainty. The uncertainty resolved, the doubt settled, the interest vanishes. To me it is an incomprehensible certainty. But there are, you know, some suspensions so lovely in music, some moves so elegant in chess that the interest remains stronger after the problem is solved. How must it be, then, when the solution of the problem is the most pointed putting of the difficulty and the incompatibility itself the answer in which you are to rest?

Hamlet is a play of this kind.

Hamlet is an existentialist tragedy, a play at once of a great uncertainty, and yet one which affirms the responsibility of man. When I say that *Hamlet* is an existentialist tragedy, I mean of course in a sense in which Jean-Paul Sartre and Albert Camus define it. By way of illustrating how close the contemporary criticism of *Hamlet* may come to the modern idea of an existentialist play I shall quote two modern critics of *Hamlet* and then from Sartre and Camus.

Professor D. G. James in *The Dream of Learning* wrote:

> Shakespeare in *Hamlet* saw uncertainty, ignorance, failure, deceit. I do not say that he saw even in *Hamlet* only these things but that he saw at least these things we cannot deny. Hamlet certainly had no unquestioning faith. He had no philosophy, natural or other, and his problems were hardly to be solved by the use of scientific method or knowledge or experiments as Bacon's were. Shakespeare was using an old, crude and violent story; he was turning it to majestic usage, controlling and mending it as far as he could, to convey the tragedy of a man caught in ethical and metaphysical uncertainties.

And Harry Levin in *The Question of Hamlet* entitles his three sections 'interrogation', 'doubt' and 'irony'. *Hamlet* is one who questions, tests and probes, an intellectual whose first impulse is to chop down his thoughts. Hamlet's thought is primarily in the interrogative mood. The graveyard scene has seventy questions in three hundred and twenty-two lines. 'Who's there?' opens the play. 'Long live the king!' is the watchword. But we are soon to ask 'Which king?'. Questions of 'What is the ghost?' haunts the play. Polonius, Rosencrantz and Guildenstern test Hamlet with questions. There are doubts of the ghost, of Ophelia's virtue, of Hamlet's intention towards her, of whether to kill the king at prayer, or whether to go on, or to seek suicide. Levin notes that Camus has written: 'Only one philosophical problem is really serious, that is, suicide. And to decide whether or not life is worth living is to answer the most fundamental problem of philosophy.'

Now, for an existentialist's statement of tragedy. Sartre in *Forgers of Myth* (1946) wrote:

> Man is not to be defined as a reasoning animal or as a social one, but as a free being, entirely indeterminate, who must choose his own being when confronted with certain necessities, such as being already committed in a world full of both threatening and favourable factors, among other men who have made their choices before him; who had decided in advance the meaning of those factors. He is faced with the necessity of having to work and die, of being hurled into a life already complete, which is his own enterprise, and in which he can never have a second chance, where he must play his cards and take risks no matter what the cost. A man is free within the circle of his own situations who chooses whether he wishes to or not for everyone else when he chooses for himself.

That is the subject matter of our play.

And this is Camus' description of Sisyphus in *The Myth of Sisyphus*:

> The gods condemned then Sisyphus to ceaselessly rolling a rock to the top of the mountain, when the stone would fall of its own weight. They have thought with some reason that there is no more dreadful punishment than futile and hopeless labour. You have already grasped that Sisyphus is the hero of the absurd. His scorn of the gods, his hatred of death and his passion for life won him that unspeakable penalty in which the whole being is exerted towards the accomplishing nothing. His is the price that must be paid for the passions of the earth. One merely sees the whole effort of a body straining to raise the huge stone, to roll it and push it up a slope a hundred times over. One sees the face screwed up, the cheek tight against the stone, the shoulder bracing the clay-covered mass, the foot wedging it, the fresh start with arms outstretched, the wholly human security of two earthclotted hands. At the very end of this long effort measured by skyless space and time without death, the purpose is achieved. Then Sisyphus watches the stone rush down in a few moments towards that lower world, when he would have to push it up again towards the summit. He goes back down to the plain. It is during that return, that pause, that Sisyphus interests me. A face that toils so close to the stone is already stone itself. That hour, like a breathing space which returns as sure as his suffering;

that is the hour of consciousness. At each of those moments when he leaves the heights and gradually returns towards the lairs of the gods, he is superior to his fate. He is stronger than his rock. The lucidity that was to constitute torture at the same time, crowns his victory. There is no fate that cannot be surmounted by scorn.

This is the ironic mood of Hamlet's soliloquies, especially of 'O that this too too sullied flesh would melt', and is the Sisyphus situation 'To be, or not to be'. Who would fardels bear?

The irony is strongest when divine vengeance overtakes the King at the end of *Hamlet*. The Prince makes the point with the harsh jest:

> Here, thou incestuous, murderous, damned Dane,
> Drink off this potion. Is thy union here?
> Follow my mother. (V. ii. 317–9)

as well as to Laertes, who acknowledges more piously and devoutly: 'I am justly caught with mine own treachery'. Chance turns into a larger design. Randomness becomes retribution, as Professor Holloway observes. There is very little incertitude possible in a world governed by such mechanisms of dark precision. But Hamlet himself does not win by deep plots. He leaves those to his enemy, except insignificantly in putting on his antic disposition, and in the trap of the play scene; but otherwise his irresolutions serve him well, while the deep plots fail. The significant pattern that emerges is not of his devising. For he does not usurp the role of omnipotence, nor take upon himself the mystery of things as if he was God's spy.

Hamlet is both a scholar and a soldier. He has friends of both sorts, Marcellus and Horatio. Yet he is perhaps the first character in English who betrays the nervous irritability of the artistic temperament. He is vulnerable, a man who can be hurt in new ways, as when his grief is misunderstood. 'Why seems it so particular with thee?' asks the Queen, and he flinches from the word because it betrays such incomprehension of his feeling:

> Seems, madam! Nay, it is; I know not 'seems'.
> 'Tis not alone my inky cloak, good mother,
> Nor customary suits of solemn black,
> Nor windy suspiration of forc'd breath, . . .
> Nor the dejected haviour of the visage,
> Together with all forms, moods, shapes of grief,
> That can denote me truly. These, indeed, seem;
> For they are actions that a man might play. (I. ii. 76–84)

At once, the old formal tableaux, the display of grief, is before us as in the earlier plays, but only to be rejected in the fluent, vehement sketch of Hamlet's critical revulsion from old, mere shapes of feeling. I thought that the performance of *Hamlet* last night brought out very clearly these changes of mood in Hamlet, and in particular the revulsion from pretence. When Ophelia returns his presents with the pious little platitude, that she must have learnt from Polonius:

> to the noble mind
> Rich gifts wax poor when givers prove unkind, (III. i. 100–1)

Hamlet responds in instant exasperation against the banality: 'I never gave you aught' as much in recoil against the memory that he cannot bear to have referred to. He recoils again from the shape of the actor's grief in playing the scene of Hecuba: 'What's Hecuba to him, or he to Hecuba?' He is not a stoic.

It is worth recollecting that the play, of itself, cannot be regarded as a finished composition which was composed by Shakespeare at one burst of easy fluency, to remain unmodified for the ten years after its composition, during which the author still remained an active member of the Chamberlain's Men. The play exists in various states and it seems probable that, like other popular forms of spoken literature, it received additions or deletions on different occasions. Speeches might be inserted, just as Hamlet asks the players to insert his speeches; or on certain occasion, omitted. The position of the soliloquy 'To be or not to be', is quite different in the Quarto and Folio texts. In the first Quarto we have an example of how badly the play could be treated by actors and how little understood. Shakespeare may have revised *Hamlet* just as Goethe spent his whole life revising *Faust*. The fascinating dynamics of *Hamlet*, the possibility of growth, the space for variant interpretations which allows such a wide legitimate scope to actors and producers may be dependent upon this original dynamic in its conception. There could be no final version of *Hamlet*. And, therefore, I think, the version given last night, which was essentially the tragic *Hamlet* with the comic scenes severely pruned and even some of the more witty aspects of Hamlet himself omitted, is a legitimate version. It is not a complete *Hamlet*, but it is a *Hamlet* which is quite legitimate and reasonable to present.

The nineteenth century saw Hamlet as an entirely pure and largely meditative character, and Claudius as entirely wicked. In the twentieth century there have been pictures of Hamlet as an egotistical Machiavelli, as a brutal and violent intruder on a peaceful citizenry. Salvador de Madariaga, L. C. Knights and Derek Traversi depicted him in this way. I have seen Robert Helpman's Hamlet played as a mere boy shattered by his first encounter with the cruelty of things, Sir John Gielgud's royal prince, scolding his mother for her failure to live up to the standard of behaviour suitable to her royal station. I have seen Hamlet in Napoleonic costume, Hamlet in late Victorian costume, and the last students' production I saw at Cambridge, the one before yours, was *Hamlet* played on a grassy bank beside a stream with a real willow tree, in a warm summer night in June; with the famous actors, Sir Lewis Casson and Dame Sybil Thorndike watching their young granddaughter playing Gertrude. So that many different Hamlets can mean different things. Yet there is a measure of continuity within these protean forms which I cannot better define than by the term with which I began, negative capability, that is, when a man is capable of being in uncertainties, mysteries, doubts without any irritable reaching after fact or reason.

What chiefly remains from the older drama in this Shakespearean version seems to me to be the figure of the Ghost. The Ghost offers Hamlet a traditional role, that of the revenger, but Hamlet is not to be confined within any simple presumption. Yes, Hamlet is a man who has seen a ghost and it is round the Ghost that the natural imagery of this play develops – and round that skull of Yorick which, in the graveyard scene, replaces it as the form of the dead. The Ghost of his father will speak only to Hamlet. The Queen thinks it, what Horatio called it at first, an illusion. Even to Hamlet it is but *like* the King that is dead. It is in fact the first character we meet, and deeply mysterious, bringing both airs from heaven and blasts from hell. The Ghost comes to tell the secrets of his prison-house, from which he has escaped to the chill glimpses of the wintry moon, beside the glittering waves of the sound where the great fortress palace stands with all its miles of cellarage, its underground fortifications. To Hamlet, the Ghost presents this image of imprisonment.

Hamlet, his own flesh and blood, learns how flesh betrayed the old King. The heavy stalk of the Ghost, the plated armour he wears, his telling monosyllabic greetings: 'List, list, O, list!', 'Mark me', 'Remember', accompany the issuing of an archaic but absolute command, 'Vengeance'. It is a compulsion, it is a *must*, laid on Hamlet by an archaic part of himself, a part which has been disturbed and reactivated by his mother's marriage following hard upon his father's death. These two shocking events, coming so close together, have roused up this commanding spectral figure with its ghostly truncheon and its final command, 'Swear, Swear, Swear' (which you left out, I noticed, last night). The compelling power of that part of ourselves, which we do not understand, can appear only in such images. Returning to daylight, Hamlet no longer feels sure what it is that has quenched for him the golden fire that adorns the firmament, covering it with vapours, and sterilized the earth to rocky barrenness. The prison of his own solid flesh, within which the prince (even at the beginning of the play) has felt depressed, is further darkened by this encounter. The whole world has become a prison for him. Yet he tells his companion: 'O God, I could be bounded in a nutshell and count myself a king of infinite space, were it not that I have bad dreams' (II. ii. 254–5). So he half acknowledges his own mood to be illusion, 'It goes so heavily with my disposition'. And it is because he knows he does not know, because at the centre of the play there are questions, doubts, disturbances, that Hamlet's part is everyman's. The unfocused, unacknowledged grief, 'the pang without a name, void, dark and drear', is common to all; and because there is a void at the centre of Hamlet the man, and the Ghost is at the centre of *Hamlet* the play, there is room enough for a whole multiplicity of Hamlets. He can be interpreted to suit all thoughts and conditions of man.

The motionless heaps that litter the stage at the end of *Hamlet* are but untenanted clay, which will be shovelled in rapidly to join Yorick, Ophelia and Polonius. Hamlet had thrice held discourse with the dead in his lifetime; once on the battlements, once in his mother's bedchamber and once, sardonically, and playfully, with the skull of Yorick; which he holds in his hand like a fool's bauble or a ventriloquist's doll, coaxing the chap-fallen jaw to utterance, putting a tongue in its mouth and sending it back to the bedchamber to speak to Gertrude the message she will not hear, that she must rejoin the Ghost one day. 'Go, get thee to my lady's chamber, tell her, let her paint an inch thick, to this favour must she come; make her laugh at that' (V. i. 187–9).

The relation of the characters with each other in this play extends not only to husbands and wives, parents and children, but to living and dead. And the relation of the living to the dead can be achieved only through that process which we call mourning. The ability to mourn is one which an eminent psychiatrist, Carl Rogers, of Chicago, has described as one of the leading characteristics of emotional maturity. And I shall conclude this account of *Hamlet*'s psychodynamics by considering it as study in mourning. I have done this in collaboration with a psychiatrist, a friend of my own, who works in London on clinical psychiatry.

According to my friend, Dr Heard, the process of mourning normally follows a fourfold development. In the first phase of shock or disaster, the mourner will not feel anything, but may be deeply numbed and almost paralysed. The second characteristic phase is anger or resentment, sometimes irrationally directed against the dead for having deserted the mourner. The third phase is one of restitution, the mourner tries to replace the dead or reincorporate them as if they were still alive. The last stage is the acceptance of loss and recovered stability.

In his first soliloquy Hamlet is still undergoing the first phase. 'O, that this too too solid flesh would melt!' This passes into the second. Grief for his father is converted into rage against his mother, the unworthy remaining half of what had been to him an inseparable image of authority and love. The Queen's failure to share his mourning is Hamlet's prime distress. The third stage of mourning (when in phantasy or imagination the dead is restored to life, preferably as a part of oneself), which the psychologist calls 'introjection', occurs between Hamlet's departure to England and his return. When he found the document that ordered his execution, he acted promptly and royally, writing an order in the royal style and sealing it with the royal signet of his father. He despatches his traitorous companions as coolly as Henry V despatches his traitorous followers at the opening of *Henry V*. And he announces his return by adopting the royal title; 'This is I, Hamlet, *the Dane*;' that is, the *King* of Denmark. Moreover, in the graveyard scene there emerges for the first time, and quite unrepressed, Hamlet's physical revulsion at the physical fact of death, as he faces it in his dialogue with the skull of Yorick. The corpse he mourns is still like his father, though there are fleeting recollections of Polonius, a politician, and Rosencrantz and Guildenstern, the flatterers that 'praise such a lord's horse when he meant to beg it'. Finally, the image of the great Alexander himself, a form of his father's military figure: 'Dost thou think Alexander look'd o' this fashion i'th'earth?' 'Even so', says Horatio. 'And smelt so? Pah!' (V. i. 192–4). The loathing that comes out here is transferred from Hamlet's original loathing, but it is much more natural and immediate. When he learns that the unsullied flesh of Ophelia is to be laid in the grave new-made, he breaks out in a passionate grief that transforms itself immediately to a passion of anger against Laertes, the two feelings appearing almost simultaneously (this, of course, because in his speech Laertes has very obviously reproached Hamlet as the cause of Ophelia's madness).

At the end Hamlet appears calm, resolute and prepared to meet death.

> If it be now, 'tis not to come – if it be not to come, it will be now, if it be not now, yet it will come – the readiness is all. Since no man owes of aught he leaves, what is't to leave betimes? Let be. (V. ii. 213–6)

And so he is content to rest in the absence of knowledge, content to accept the uncertainty of his too-likely end. And there are no thoughts of anything dark or uncertain after death, which to the dying Hamlet represents felicity ('Absent thee from felicity awhile'). By what pain and through what havoc this calm has been achieved and how much is left for the mutes and audience to this act to piece out with their thoughts! For here, as a later poet (almost in Hamlet's last phrase) has said, is where 'Words, after speech, reach into the silence'.

XII

Othello, Webster and the tragedy of violence*

Eloquent and spectacular, *Othello* is now the least discussed of Shakespeare's major tragedies, yet in his own day it was the most innovatory. It is more than half a century since the hero was condemned by T. S. Eliot; I don't believe that today anyone would imagine that in his last speech Othello is 'cheering himself up' – a remark that from the future author of *Sweeney Agonistes* and *The Family Reunion* tends to rebound against him. Leavis intensified the charge to 'brutal egoism'; Auden thought Iago more interesting than Othello. Certainly today he inevitably becomes the centre of dramatic interest. Othello as a role defeated Garrick; some think he defeated Olivier; and today on stage the helpful plainspeaker who turns out to be a killer by remote control calls out a response that mere wife murder cannot evoke in those who have supped full with the horrors of the large and small screens. He is brainwashing.

Yet Rymer, in the first attack on this play, hardly mentions Iago, and Leavis considers him but a plot device. The attempts at intervention from the audience have usually been directed to Othello, either to enlighten him ('You great black fool, can't you see?') or the Russian justification 'He wasn't to blame. A love like that could burn up a City'. Shakespeare has built both these responses into the final scene; the first is Emilia's, the second Cassio's.

Desdemona's piteous look as she lay at his mercy was noted for its great effect by an Oxford spectator as early as 1610; Samuel Pepys recorded gratification when a pretty lady sitting next to him 'cried out' as Desdemona was murdered. In his *Lettres Philosophiques* Voltaire cited the scene as the greatest of Shakespeare's barbarisms; in 1822 in Paris the curtain had to be rung down, and Talma was forced to supply a happy ending.

*The Folger Shakespeare Library's annual Shakespeare birthday lecture, 1981.

This scene has always been a favourite with painters, for its purely spectacular appeal is both to tenderness and violence and the picture therefore 'vibrates' naturally. 'The grieved Moor' was a contemporary tribute to Burbage's acting; 'Nay, lay thee down and roar' is Emilia's comment. Othello uses no weapon but his own hands to destroy Desdemona. Pity or sympathy is also essentially a tactile impulse, a movement to touch; pity or sympathy was what Desdemona evoked very strongly in the first audience. In contrasting the violence of wife murder with the atrocities of modern films I have blurred an important distinction. Violence implies the rupture of an existing relationship, with one partner seeking the absolute domination of the other. Perhaps to annihilation. Thus the violence involved in law enforcement represents the absolute domination of the general will upon the transgressor; such violence is authorized, again even to annihilation. War, a second form of legalized violence, represents for Othello the tranquil mind, it represents content.

An atrocity is a gratuitously criminal act between two without previous relationships; it is strictly a meaningless act. Iago may be committing violence on some opponents; but he appears incapable of relating to anyone reciprocally and therefore atrocious. To Othello's 'Why . . .?' no answer is given. Othello, in assuming the role of judge first on Desdemona, and then on himself, combines also the roles of prosecutor, executioner and finally victim. Yet paradoxically he pleads not guilty too: 'an honourable murderer, if you will'.

For violence in art, an equal combination of savagery and tenderness is therefore needed; without tenderness the situation is not tragic. The act of violence then becomes an act of self-violence also, since part of the self was denied. In Heywood's *Woman Killed with Kindness* which appeared in the same season as *Othello*, 1604, the pious husband severs relations with his guilty wife utterly, telling her she is the murderer of the relation between them:

> It was thy hand cut two hearts out of one.

Desdemona is the first to use the term – 'my downright violence and storm of fortunes' she tells the Senate, in marrying Othello has cut her off from the life she had known, to share that of 'an extravagant and wheeling stranger/Of here and everywhere' (I. i. 137–8). She wants to plunge into the sort of Marco Polo wanderings he had recounted; to share dangers; 'she wished that Heaven had made her such a man' as Othello. He has opened a new world to her, as she created one for him. When he thinks her false, Othello's occupation's gone, chaos is come again, heaven mocks itself; in his mind her death effects a huge eclipse in the cosmos.

As they land together in Cyprus, first stage of the wandering, he reaches an inner harbour of the spirit;

> If twere now to die,
> 'Twere now to be to be most happy; for I fear
> My soul hath her content so absolute
> That not another comfort like to this
> Succeeds in unknown fate.   (II. i. 187–91)

At the end of an agonizing interior journey, he finds himself in another harbour: and anchors upon the marriage bed.

> Here is my journey's end, here is my butt,
> And very seamark of my utmost sail . . .
> Where should Othello go?   (V. ii. 270–1, 274)

Recent studies have stressed Othello's insecurity, from B. McElroy, *Shakespeare's Mature Tragedies* (Princeton, 1973) to Jane Adamson (*Othello as Tragedy, a study in Judgment and Feeling* (Cambridge, 1980), who decides that in this play everyone misjudges everyone else because in defence of their own precarious identity they are so impelled; it is less painful for Othello to believe the worst than in his basic insecurity to tolerate a state of doubt. 'Away at once with love or jealousy!' Miss Adamson's own psychological and permissive approach makes her try 'to govern our loathing for Iago' (p. 202) and to place Bianca as only another woman. Her version is not related to performance, but well designed for those in analysis; blood is replaced by trauma; there are no spectators to cry out.

In attempting to present the kind of Othello that Heywood might have perceived, a Jacobean Othello, some paradoxes are encountered. The only tragedy by Shakespeare set in roughly contemporary times, it is also the only one in which he went straight to an exotic foreign tongue, the Italian of Cinthio. It deals with a limited domestic subject (tragedy being traditionally about the fate of kingdoms and the fall of princes), yet links this with the order of society and of the cosmos, in the manner that in his great marriage hymns Spenser had involved the eternal powers in two London marriages. Shakespeare had displayed this at the end of *As You Like It* when he brought in Hymen, 'God of every town'.[1] The sacramental theory of marriage, which St Paul terms *enosis* or unification – 'they shall become one flesh' – has joined the young Venetian noblewoman so completely to the mature black stranger that when asked on her deathbed 'O, who hath done this deed' she can reply quite truthfully 'No body, I myself'. She will not allow Othello to cut two hearts out of one. It is he who sees himself as separated and calls her a liar.

A few Blackamoors could be found in the City of London as in any great port,[2] but Shakespeare may have first met them as he was working on the play, when in August 1604 he was commanded with his fellow actors by his new master, King James, to attend on the Spanish Ambassador, the Constable of Castille. Two hundred followers, including perhaps some Moors and negroes, were in the train, the first Spanish embassy to be seen since 1588. He might even have learnt something of Spanish drama and the code of honour that sustained its violence.

In 'A Hispanist looks at *Othello*',[3] Edward Meryon Wilson pointed out that the Spanish code demanded death for any woman who by adultery contaminated the purity of noble blood. As a public duty a noble *must* so punish any of his female kin who offended, for the whole family were polluted by her unchastity. It is a stock-breeder's view of family life, an archaic and familial conception (with perhaps a dash of Muslim male dominance) incompatible with the British rule of law.

However, a Spanish lady who denied adultery must be given a careful hearing. Calderón's *El medico de su honora*, where an innocent woman was bled to death, convicts the husband of rashness but not of murder. Othello who claims that 'Naught did I in hate but all in honour' had been pitied by Ludovico as 'this rash and most unfortunate man' (V. ii. 298, 286).

He had never brought a rational accusation against Desdemona, for he breaks out not into accusations but laments and curses; she, while denying with oaths the charges she is so slow to conceive, does not press her demands for evidence till too late. She knows obscurely that he will probably kill her, yet she will not abandon that image of him that unconditionally she carries with her. She knows 'his unkindness may defeat my life' and although she protests against the injustice of her death ('O falsely falsely murdered') her last words are 'Commend me to my kind lord'. To this second trial (Cassio's having been the first) the Governor of Cyprus had brought the sword but not the scales of justice, and in two lines Emilia can destroy his case.

> O thou dull Moor! That handkerchief thou speak'st of
> I found by fortune and did give my husband.   (V. ii. 228–9)

Emilia's death bears witness that the 'universe of two' – the new freedom of hazardous choice, dangerous service and committed union made by Desdemona – won at least one convert. Emilia's death is of prime significance as validating this violent and catastrophic choice. An impulse of trust in the faithful service of her woman links this intimate tragedy once again to the larger world. By contrast the faithful servant in *A Woman Killed with Kindness*, Nicholas, who senses the collective wrong, the offence to the whole household, in the guilt of his mistress, refuses to do more than weep at the catastrophe, 'I'll weep, but by my faith not die'. Here the wronged husband having actually taken his wife and her lover abed, by Christian restraint drives the man away 'to the devil' and converts his wife to a state of contrition that constitutes a slow suicide.

The early Venetian scenes of *Othello*, which as has been observed, develop in the manner of a comedy,[4] present Othello facing someone very like the lord mayor in his capacity as chief magistrate. For Shakespeare Venice was not one of the interchangeable Italian cities like Verona, Padua, Milan or Mantua; the great international sea-port presented to him as to others a particular, enlarged image of London itself (as he had already shewn it in *The Merchant of Venice*). If in one perspective, London was Troynovant, in modern terms, like Venice, it was 'seated between the old world and the new'. Every year the republic of Venice was wedded to the sea by the Doge casting a gold ring into the Adriatic. Webster was later to recall this in the opening words of a Lord Mayor's Triumphal Entry: Thetis addresses Oceanus

> What strange sea music bids us welcome, hark!
> Sure this is Venice and the day St Mark,
> In which the Doge and Senate their course hold
> To wed our Empire with a ring of gold.
>
> (*Monuments of Honour*, 1–4)

The mayoral triumph was sometimes headed by a king of the Moors scattering fireworks or flourishing a great sword to keep back the crowd, a figure both of splendour and some terror. He was followed by the pageant or float that always led the procession – a beautiful girl, richly clad and decked with gems which she was permitted to keep against her wedding day. The Mercers' maid, 'device' of the Senior Company of the Livery, borne aloft by the bachelors of that company, doubtless represented a more exalted Virgin from an earlier age. Her image must have sunk deep in the popular mind.

Another pageant, the ship, sometimes scattered spices, or brought wine or (if the Lord Mayor were of the Fishmongers') live fish as gifts to the crowd. At the end of *The Merchant of Venice* the ships, described as 'the portly burghers of the Flood' have been replaced by Portia, entering once more in farthingale like a stately ship and scattering largess to Lorenzo and Antonio.

The equation of a beautiful bride with a great captured treasure ship is made when Iago says of Othello:

> Faith he tonight hath boarded a land carrack.
> If it prove lawful prize, he's made for ever.   (I. ii. 50–1)

and his interlocutor Cassio, greeting Desdemona at Cyprus, cried:

O behold,
The riches of the ship is come ashore.   (II. i. 82–3)[5]

The image of a ship bringing riches up the Thames was traditional in many popular stories and dramas. Only that spring of 1604, their ships had come home in the grandest way for London, for Shakespeare and for King James.

On 14 March 1604 his three kingdoms of England, Scotland and Ireland were united in London for the triumphal entry of James I from the Tower to the palace of Westminster to open his first Parliament. In his train, with a golden crown on the breast of their scarlet royal livery, marched the King's Players, including William Shakespeare. For him, a month short of forty, as for the king, two years younger, this daylong progress forged a new relationship with the City that crowned a lifetime's expectations. It followed in an enlarged form the annual mayoral procession of installation, in which the City expressed its sense of identity and its power; the City had stood firmly for James at his accession, when the Lord Mayor became temporarily the most powerful officer in the realm, all court offices being vacated at the monarch's death till reconfirmed. The King was the City's choice; they had averted the country's worst dread, civil war, so that to the sense of identity and power the City added a magnetic force of union. London epitomized the whole realm, as Dekker put it in recalling Shakespeare's great speech on England of *King Richard II* (II. i. 40ff) and transferring its sacramental grandeur to London:

> This little world of men, this precious stone
> That sets out Europe . . .
> The jewel of the land; England's right eye . . .

In the Lord Mayor's triumph, the metaphor that he was wedded to the City (Londinium, a woman crowned with towers) meant that like Peleus or Anchises he had married an immortal, thus ensuring his own immortal Fame. Imitating Queen Elizabeth, James was to use the image of marriage to his kingdoms ('I am the husband and the whole isle is my wife'); in his masque of *Hymenaei* Ben Jonson was to develop a magnificent variation on this image, enlarging it to cosmic proportions, where the king was the priest who wedded the kingdoms with the ring of the encompassing sea.

The Renaissance jewel offered a 'little world' in itself, often an exquisite and complex piece of goldsmith's fantasy, as in the work of Cellini; but gems also carried sovereign 'virtues' or powers – what we should call radiating influences – which warned of poison or averted its effects. Jewels were associated with black men because they came generally from India or Africa. One of the most famous is the

Armada Jewel given by Queen Elizabeth to Sir Francis Drake. On the outside of the pendant is the profile of a Negro of full African-type – behind him and half-eclipsed by him, an image of a white woman. Within, there is found a picture of the Queen herself and her emblem, the phoenix. Earlier Elizabeth had given to Thomas Walsingham's daughter on her marriage to Thomas Greasely the Greasely Jewel. This displayed an image of a full negro and two black cupids, opening to reveal double portraits of the bridal pair. From the imperial treasury at Vienna come fourteen cameos of black gods, the most striking being a black Diana, with a rich pearl suspended from her Ethiopean ear – as Romeo characterizes Juliet! (I. v. 47–8; cf. III. ii. 21–5)

The ultimate Biblical justification came from the *Songs of Songs* ('I am black but comely, O ye daughters of Jerusalem', 3. 6) where the black bride becomes identified with the whole human race united to Christ. Some years later, when the Chancellor of Cambridge, Francis Bacon, sent a diamond to the Public Orator, George Herbert, the poet replied by sending back 'a blackamoor' – some verses in black ink in George's best Latin, afterwards translated as 'A Black Nymph wooing a Fair Boy'. He replied with Iago's arguments.

> Black maid, complain not that I fly,
>   Where fate commands antipathy,
> Prodigious might that union prove
>   Where day and night together move,
> And the conjunction of our lips,
>   Not kisses mark, but an eclipse
>   (*Poems of Henry King*, ed. M. Crum, 1965, p. 151)

Here are the *disjecta membra* of images from *Othello*.

There were two paradoxical and opposite images of black men on the Elizabethan stage, as George Hunter and Eldred Jones in different ways worked out.[6] The treacherous evil Moor, the 'infidel' often coupled with some other infidel, such a Jew (as Ithamore with Barabas in *The Jew of Malta*) had been sketched by Shakespeare in Aaron of *Titus Andronicus*. The noble black warrior, from Peele's *Battle of Alcazar* (1589) descends through Marlowe's Calymath, Shakespeare's Prince of Morocco (in *The Merchant of Venice*) and Heywood's Mullisheg in *The Fair Maid of the West* to the union of the two in the disguised Machiavel, the Duke of Florence, in Webster's *The White Devil*.

The symbolic use of black and white imagery in *Othello* is too familiar to need any stressing now; Iago proves the black devil in the end; Desdemona appeared blackened in Othello's eyes, whilst Emilia stresses crudely the theological implications in rebutting Othello's accusation:

> The more angel she,
> And you the blacker devil!   (V. ii. 33–4)

an antithesis that Othello re-echoes in his own speeches of despair
(V. ii. 273–80). It is more significant now in tracing the submerged
images that make the play at once exotic and familiar, that bring
violence close to tenderness,[7] to observe the use of negroes with love
tokens and to see the variant here. A love token or indeed a token of
any kind is an activating gift of great potency for any dramatist in the
structure of his play. As symbol of the deepest exchange, of *enosis*,
the ring appears in many of Shakespeare's comedies.[8] Troilus' sleeve
and the love gifts which Ophelia returns are the chief tragic uses of
such tokens.

As he loses her, Brabantio recognizes Desdemona as his 'jewel' (I.
iii. 195) and so does Othello.

> Had she been true,
> If heaven would make me such another world
> Of one entire and perfect chrysolite,
> I'd not have sold her for it.   (V. ii. 146–9)

and in his death speech he characterizes himself as 'one whose hand

> Like the base Indian, threw a pearl away
> Richer than all his tribe.   (V. ii. 350–1)

The chrysolite, an infrangible stone that could never be flawed or
broken, represents the new world that neither he nor she could find
except in each other; it represents also the unflawed virginity that she
brought him. She was the pearl of great price but she could not
protect Othello from Iago's poison, the deadly 'medicine' he set to
work in Othello's veins.

Instead of a jewel, the actual dramatic object is the handkerchief
upon which so much of the action turns, which caused so much mirth
to Thomas Rymer and other classicists ('Let this be an example to all
housewives, that they look better to their linen'). However, in his
attendance on the Spanish Ambassador Shakespeare may have seen
the Spanish ladies with their ceremonious handkerchiefs. Any Spanish painting is likely to show a fine handkerchief prominently
displayed (as at the wedding of the Infante Isabella to Francesco de
Medici). In a Mediterranean climate a handkerchief, like a fan, was a
necessary piece of equipage, and could be as obvious as royal regalia.

In Shakespeare's very first tragedy, the napkin spotted with the
blood of the murdered boy Rutland is given to his father Richard of
York tauntingly by Queen Margaret and calls out the celebrated
tirade 'O tiger's heart wrapped in a woman's hide!' (*3 Henry VI*, I. iv.
110–49). (Here the religious analogue is of course the Veronica

napkin.) Othello's handkerchief, spotted with strawberries, is noted only when it is dropped (or possibly cast away by Othello himself) and picked up by Emilia, initiating the start of the tragic movement in the second half of the play

> She so loves the token
> (For he conjured her she should ever keep it)
> That she reserves it evermore about her
> To kiss and talk to.   (III. iii. 297–300)

Later only is it revealed that the magic in the web 'dyed in mummy which the skilful Conserved of maidens' hearts' (III. iv. 73–4) is to work magic not on the bride but the bridegroom. Othello's witchcraft if any is originally directed against himself. In a pathetic attempt to counter the lost magic, Desdemona asks Emilia to lay on their bed the wedding sheets (a delicately wrought work that every young girl prepared for her own bridal) spotted not with blood from maiden hearts but with the hymenal blood that had witnessed to her virginity, to the integrity of 'the perfect chrysolite'. Desdemona asks to be buried in one of these sheets. If the handkerchief represents all that Bertram's ring does in *All's Well That Ends Well*, Desdemona exchanged what Helena also offered. These tokens are more fragile and more intimate than jewels.

Iago had opened the action with a most offensive description of Othello ('an old black ram', 'thicklips') with the implications of fornication but none of marriage rites, only 'the beast with two backs'. It was commonly believed that Africans were more fierily volatile and emotional than the Mediterranean races, because they were born nearer the sun. Yet in these opening scenes Othello shows a calm patience, an ability to absorb shock and insult rendering it insignificant, that is truly African. 'Big Otto' uses without inflation the natural voice of command, as Desdemona addresses the Senate in a rhetoric as dignified and judicial as Portia's. In a quiet aside, Othello indicates to a subordinate his royal descent.

But when passing through the tempest, they reach Cyprus (or the London expedition, shall we say, reaches Ireland?)[9] what follows happens outwardly but also within Othello's mind, in 'the small circle of pain within the skull'. Each character casts a double shadow, and the shadows change erratically. The one real object remains the handkerchief; so that in the scene of shadow play where Othello is deceived by seeing it in Cassio's hand and tossed to Bianca, he then enters a living dream, a state of madness where all actions are profoundly unreal.[10] The audience must move at once in empathy with, and in judgment upon, what is happening. Desdemona is never as explicit as Hermione in *The Winter's Tale*:

> My life stands in the level of your dreams,
> Which I'll lay down.   (III. ii. 78–9)

but in the willow song she implies that he is mad – and therefore she
is mad too. Adopting the language of Iago, Othello imagines Desdemona copulating with his entire command down to the blackened
'pioneers', the sappers. In the last scene he too for the last time 'tastes
her sweet body' whilst invoking external codes to legitimize his
violence as husband, commander of the troops, governor of the
isle.

> O balmy breath, that almost doth persuade
> Justice to break her sword!   (V. ii. 16–7)

These perhaps the most purely sensuous lines of love in the play,
initiate an epitome of that firm structure in which Othello develops
from the African calm of Act I to the African frenzy of Act V. The
disjunctive technique of a series of scenes in which tableaux punctu-
ate long speeches, and quick exchanges suggest continuity is sustained by the two time-clocks that make the pace seem both gradual
and violent. Iago, who like Othello lives by creating an imaginary
world for himself, transmuting actions, treats his own wife as
messenger, decoy or catspaw; although she holds all the clues,
including the name of Cassio, which Othello gave her in the brothel
scene, Emilia never suspects Iago. The hapless Roderigo, never seen
anywhere but in Iago's company, serves to mirror his success with
Othello, Cassio and lastly with Desdemona herself; the first blood he
draws is upon Roderigo, until finally by killing his wife, Iago puts
himself on an equality with Othello in the eyes of the law, where
authorized violence decrees that his death be prolonged by tortures.

Although it was not printed till 1622 and therefore could have
been known only in the theatre, *Othello* is a central influence on the
two tragedies of John Webster, *The White Devil* (1611) and *The
Duchess of Malfi* (1613). *The Duchess of Malfi*, his masterpiece,
given by Shakespeare's own company, evoked the same pity for the
Duchess that had been called out by Desdemona;[11] her momentary
revival after strangulation, and the conversion which the sight of her
dead face miraculously works in her murderers, intensify the local
effect of the scene, yet the structure of Webster's tragedy, though
related, is different, and far more disjunctive. Webster's Italy is not a
blend of the exotic and the intimate, of London and her wedding to
King James and Shakespeare, with the country of dreams. The Italy
of Jacobean tragedy was a literary convention, a country of the mind
that Webster shared with Marston and Tourneur. It is a dreamworld
where the struggle for power is played out by characters whose force

is evinced not in any political dimension – each moves in a bubble world of his own, of brightness or darkness, mist or brilliance. It might be said they are all mad, and like the vision of the madmen in Act IV of *The Duchess of Malfi*, this vision works collectively.[12]

The Duchess cannot reconcile her regal and her feminine selves; she moves first within her own dream of security, then in the prison of her insane brother's fancy. Her faithful woman says at the first proposal of the second marriage to her steward:

> Whether the spirit of greatness or of woman
> Reign most in her, I know not; but it shows
> A fearful madness: I owe her much of pity.   (I. i. 576–8)

Social distinctions operate here as powerfully as racial ones, with the added violence to natural sequence that the widow is here the active partner, wooing more directly than Desdemona. Antonio, her 'disqualified' choice, plays a feminine, passive role; it is she who plans the union, directs the flight and then unwarily exposes all to one who betrays her. We never meet her by her personal name Giovanna; she is Duchess of Malfi still. Except possibly in the echo scene after her death where Antonio recognizes the voice of 'my wife'. This homeless voice had been heard once before, offstage, crying out in the night in the pains of childbirth. The echo tells Antonio he will never see her more. Webster added the pathos of infants, a proof of tenderness that counterbalances the extreme horror of his mad Spanish royalty, the princes of the House of Aragon, or his cold Medici in violence directed onto women who here first give their names as title roles to tragedy.

The violence in Webster is continuous, and his language is no more diluted by the commonplace than his princes are restrained by precepts of morality. 'Tush for justice!' is the comment of the Duke of Florence on learning that his revenge is authorized by his sister's having been murdered. The power game is played out in a setting which like that of the drug addict is compulsorily attractive or repulsive. Bosola, the professional spy who betrays the Duchess wears many disguises, betrays and then doublecrosses his betrayer, dooming himself in the act. He is inevitably a masquer, an actor of roles, who never till the end finds true 'integrity of life'.

The Spanish code of honour is assumed but not accepted. The Duchess's brother finally asks Bosola:

> By what authority didst thou execute
> This bloody sentence?
> *Bosola:*   By yours.
> *Ferdinand:* Mine? was I her judge?

> Did any ceremonial form of law
> Doom her to non being? did a complete jury
> Deliver her conviction up i' th' court?
> Where shalt thou find this judgment registered
> Unless in hell? (IV. ii. 298–304)

Webster, a student of the Middle Temple, wrote no play without a trial scene, but the sword of heaven replaces the imperfect legal cruelties of men. Of the negative vision in Bosola and in Flamineo, George Hunter said: 'These patterns (of negation) are important if the author can convey some sense of the value they exclude.'[13]

The deepest insights come near to madness; in an insane world, madmen can see some things more clearly. Webster's scenes move by flickerings, jumps and reversals; his characters also develop in this way. There may be brief moments of absolute security as when Brachiano first meets his White Devil, and they exchange jewels as love tokens.

> Give credit, I could wish time would stand still,
> And never end this interview, this hour. (I. ii. 192–3)

As her Moorish maid spreads a rich carpet and cushions for the encounter, the words are stately or emblematic but the actions intimate, Flamineo, her treacherous brother, providing the innuendo:

> 'His jewel for her jewel'; well put in, Duke . . .
> That's better; 'she must wear his jewel lower' . . .
>
> (I. ii. 215, 218)

Heroic in pride and energy Vittoria (described as 'the famous Venetian courtesan' though she is not Venetian) surmounts her subsequent trial for adultery; whilst Brachiano's Duchess, who like Desdemona has taken his guilt upon herself, has been divorced with a kiss and murdered for reward. Built from opposing beauty and evil, the sharply disjunctive scenes of Vittoria's life end in

> O, my greatest sin lay in my blood,
> Now my blood pays for't. (V. vi. 240–1)

These broken forms carry the possibility of character development which, as modern psychologists observe, proceeds by vibrations, leaps and jumps. Webster's 'poetry of the gaps' allowed his actors to breathe inside their parts, insert their own contribution and make their own interpretation. He worked very closely with the men of Queen Anne's troupe, and with the King's Men. Any actor will recognize the expertise of this 'poetry of the gaps'.

The Duchess of Malfi is subjected to tests of mockery and torture, through the grisly parody of an exchange of love tokens, when she receives the dead man's hand with a wedding ring upon it which she had given; Ferdinand's first gift to her had been a dagger of their father, his last the gift that 'brings last benefit, last sorrow' of the coffin and cords.

Ritualized cruelty (a kind exploited in such Spanish dramas as *Justice without Revenge*) culminates in grotesque parody as the Duchess's waiting maid is killed beside her mistress.

Other features of Webster's earlier life are reflected in the darkness of these tragic visions,[14] which have been revived with such powerful effect upon the modern stage. The sometimes gratuitous atrocity in Webster (as Flamineo's murder of his brother) can provoke the crazed tenderness of their mother's dirge.

> Call for the robin redbreast and the wren . . .

and in the darkness of her 'last presence chamber' the Duchess finds freedom. Iago's words on Othello

> Not poppy, nor mandragora,
> Nor all the drowsy syrops of this world
> Shall ever medicine thee to that sweet sleep
> Which thou owedst yesterday.   (III. iii. 334–7)

become transformed by her to

> Come, violent death,
> Serve for mandragora to make me sleep.   (IV. ii. 241–2)

The affirmation of Shakespeare and of Webster is that such beings have witnessed to their faith, so that the final act still carries tenderness. The hope may be eschatological only, yet in both of Webster's tragedies the last murders spring from devotion to two good women, whose young sons survive the general holocaust.

Notes

1 See D. J. Gordon, *The Renaissance Imagination*, ed. Stephen Orgel (Berkeley and Los Angeles, University of California Press, 1973), p. 115.

2 See Eldred Jones, *Othello's Countrymen* (Oxford, Oxford University Press, 1965), p. 12, for an order to a Lubeck merchant in 1601 ordering the return of 'Negars and Blackamoors' who had come 'since the troubles between her Highness and the King of Spain'.

3 In *English and Spanish Literature of the Sixteenth and Seventeenth Centuries* (Cambridge, Cambridge University Press, 1980).

4 See e.g. Barbara H. C. de Mendonça, in *Shakespeare Survey*, 21 (1968), 31–8. Susan Snyder has also made this point.

5 The riches of the great carrack, brought to Plymouth in 1592 had included a great diamond, bartered in a London theatre. Heywood in his *Fair Maid of the West* had displayed the riches of Barbary; the story of Dick Whittington has survived to this day.

6 George Hunter 'Othello and Colour Prejudice', in *Dramatic Identities and Cultural Tradition* (Liverpool, Liverpool University Press, 1978), (originally presented 1967); Eldred Jones, *op. cit.* note 2. Cf. Marvin Spivack, *The Anatomy of Evil* (Oxford, Oxford University Press, 1958) for black Iago, and also Leah Scragg, *Shakespeare Survey*, 21 (1968), 52–65.

7 Since the craft plays, the black king of Ethiopia, Balthazar, had been linked with rich gifts at the epiphany; in Heywood's *Golden Age*, Pluto, the black king of Tartarus, is made King of Tartary, associated with rich camel trains, evidently on the Venetian trade route from the East! The most famous image is the Daughters of Niger in Jonson's *Masque of Blackness* (1604/5) played by the Queen and her ladies at Court. Compare the older use of spotting the face with ink to denote sin in Morality plays e.g. *Three Ladies of London*.

8 Love tokens range from the rings of *Romeo and Juliet, Merchant of Venice, All's Well* and *Twelfth Night* to the absurd dog of *Two Gentlemen of Verona*, the shower of pearls, gloves, diamond studded pictures of *Love's Labours Lost*, the rain of gifts in *Timon* to the ring and bracelet of *Cymbeline*. Florizel buys no fairing for Perdita, but the 'fardel' supplies identity proof and includes a jewel. There are no gifts in *Comedy of Errors, Taming of the Shrew, Midsummer Night's Dream*, or *Merry Wives of Windsor* since all are farcical in some degree.

9 Cf. the hopeful expectation of a triumphal entry of a victorious Essex returning from the Irish wars (*Henry V*, V, Chorus) and its tragic sequel.

10 He emerges most clearly in the brief exchange with Cassio, 'Dear General, I did never give you cause' [to kill me] 'I do believe it, and I ask your pardon' (V. ii. 301–2).

11 See Middleton's commendatory verses for the play: 'Thy epitaph, only the title be Write *Duchess*; that will fetch a tear for thee.'

12 A subtle treatment of madness in *Othello* is Arthur Kirsch, 'The Polarization of Erotic Love in *Othello*', *Shakespeare and the Experience of Love* (Cambridge, Cambridge University Press, 1981).

13 George K. Hunter 'English Folly and Italian Vice', *op. cit.* p. 125.

14 See M. C. Bradbrook, *John Webster, Citizen and Dramatist* (London, Weidenfeld & Nicolson, 1980) for the story of the Princess of Eboli and Antonio Perez. For Overbury's murder see Beatrice White, *Cast of Ravens* (London, John Murray, 1965). Webster could have met the young Duke of Brachiano, who closes *The White Devil* on a strong note, for in 1601 he visited London after escorting his cousin Marie de Medici to France to wed the French king.

Acknowledgements

Many of the articles collected in this edition were originally published elsewhere. I am grateful for permission to include them in this collection, and would like to express thanks to all concerned.

'No Room at the Top: Spenser's Pursuit of Fame', *Elizabethan Poetry*, ed. John Russell Brown, Stratford-upon-Avon Studies II (London, Edward Arnold, 1960), pp. 91–109; 'Beasts and Gods: the Social Purpose of *Venus and Adonis*', *Shakespeare Survey*, 15 (1962), 64–72; 'John Webster and the Power Game', *The Times Higher Educational Supplement*, 31 October 1980, pp. 11–12; 'Marvell and the Masque', *Andrew Marvell 1678–1978*, ed. K. Friedenreich (Shoe String Press, Hamden, Connecticut, 1979), pp. 204–23; 'Marlowe's *Doctor Faustus* and the Eldritch Tradition', *Essays on Shakespeare and Elizabethan Drama in honor of Hardin Craig*, ed. Richard Hosley (Columbia, University of Missouri Press, 1962), pp. 83–90, reprinted by permission of the University of Missouri Press, copyright 1962 by the Curators of the University of Missouri; 'Shakespeare's Primitive Art', *Proceedings of the British Academy*, LI, published for the British Academy by Oxford University Press (1965), 215–34; 'Dramatic Role as Social Image: a Study of *The Taming of the Shrew*', Shakespeare-Jahrbuch, 94 (1958), 132–50; 'King Henry IV', *Stratford Papers on Shakespeare*, ed. B. W. Jackson (McMaster University, Hamilton, Ontario, 1965), 1–16; 'What Shakespeare did to Chaucer's *Troilus and Criseyde*', *Shakespeare Quarterly*, IX (1958), 311–9; 'The Balance and the Sword in *Measure for Measure*', (Kinokuniya Bookstore Co., Tokyo), pp. 21–32; 'An Interpretation of *Hamlet*', *Hiroshima Studies in English Language and Literature*, XI (1964), 27–39.

Thanks are due also to the National Humanities Center, N. Carolina, where the Introduction and the final paper were prepared, and to the staff of the Harvester Press for their kind assistance.